# Celestial Navigation for the Clueless

Written and Illustrated
by Jeremy Bernal

Version 9.1b
Copyright 2006 Monitor Studios. Printing for personal use permitted; all other rights reserved. Portions of The Nautical Almanac are reproduced with permission of HM Nautical Almanac Office @ Copyright the Council for the Central Laboratory of the Research Councils. Portions of the Compact Sight Reduction Tables are produced by the US Naval Laboratory, used with permission.
ISBN-10: 1442114355 / ISBN-13: 9781442114357

## IMPORTANT:

Before you leave the book store, get a copy of this year's Nautical Almanac. You'll need it. Really. I'm trying to make the whole learning experience easy for you here. It will cost about $25 but you NEED it. You cannot learn or do Celestial Navigation without it.

The tutorials in this book are for the summer of 2005, and all the almanac pages you'll need to follow along are provided. But for you to actually go out and practice on your own, as well as learning the anatomy of the almanac, you will want your own up-to-date copy.

Don't procrastinate. Get it NOW or you'll be really confused and waste time, and have to go back to the book store, back into traffic, etc and your hair will start turning gray like mine is.

If you ordered this book and forgot to get the almanac, then you'll probably be OK learning how a sextant works, up until the part where you actually learn to compute sights. But beyond that, you'll be lost. You'll see. I'd advise ordering your almanac right now and practice using your sextant until your almanac arrives, and then moving on. Otherwise you'll just be extremely frustrated.

## Legal Claptrap:

Niether this book, nor the author, can nor should be held responsible if you do something dumb like get lost and/or wreck your boat somewhere, burn your eyes out looking into the sun, injure yourself (brain or body), or fail to follow the common sense that kept your ancestors in the gene pool up until present day. Take some bloody responsibility for your own actions for once, people! It's a shame I have to put this part in here at all. Be a good example to the rest of the gene pool!

Any appearance of dead historical figures is strictly intentional. Any reference to living historical figures is, too, but it's all in good humor so hopefully Margaret Thatcher and Mikhael Gorbachev won't be too terribly insulted.

Now that we're done covering our butts from flesh-eating zombie lawyers, let's get on with the show, shall we?

# What this book will do:

I'll teach you just what you need to know as you go. I'm not going to gum up your brain with useless trash you don't need. You learn as far as you want to. Knowing how the universe works is not important at all. You just need to follow step by step instructions, look through tables in a book, and do basic grade-school math. It's wonderfully mindless yet satisfying busy-work!

For more advanced stuff, like plotting lines of position and getting fixes at times other than noon, however, you'll need to learn some spinning planet and time concepts, but that's only if you want to go that far. If you can calculate time and degrees on a circle, then you'll be ok. Even then I've tried to make it as easy as I can, since I'm lazy and like to do things the easy way. The learning curve is steep, but not impossible.

A note on learning and innovation (paraphrased from Heinlein, who probably paraphrased it from some other wise lazy person): The innovators of our society never got ahead by being hard workers. They got ahead by finding better and more efficient ways of doing things so they could stay lazy.

So relax, crack open a beer, and lubricate your brain for the thorough reaming it's about to receive!

*For Kristen,*
*without whom I would be truly lost.*

# Table of Contents

| | |
|---|---|
| 06 | Foreword |
| 08 | Why Learn Celestial Navigation |
| 13 | Taking Your Sight |
| 15 | Index Error and Index Correction |
| 16 | Dip Correction |
| 17 | Apparent Altitude and Atmospheric Refraction |
| 18 | Altitude and Semidiameter Correction |
| 19 | Parallax / Complete Sight Summary |
| | |
| 20 | How the Earth is Measured |
| 22 | Basic Latitude Fix |

**The Noon Sight**

| | |
|---|---|
| 24 | Longitude by Noon Sight / GMT |
| 25 | GP |
| 26 | Finding Local Noon |
| 28 | Equation of Time Correction |
| 32 | Latitude by Noon Sight |
| 32 | Declination |
| 41 | Using Calculators for Celestial Navigation |

| | |
|---|---|
| 42 | **Perfecting your Polaris Sight** |
| 43 | LHA Aries |
| 44 | GHA Aries |
| | |
| 49 | **LHA, GHA, and GMT explained** |
| | |
| 51 | Using Universal Plotting Sheets |
| | |
| 54 | **Advanced Navigation: Sight Reductions and Plotting Great Circles** |
| 59 | Gathering Information |
| 62 | Breaking it Down |
| 63 | SR Tables, First Run |
| 65 | SR Tables, Second Run |
| 66 | Aux Tables, First Run |
| 67 | Aux Tables, Second Run |
| 68 | HC |
| 69 | Zenith / Azimuth |
| 70 | LOP Plot |
| 73 | How to use HO229 |
| 76 | Reality Check |

**Sighting other Celestial Objects**

| | |
|---|---|
| 77 | Stars |
| 79 | Planets |
| 81 | Moon |
| | |
| 83 | Sun-Run-Sun and Running Fixes |
| 84 | Geek Trivia and Online Resources |
| | |
| 86 | Worksheets |
| 94 | Almanac Page Samples |

# Foreword:

Honestly, I don't know why the other guys make it so hard to figure out, because it's not. Do yourself a favor—put the other guy's book down and buy this one. I guarantee mine will help you more. Here's why:

I'm no genius, and I've figured it out in a way that is easy to understand, enough that I feel that it's safe to teach YOU, the reader. I am descended from a long line of effective but grumpy bitter teachers (and Chicago bootleggers), so you're in good hands! I believe the reason we are grumpy and bitter is because things are *not* hard to learn, they are just made that way by lousy teachers!

You've probably looked at other books by brainy smarty-pants authors who like to yammer on about Kepler's orbits, Newton this and Spherical Trigonometry that, Sine, Cosine, Tangent, etc. They probably confused the heck out of you. They STILL confuse the heck out of me. They were written by people who know celestial navigation through and through, and they assume you know how to take sights and break them down, and they must also assume that you still remember a single thing from the algebra class you slept through in high school. Let alone trigonometry. Then let alone spherical trigonometry! I can safely say now that all you need to know from those brainy geek books is that YOU DO NOT NEED TO KNOW THAT STUFF! Hopefully you haven't spent money to buy those books like I did.

I read through those books. They confused the heck out of me. I have them here and I'm tearing them to bits finding the few meager useful tidbits of how-to-learn that they contain. They didn't contain much, and the few that did seemed to miss a few concepts that I think are bloody important.

I'm a stubborn guy. When I run into something I do not understand, I go for the problem's throat and bite down until it bleeds its workings out in a clear, concise format. Having run into these horrible books, I felt it was my God-sworn duty to filter through the nonsense for you folks and bring you something you could read and understand the first or second time.

I wrote this book *as* I learned celestial navigation (it started as a notebook and grew out of control). Why? Because in theory, it should give a better step-by-step perspective on just how it works, from the learner's point of view. I've already sorted through a lot of the complaints and grievances I have with the OTHER BOOKS. Yeah, you guys know who you are.

Celestial Nav is like driving a car—you don't need to know how the valves and cylinders and gears work, internal combustion processes, etc—you just want to know how to press the gas pedal to accelerate, the brakes to slow down, why turn signals are good things, and what hand gestures work best to tell others what you think of their driving. If you want to get into the nitty-gritty and tweak your car to give you more, well, Celestial Nav has that option too.

If you've got even the slightest interest in celestial navigation, it's probably good that you learn how to do it, at least on a basic level (Polaris sights and Sun sights) to use it as a backup to GPS.

You're probably a boaty person and you probably go on long trips, and you've gotten caught with your pants down in one way or another in regards to relying on electronic gadgets or battery power. You may dream of crossing an ocean someday, visiting the far-flung third world with all its flavors and culture, and you're afraid Uncle Sam will flip his lid and turn off your GPS signals right when you're skimming through that narrow reef passage halfway across the globe. Or maybe you're a grumpy curmudgeon who hates computers and prefers things that don't crash and fill your view with vague hexadecimal error code messages.

I could cite many an example of beautiful boats meeting their demise on a beach or reef because the captain was looking at his newfangled plotting gps computer program, watching the little boat icon clear the passage perfectly while in the real world he wrecked, and the chainsaw salvagers came out like wolves to the kill.

Well, that's part of my list of reasons for wanting to learn it, and maybe you're not far off, or maybe you are. It doesn't matter, because I'm going to teach you how to un-lose yourself with a sextant, pencil, paper, and basic math. When it's all over, you'll eye your GPS with the suspicious distrust that it so rightly deserves!

Celestial Navigation need not be limited to the sea; it can also be used to navigate on land or in the air.

# Why learn Celestial Navigation?

## What Celestial Navigation CAN do:

Give you a rough idea of where you are, allowing you to stumble around on the globe from sort of where you started to sort of where you're headed, and have a pretty good chance of getting to your destination. All with a paper, pencil, and sextant. All things not requiring batteries!

## What Celestial Navigation CAN'T do:

It can't thread you through narrow reefs like a GPS can. It's not fast like a GPS. It's not as accurate as a GPS. It can't provide instant gratification in the way a GPS can. It's slow, cumbersome, and not that accurate. So if you want accuracy, get a GPS. If you want reliable face-first-into-the-waves salty pegleg arr matey "When I spits, I spits tar!" kind of stuff that will get you where you need to go no matter what, then Celestial Nav is for you.

BUT...

Little electronic boxes can tell you all sorts of neat things right away, with no need to think or wait. But as a caveat, little electronic boxes:
- Need batteries to eat.
- Do not cope well with salt water.
- Sometimes have a mind of their own, especially if the above two needs have not been fulfilled.
- Need satellites to see by. Said satellites are owned and operated by the US government, who is extremely neurotic about terrorists these days, and has been known to shut down and/or scramble the satellite signals at a whim. Said satellites also need batteries to run. And though they wouldn't be fired into orbit if they weren't reliable, if they do ever break-- well, they're very far away and won't be repaired quickly, I assure you.

It's the same reasons you shouldn't navigate with purely digital charts. If your computer fails, you're SCREWED. Paper, pencil, and books never crash or run out of batteries, and they are not afraid of people in dynamite vests.

Now I've got nothing against little electronic boxes. They are wonderful inventions. They save me lots of toil, and torment. But when the chips are down, I want something old fashioned and hardcore to rely on. Salty old farts got around with a sextant for centuries, and GPS has only been around for a few decades.

There's also a sense of satisfaction, like sailing itself, that comes from knowing you can get from Point A to Point B with nothing more than a trusty boat, the wind and sky, and your own sheer brain power. It's just good and salty, it is!

Now, I may sound like a hypocrite when I start in on the virtues of the digital wristwatch. Oh well, string me up and prepare the flogs! They are cheap and reliable, and 'they' are making ones now that recharge their batteries via mini solar panels. Buy a case of them; they'll give you better service for half the price of a 'marine grade' GPS. If there was just one single electronic thing I could choose out of the whole assortment to go with me on a voyage, it would be a waterproof digital wristwatch.

## What do I need to know before I start?

Well, for starters, you need one working hand and one working eye (most pirates worth their salt still have these). You should know how to navigate by a nautical chart. You should have a basic grasp of Latitude and Longitude and how they are measured. You should know how the compass works, and how to chart a bearing on a paper chart using a parallel ruler. You should know basic dead reckoning skills. And you should know how to add, subtract, multiply, and divide. Anyone who's ever been out on a coastal sail probably knows this stuff. I can't explain these things to you because that's what other books are for (I highly recommend "The Complete Sailor" by David Siedman). Fortunately that book is good, otherwise I'd be writing a general sailing book that didn't suck to go along with my celestial nav book ☺

## What are the toughest parts to learn?

Don't be intimidated by doing math. It's never harder than grade-school add/subtract/multiply/divide, carrying numbers to make sure 6 hours 100 minutes is really 7 hours 40 minutes, and that when you pass 400 degrees around a circle, you are still only 40 degrees from the point of origin.

The biggest problem I ran into with learning Celestial Nav is that it has seemingly 2 or more names for each concept, measurement, angle, etc and a shorthand abbreviation which may or may not seem related to the real names at all. It's tough to sort them all out. In time you'll learn them by heart, but in the meantime please bear with it. I've tried to make it as easy as I can.

The Nautical Almanac may seem intimidating at first, but once you've used it a few times, it's completely friendly. There are a myriad little corrections and numbers to look up in the almanac (the most time consuming part of Celestial Nav is looking up those little numbers and corrections!) but if you have a form to fill out (those are included in this book), you'll never have to remember what they all are; the form will prompt you for everything you need to look up.

## What tools do you need to find out where you are?

Not much! These are the basics. We'll go into them at greater depth below.
1. A clear sky, day or night.
2. A sextant.
3. This year's Nautical Almanac.
4. An accurate wristwatch.

Let's go over the list in more detail:

1. This should go without saying, but obviously you need a clear sky and horizon, enough to at least see the star or celestial body you are using for your sight. As we all know, Mother Nature is moody, and you just have to hunker down and use your Dead Reckoning skills until she is clear enough to allow you a proper sight.
2. A sextant. It doesn't need to have flashy bells and whistles, but it SHOULD have a set of filters that swing to block the mirrors for sun sights. Otherwise you'll be firing the concentrated rays of the sun directly into your soon-to-be-smoldering eye socket. It is possible to take a sight with a protractor, string, and fishing sinker for the sake of learning, but a real sextant will give you much better readings. It's up to you what your budget is, and how much you want to use your new skills.
3. Nautical Almanac. It's usually blue, with white letters, and available in 2 versions. The commercial version is the same information, just made cheaper because boat-stuff companies place ads in the front and back pages, thereby reducing the cost of publication and passing those savings onto you. No, they don't stuff ads in the middle and make it hard to read—it's all at the very front and back, nice and tidy.
4. An accurate watch. Something digital, waterproof, with a digital readout, date-keeping (with leap years), and preferably a 'dual time' function. If you don't have or can't get a watch with dual time settings, get two watches. Keep one set to your local time, and set the dual time (or second watch) to GMT (Greenwich Mean Time). Synchronize both time settings down to the second. Really. It's important that you do so, so that your readings are as accurate as you can manage. You would not believe the headache that could have been prevented learning this stuff if a SINGLE ONE of these book writers had thought to mention setting a watch to GMT and keeping it that way. It makes it so much easier, trust me. The date-keeping function is nice to have if you're a forgetful idiot like me who often loses track of what day it is.

Not all watches are created equal. Don't cheap out—get a durable one. If you need to get two, get both the same kind. I am not receiving a royalty for this, but I should! I highly recommend the Casio AQ-150W. It has an analog face, with digital readout for 2 time settings, a stopwatch, and good night illumination. Its time setting method also lends itself well to synchronization with timecode and/or the atomic clock. It's waterproof up to 10 bar of pressure, and its cost is around US$25.00, commonly available at WalMart and Target stores. There are a variety of ways to find what the real, honest time is. Radio timecodes, Atomic Clock websites (nist.time.gov), and shareware computer clock-sync utilities are freely available to help you sync up your time.

Quartz movement digital watches are so accurate these days that unless they get frozen, you should not have to worry about them slacking off or running too fast. Just to be sure, though, check and adjust your time before you begin your passage, and you should be ok.

## What does a sextant do?

It measures the angles between your eye, the horizon, and any object in the sky.

## So how can a sextant be used to find my position?

The Great Geeks of History have done all that work for you over the centuries, and offer it to you condensed into what we call the Nautical Almanac. This book can tell you at any given time where any celestial object will be in relation to the earth's center. Your viewpoint, through the sextant, will give an angle of observation, which, when compared to an angle from a real-world location, tells you how far you are from that location. 2 or more of these angle comparisons can be crossed to give you a 'fix' on your position.

There are many different ways to find out where you are, from easy to hard, and we'll go over them in that order. You don't have to know HOW it works, only that it DOES. Simply following directions on the worksheets included will get you through Noon Sights and advanced Polaris Sights. If you want to learn past that, it's in here too, but I won't fault you if you don't want to.

The first, most basic way to use a sextant is to determine your Latitude by sighting Polaris, the north star (which you don't necessarily need to have the Almanac for unless you're a stickler for details). The second is finding Longitude through a Noon Sight of the Sun. This requires a series of sextant sights and watch set to Greenwich Mean Time. Then we'll do Latitude by Noon Sight of the Sun, which requires the Almanac and data from the same Noon Sight taken for Longitude.

The above stuff is plenty to get you going, and very adequate to get you fixed on just where the heck you ended up at least once every 12 hours. Beyond that, if you really feel like learning, is where it gets more difficult but useful, allowing you to figure your position any time 2 or more celestial objects are visible.

# A note on old Nautical Almanacs:

You may want to save your out-of-date Almanacs. Every 4 years, the cycle of numbers starts over for the Sun and Stars, so that data is still good. The Moon and Planets tables, however, do not follow the same cycle and will be useless.

Small post-it notes or stick-on filing tabs from the office supply store make excellent page markers for quick reference.

*The best reference book in the world! The first one was published by the fifth Astronomer Royal Nevil Maskelyne in 1766, and since 1832 it has been kept up by Her Majesty's Nautical Almanac Office at the UK's Rutherford Appleton Laboratory.*

# Taking your sight:
## How do I read it?

When looking through the eyepiece, facing your target sun/star/planet, you find the horizon in one view, while you locate the target object in the opposite view. Finding the angle is as simple as manipulating the index mirror so as to line the target object up with the horizon. Wag the sextant side to side, and 'swing' the object, making sure it just brushes the horizon at its lowest point. Then read the angle off the sextant. Not all sextants are the same, so refer to your owner's manual on how to read the increments on your fine-adjustment knob.

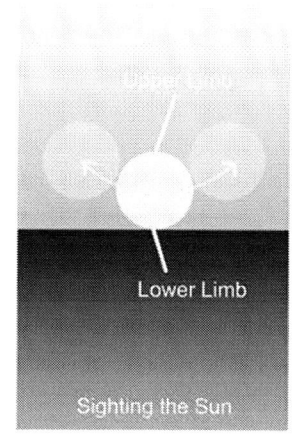
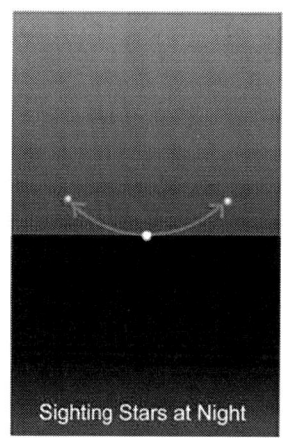

Since it is tough to figure exactly where the center of the sun (or moon) is to line it up, we typically (because it's easier to see) line it up by dropping the bottom edge of said object to where it just touches the horizon. Touching the bottom edge of the object to the horizon is referred to as using the Lower Limb of the object. For the sake of sanity, we'll always do Lower Limb sights.

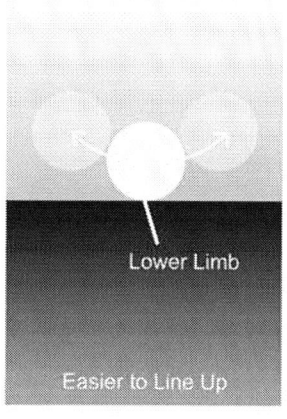
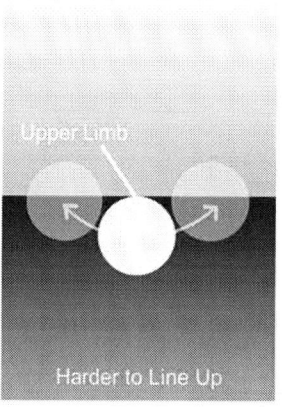

The sextant should have a rough adjustment for large movements, as well as a fine adjustment knob at the bottom of the index arm. If it has no fine adjustment, don't worry—you can still learn how to do this, there will just be a larger margin of error in your fixes (which is fine!).

When taking sights, it is best to take three sights and average the results. This will make up for minor errors in adjustment, as well as point out if you're making any major mistakes.

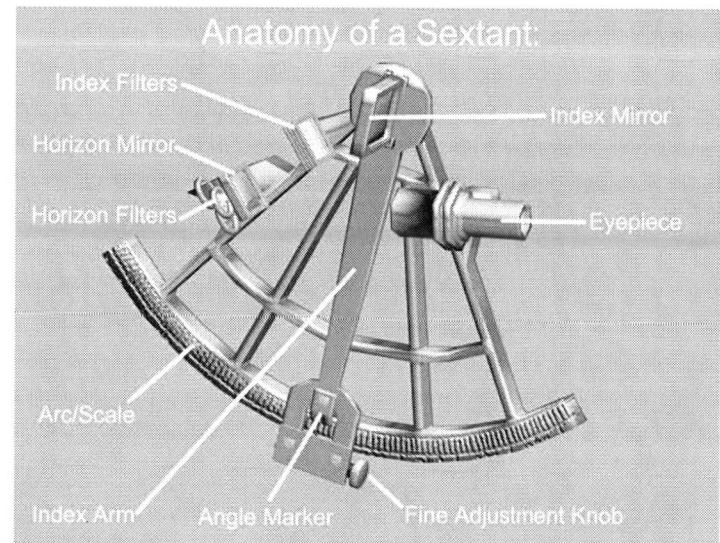

A sight consists of 3 parts: an angle, a celestial object, and a time. It helps to have an assistant ready to note the exact time the sight is taken. Once your sextant is aligned, say "Mark", and have them note the time. Then look at your sextant and tell them the measurement, and what you were looking at (Sun, Polaris, etc).

If you're on your own, the fastest way to do it is this: Line your sight up. Have a pencil ready. Bring your watch up in view and look at it with your free eye. Note the seconds first. Now put the sextant aside and write down that seconds reading. Then the minutes, then the hours. Mark down the sextant measurement last, as it's there to stay until you take your next sight.

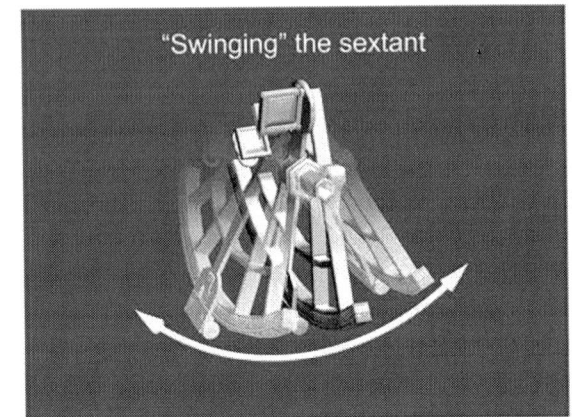
"Swinging" the sextant

There are naturally things that will affect your reading. These are:
- Your sextant may need adjustment or may always be off a bit (don't panic—this is ok, read on).
- Your eye may be at different heights when you take sights.
- The atmosphere acts like a lens and bends light.

Fortunately, once again, the Great Geeks of History in their vast triangular genius have calculated how to make up for these issues, and the solutions are all in that fantastic Nautical Almanac.

# Index Error and Index Correction:
## Not all sextants are created equal!

In order to get an accurate reading, you will need to find out the Index Error (so you can correct it with the Index Correction) of your sextant. This is easy to do—go anywhere you can see the horizon clearly in both mirrors, line them up, and see what the sextant reads. This number is your Index Error. No, your sextant is not defective. Every sextant has tiny differences, and their readings can be affected by age, temperature, number of times it's been dropped, etc. This is an important number to know, and you will need to compensate for it in every one of your calculations.

- *Index Error* is the amount "off center" your sextant is.
- *Index Correction* is the number you need to compensate and bring the sextant back to Zero. It is the exact opposite of Index Error. If your sextant is 1 minute in error, then the Index Correction is –1 minute. If your sextant is –2.3 minutes in error, your Index Correction is +2.3 minutes.

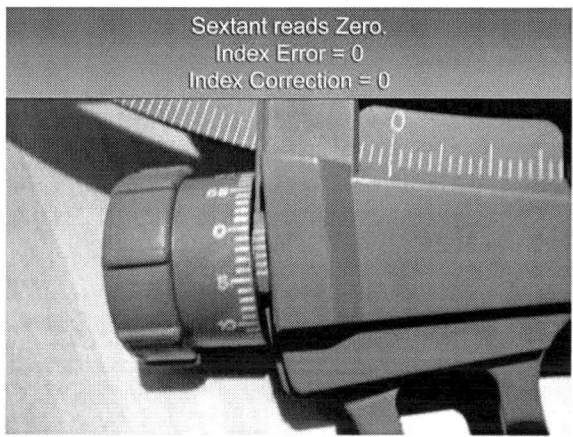

Sextant reads Zero.
Index Error = 0
Index Correction = 0

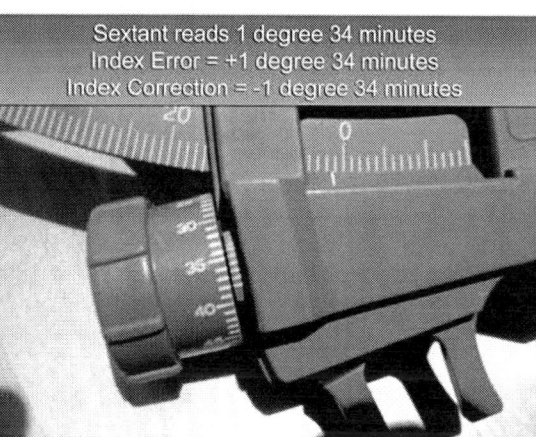

Sextant reads 1 degree 34 minutes
Index Error = +1 degree 34 minutes
Index Correction = -1 degree 34 minutes

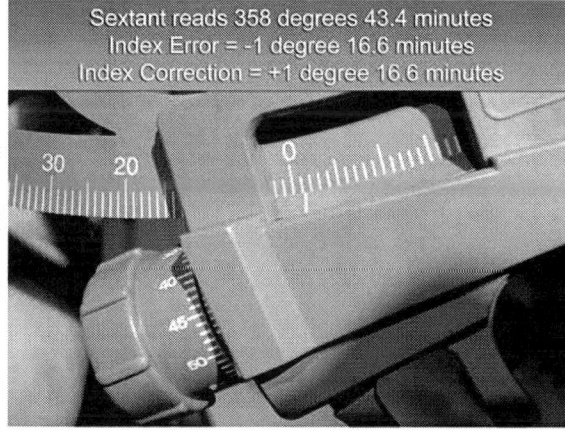

Sextant reads 358 degrees 43.4 minutes
Index Error = -1 degree 16.6 minutes
Index Correction = +1 degree 16.6 minutes

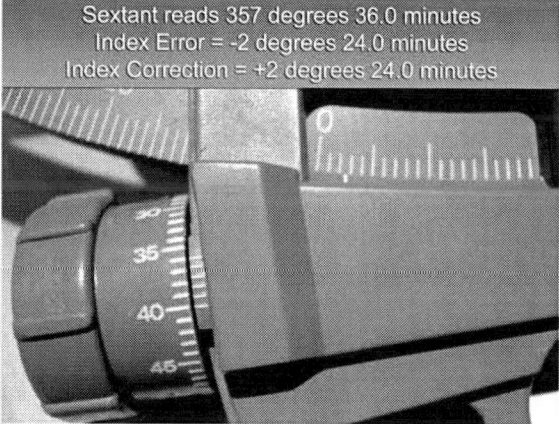

Sextant reads 357 degrees 36.0 minutes
Index Error = -2 degrees 24.0 minutes
Index Correction = +2 degrees 24.0 minutes

Some sextants have adjustment screws on their mirrors that can be used to 'zero' the sextant's measurement thereby removing Index Error from the equation. You should zero your sextant or re-calculate your Index Correction every week or so as the seasons/temperatures change to make your readings the most accurate.

Plastic sextants expand and contract quite a bit depending on temperature. Metal sextants change less, but are more expensive. They still measure the same things; it's just a matter of preference and how you'll be using your sextant. If you only want it as backup, or just to learn, go with a cheaper plastic one. If you are really jazzed about the whole concept of Cel Nav later on, then you may want to invest in a metal sextant.

*Helpful hint:* While we're at this point where we begin discussing what we call Sight Corrections, write down your Index Correction (not index error) on a card or slip of paper, and tape it to the inside of your sextant case.

# Dip Correction :
## Where are you taking the sight from?

Sextant sights are full of little Sight Corrections depending on time of year, atmospheric refraction; the list goes on and on. The higher your eye is above sea level, the larger your angle will be when sighting your celestial target. This needs a correction in your calculations, and this is called your Dip Correction.

The first thing you need to know is how high your eye is from the ground (sea). It should be pretty easy to figure out, and it doesn't have to be super-accurate, just a rough guess. For example, if you're on the deck of a boat that is 4 feet above sea level, and your eye is 5 feet above that, your eye height will be 9 feet.

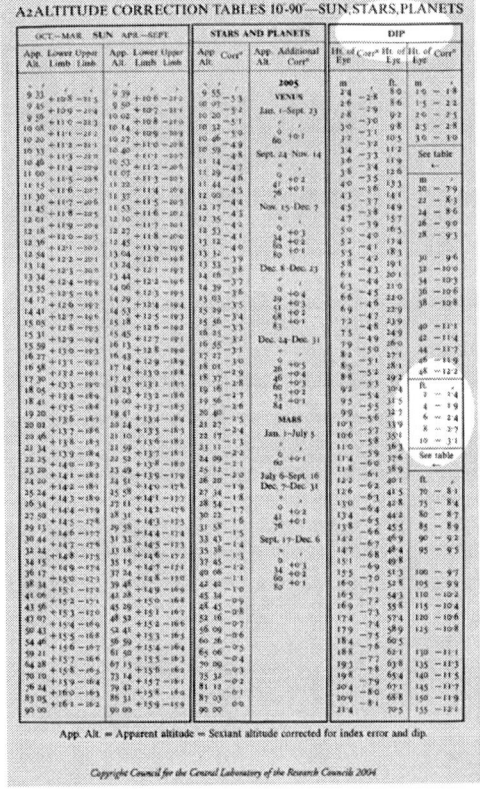

There is a table in your Nautical Almanac which tells you your Dip Correction based on that height. It should be a yellow page, near the front of the book, and it is usually on a heavier grade paper than the rest of the pages. If you do not have the yellow page, this table will be on page A2 in the front of your almanac.

The top of the page should read "Altitude Correction Tables – Sun, Stars, Planets". It has 3 columns, the right-most of which is "Dip". Find your eye height, and then find your dip correction next to it, in minutes and seconds.

Take a moment to find your 2 common Dip Corrections for, say, standing on your front deck and sitting in your cockpit, and write them down on the paper you taped inside your sextant case.

**Dip corrections are ALWAYS SUBTRACTED from your sextant angle.**

# Apparent Altitude (with semi-important vague geek trivia):

Your sextant sight, corrected for Index Error and Dip, is called "Apparent Altitude." Why it is done this way *before* the Refraction and Semi-diameter corrections were included is beyond my knowledge and understanding, and it is likely that some dead famous Geek of History took the secret to his grave. Nonetheless, you cannot determine your Refraction or Semi-Diameter corrections unless you first have your Apparent Altitude.

# Atmospheric Refraction :
## The curvature of the Earth's atmosphere bends light.

As light enters the Earth's atmosphere, it bends (refracts), meaning that the source of the light is not really located in the exact direction you are looking at it from. Don't worry—it's easy to figure out how to correct for this. It's all written down in that handy Nautical Almanac.

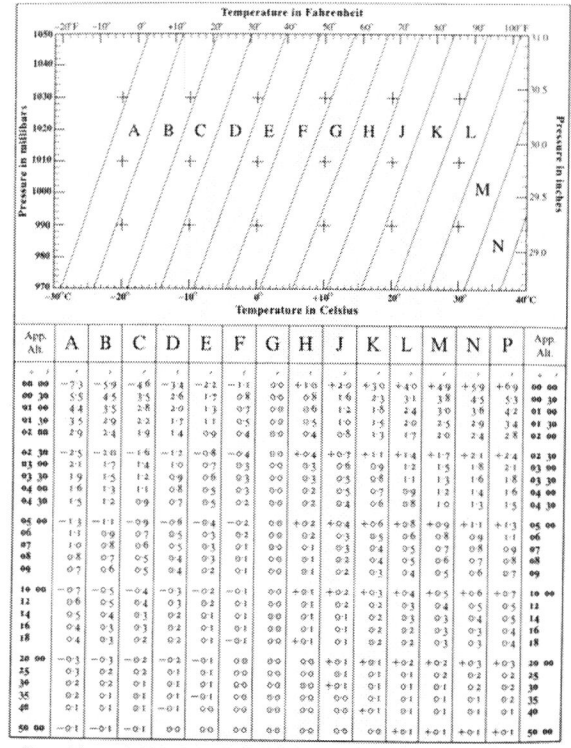

In the front of your Nautical Almanac is a page (page A4) with tables to find your atmospheric refraction correction. The top of the page reads, "Altitude Correction Tables – Additional Corrections"

The top table is for temperature and barometric pressure adjustments. The temperature and pressure should coincide with a letter-coded zone on the chart. If you don't know your barometric pressure, just use the letter in the column for temperature. Keep that letter in mind for the next table.

The chart on the bottom is what is important. Basically, the more atmosphere you have to look through, the more light bends. When you are looking at an object near the horizon, its light is bent the most—you are looking through much more air at the horizon. The light from directly overhead is bent the least.

Your apparent altitude is what you use to look up this atmospheric correction. Use the columns at either side to find your apparent altitude, then work your way across to the column that coincides with the letter you found in the top (temperature/pressure) table. Write this number down on your worksheet.

# Altitude/Semi-Diameter Correction:

The Sun is fat. So is the Moon. Since they consume space in our eyepiece, and because of how the sextant works, we find it easier to match their edge to the horizon, rather than their center. The angle you measure with the object's top edge on the horizon will obviously differ from its bottom edge touching, and this difference is called Semi-Diameter Correction.

Stars and planets, since they are so far away and appear so tiny, do not require semi-diameter correction.

Now, on Pages A2 and A3 in your Nautical Almanac, "Altitude Correction Tables – Sun, Stars, Planets", you will see a column for "Sun" with 2 columns denoting monthly ranges on either side. Find your month's side, and read down the Apparent Altitude column until you find the number closest to your Apparent Altitude. Note that the corrections are listed for ranges of numbers (for example, An Apparent Altitude of 85 degrees during Apr-Sept will have a +15.8 minute correction for the sun, and a –0.1 correction for stars.)

You'll notice that the Sun's correction hovers around +16 or –16, and changes as it gets closer to the horizon (this is due to our old friend Atmospheric Refraction). The "Fat" objects in the sky are the Sun and the Moon. Since the Moon is so close, so fat, and has its own special goofy orbit, it has its own special page of corrections in the back of the Almanac.

So why do we even need Upper Limb? Well, if the sun or moon's Lower Limb is obscured by clouds (or if you can't see the Moon's lower limb due to its current phase), you can still measure it by its top edge.

Find where your reading falls in the column, and add that number to your now full-grown list of onerous corrections.

## Parallax:

While learning, you may find references to "Parallax Correction". Parallax defined is the angular difference in direction of a celestial body as measured from two points on the earth's orbit. You shouldn't have to worry about it with stars, since they are tiny points in the sky, *very* far away and therefore the measurements are microscopically negligible. It is an issue present with the sun and moon, however, since they are close to us. Modern almanac data includes this amount in the Semi-Diameter corrections for the Sun. The Moon has its own page of Parallax corrections in the back of the Almanac.

So don't get worried; just know that it's there, hiding—this explanation is just so you don't panic, thinking you are forgetting to calculate something.

## Complete Sight Summary:
1. Take your sight.
2. Add Index Correction (if applicable).
3. Subtract Dip correction.
4. Add Refraction correction.
5. Add Altitude/Semidiameter (SD) correction
6. Add Parallax correction (if applicable)
7. All done!

## Beginners' tips for getting the aim right:

You may find it hard at first to get your target object lined up in the mirrors. It's a lot of sky to scan and small mirrors to fit it into. Don't worry, I had that problem too, still have it sometimes.

Set your sextant to 0 degrees, with the horizon in both views. Then, with both index and horizon filters on, look up directly at the sun. If it's too bright, flip down some more filters until it's easy to see but not burning holes through your skull.

Now hold the index arm steady, and tilt the sextant instead. Slowly tilt the sextant down while opening the angle, keeping the sun in your index mirror as you bring the horizon into view. If you have to stop halfway to get the horizon filter out of the way, it's ok. Voila! Much easier.

# How the Earth is Measured:

The Earth is divided top-to-bottom by horizontal lines of Latitude (like a sandwich), and cut into vertical wedges by lines of Longitude (like an orange). The diameter of Latitude sections varies, while diameter of Longitude remains the same.

The Equator is 0 degrees Latitude. Counting from there, each degree of Latitude increases, until it reaches each of the poles at 90 degrees, North and South, respectively.

Longitude lines split the Earth vertically into wedges, like the segments of an orange.

Counting the lines is slightly more complex than Latitude: Since the lines branch from the poles, how do we determine where the counting should "start" from? We need a zero, a point of origin, known as the Prime Meridian. Who decides where it is?

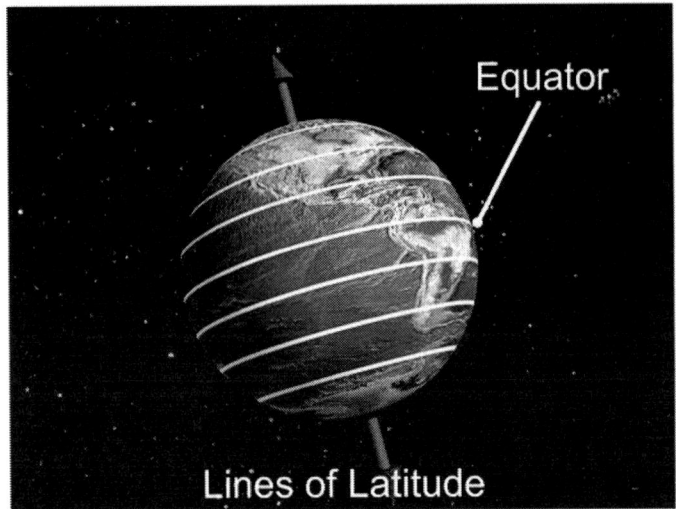

Back in the old days of early exploration, every country had its own idea of where the Prime Meridian ought to be located. Eventually they all got tired of running their expensive galleons up onto the rocks halfway across the world so they all jumped on the bandwagon with the British, who declared that their Prime Meridian, 0 degrees, is at Greenwich. And there it lies to this day.

Except for the stubborn French, big surprise, who finally gave in only 150 years ago and changed their Prime Meridian from Paris to Greenwich.

Starting from that point in Greenwich, the wedges of Longitude count to 180 degrees East or West respectively, where they meet at the opposite side of the Earth at the International Date Line.

As the lines of Longitude approach the poles, they get mashed closer and closer together. Lines of Latitude, however, always remain the same distance apart no matter how close to the poles you are. Thus, the actual counting of distance East to West decreases the farther North or South of the Equator you are traveling. Keep this in mind for chart navigation as well as advanced celestial navigation later on.

International Date Line

Prime Meridian

# Basic Latitude Fix:

Beginning with the easiest,

## Latitude by Polaris (generic format)

Remember the rhyme Lat is Fat! The sandwich stacking concept might help nail this one into your brain.

Your Latitude, the lines that fatten at the equator, splitting the earth into 'horizontal' discs, is the easiest fix to figure out with a sextant sight. Fortunately, there is a star (Polaris) that is almost perfectly aligned with the polar axis of our planet Earth, and if you can see it, you can measure your latitude. You don't even need to know the time.

You can only do this easy sight, however, if you are in the Northern Hemisphere, i.e., north of the Equator, as Polaris is otherwise hidden by the curvature of the Earth.

The easiest way to find Polaris is to find the end of the Little Dipper's handle. Or, trace a line from the pouring edge of the Big Dipper. Imagine it is pouring a perfect straight line upward (from the bottom to the rim). The imaginary line will run right into Polaris. The Big Dipper spins around Polaris, so be prepared to see the following diagram in any position.

*How to find Polaris*

To make the most generic of generic celestial sights, line up Polaris with the horizon in your sextant. Add (or subtract) your Index Error and Dip Error, and there you have it. This number is your general Latitude, and should be accurate to an average of 55 miles. This is how they did it in the old days before timepieces, when voyaging ships would travel north or south first, lining themselves up with the known Latitude of their destination, and then sail east or west until they arrived.

But a whole 55 miles of error! Possibly more!?! Well, it's enough to keep ancient mariners from running into most charted islands (give 'er a good wide berth there, matey!), and enough to get them reasonably close to the port they wanted. Beyond that, like Captain Ron navigates, if they needed to know where they were, they just stopped somewhere and asked directions, or skewered the locals with rusty cutlasses until they pointed the way.

Until the age of clocks and Isaac Newton and the Great Geeks of History, though, you were pretty much stuck with Polaris and its potential error margin. Here's why: Polaris isn't 100% perfect. Even though it's closely aligned to the Earth's pole; It has a slight wobble which can be corrected for in more advanced sighting calculations, which we will cover later (If Polaris were attached to the Earth, it would be about 47 miles from the North Pole). But for now, hopefully you understand the basic concept of Latitude by Polaris and how your sextant measures the angle of a celestial object.

*Polaris is lined up nearly perfectly with Earth's axis.*

# The Noon Sight

## Longitude by Noon Sight.

Finding Latitude by a star that "never moves" is easy enough, but how do we figure out Longitude when the planet is spinning and there is no object in the sky around our equator that "holds still?" Fortunately for the lost souls of the world, the sun is absolutely guaranteed be overhead once every 24 hours for the next few hundred million years.

One benefit to the Noon Sight is that you don't need any Dead Reckoning or Assumed Position (explained later on) in order to build a fix. You can be absolutely 100% lost; so long as you have the correct date and time, you can take a noon sight and un-lose yourself.

It's easier to understand just about all of Celestial Navigation if you think of the earth as the center of the universe, with the sun and stars spinning around it. We'll speak in these terms to keep it easy.

Every 24 hours, the Sun "orbits" around the Earth one time. The earth is divided into 360 degrees of Longitude. Divide 360 degrees by 24 hours and you find that the sun passes 15 degrees around the earth for every hour. The old guys in funny wigs discovered that if you had an accurate way to measure time, you could find out your Longitude by calculating where the sun passes over. But how do we find the time if noon happens 24 hours a day anywhere on earth wherever the sun is directly overhead (and like Alan Jackson and Jimmy Buffett sing, "It's 5 o'clock somewhere")??? We need some point of reference to time things by. This is why, in the beginning, I stressed the importance of having a watch set to…

## Greenwich Mean Time:

At some point, the old guys in funny wigs decided that the Royal Observatory in Greenwich (London) ought to be that reference point: the standard for true Noon, because hey, if we're figuring out all this stuff, the center of our observations may as well be right where the geeks are doing the research. It's not important how or why, really, only that a center point had to be decided and it's been declared that Noon at Greenwich is "True Noon". Noon at Greenwich is 12:00 GMT (Greenwich Mean Time). This line of Longitude where Greenwich lies is also called the Prime Meridian, or Zero degrees. On the opposite side of the earth, 180 degrees away or 12 hours of the sun's passage, is the international date line: 24:00 hours and 0 hours simultaneously.

Other books will tell you all sorts of tricky stuff about calculating time to account for Longitude differences, but it's all 100% garbage and you can throw it all away if you set a watch to GMT. All your calculations are going to be based on GMT, so why add the burden of extra math? Save your brain!

# Geographic Position (GP):

If the sun were attached to the earth on a stick, like the knob at the top of a flagpole, the base of that flagpole would be its GP, or Geographic Position (the actual pole part, for you trivia geeks, is called the Zenith). In our simple Geocentric model of the universe, of course, the sun spins around the earth, so the flagpole's base is going to move. And since the earth is on a tilt and doesn't exactly sit straight, the sun's 'base' will be at different places at different times of the year, different Latitudes and Longitudes. This is why we have the Nautical Almanac—it tells us when and where the base will be at any given hour, minute, and second during the year. This flagpole base/GP also tells us on what meridian (Longitude) Local Noon is, since the sun is at its highest point overhead.

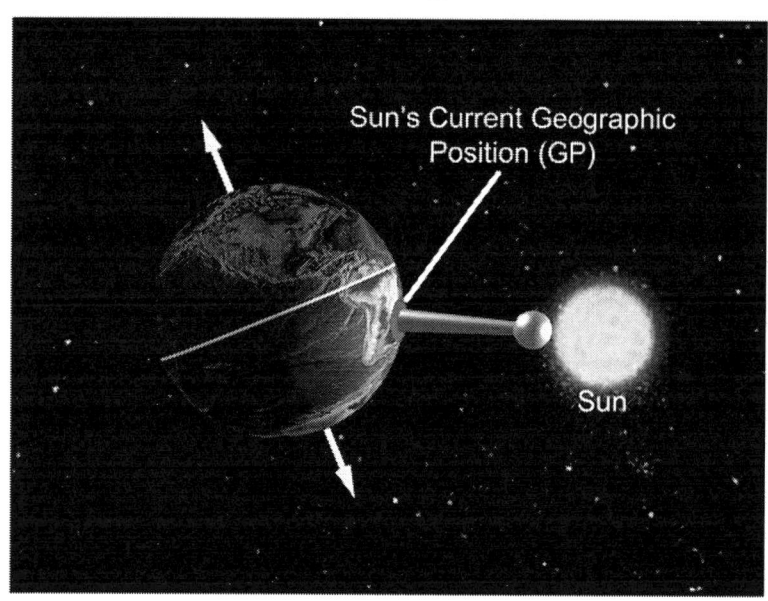

Since we have a base of standard time to go by (Greenwich time), we know the sun was directly overhead there at 12:00 GMT. Now suppose we're halfway across the globe, in uncharted seas, and we have no idea what our Latitude is. We've got a clock set to GMT. All we have to do is find out our Local Noon, and compare it to Greenwich's noon, and the difference will tell us our Longitude.

The Sun isn't the only thing with a GP. Every celestial object spins "around" the earth, each attached to its own 'flagpole', the base of which is that object's GP. The GP of each of these objects for every day, hour, minute, and second can be looked up in the Nautical Almanac.

## Finding Local Noon:

How do we find Local Noon? Easy, with the sextant and our trusty clock (which is set to GMT). Using your sextant, start taking sights around when you think noon will be, say, every 5 minutes, for about 30 minutes before and 30 minutes after. Your measurements should rise, then plateau, then begin to decrease again. Your highest sight will be the moment Local Noon occurred (or close enough to it to get a fix within a few miles of your actual location), and should have a time written next to the sight. Now you know your Local Noon.

For figuring out Local Noon, it's not even important what your sextant reading *is*, so much as that you know which time you took your highest measurement. You can do this by measuring shadows if you like. If you're ever marooned on a desert island with a single tree for shade and your GMT watch, you can at least figure out what your Longitude is, so you have something logical to scream out over the empty ocean.

OK, so now we have this sight of the Sun from Local Noon- with angle and time. What do we do with it?

## How to break it all down into a Longitude measurement:

The measured angle is not important right now except for knowing that it was at its highest, which marked noon. We'll use the actual measurement later to find your Latitude.

What did your GMT clock say? Let's suppose it said 04:55:30. This means there is a 7 hours 4 minutes 30 seconds difference between Local Noon and Greenwich Noon. It's easier to break it all down to minutes to do the math.

How many minutes away is Greenwich noon?
7 hours = 420 minutes
4 minutes = 4 minutes
30 seconds = .5 minutes.
**Total = 424.5 minutes until Greenwich Noon.**

Always use GMT Noon as your reference point for noon sights—it's much easier this way! If you took your noon sight *after* GMT Noon, then count backward to find out how many hours it was since then.

The sun passes 15 degrees of Longitude for every hour in orbit.
15 degrees / 60 minutes = 0.25 degrees per minute = 15 minutes of Longitude arc per minute of time

In essence, for every minute of time, the sun travels across the sky 15 minutes of Longitude. Yes, this is a little confusing, comparing minutes of time to minutes of Longitude. Just keep in mind that Time Minutes are not the same as Longitude Minutes. They are not related in any other way than that they share the same name. Those old guys in funny wigs liked to confuse people.

**424.5** *minutes of time* **x 15** *minutes of arc per minute* = **6367.5** *minutes of arc from Greenwich.*
**6367.5** *minutes of arc / 60 (minutes/degree conversion)* = **106.125** *degrees of longitude from Greenwich.*
**.125** *degrees* **x 60** = **7.5** *minutes of longitude.*

*In a logical world, our Longitude **would** come to **106 degrees, 7 minutes, 30 seconds**. But it **doesn't**! Read on to find out why!*

The universe isn't perfect and it's determined to foul up the accuracy of your reading, which can be a long way off. Here's how to fix it--

# The Equation of Time Correction

"Why are you telling me this NOW?" you ask. Because to understand the concept of Equation of Time, you need to first understand how time relates to the turning of the earth and its measurements of longitude. Which we just covered on the preceding pages. Now for the shocking truth that will ruin your day:

Just because it's noon at Greenwich does not mean the sun is always at its highest point there. The Earth's orbit isn't a perfect circle; it's egg-shaped. It causes noon to shift early or late up to 16 minutes depending on the time of year.

Longitude is, theoretically, sort of set up like a clock. As the Sun spins around the Earth, the lines of Longitude tick away. Or so your brain would make you think. Averaged out over the long term, it makes sense. To understand this concept, the easiest way to think of it is that we have a Sun with a split personality. One is the Good Sun, and one is his evil twin, the Bad Sun.

Long ago in a Happy Land with rainbows and world peace, the Good Sun passed overhead at Greenwich every day at 12:00GMT, without fail. Clocks were set to the Good Sun. Everyone cheered and held ticker-tape parades, beer was always cold, there were real virgins to sacrifice, and life was good and wholesome.

But then evil struck Happy Land! Their leaders brought about income tax and spoiled Happy Land for good. The planets fell out of alignment, the Earth's perfect circular orbit became egg-shaped, and the Sun went Bad! He shaved his head, wore a leather jacket, and became a chronic underachiever: always late or always early, and he only arrives right on time a few days every year. To this day, though, we still keep our clocks accurate in the hopes that the Bad Sun will see the error of his ways and become the Good Sun again. The only consolation is that the Bad Sun's fashionable lateness or earliness is very predictable, and his habits are kept track of in the Nautical Almanac.

Our time is based on where the Good Sun would be. The Good Sun would be the equivalent of a clock. We can't follow that clock around in the sky, though. Cruel reality dictates that when you are finding Local Noon, you're finding the Local Noon of the Bad Sun. Since the Bad Sun is always late or early, you will be too, and this will throw off your Longitude fix.

The Great Geeks of History, in their vigilance to rid the Earth of fashionably late rebels who woo their girls away, have figured out how to shape up the Bad Sun's mistakes and the corrections are in the Nautical Almanac. The Equation of Time correction makes up for the difference in how early or how late our Bad Sun is, and therefore makes up for the fudge in your Longitude. It is measured in units of time, not units of Longitude.

## Where do I find it?

Let's say today is June 10, 2005. Open your Nautical Almanac to that page. In the lower right hand corner of each page is a small square area with the Sun, Moon, and Equation of Time. We have the date in the left column, and three more columns under the Sun of 00h and 12h, and Mer.Pass (Meridian Passage).

Let's talk about the Meridian Passage first. Meridian Passage tells us just what time it was in Greenwich when the sun was directly overhead.

The 00h column represents the difference in time between Greenwich midnight and where the sun will be in relation to the International Date Line.

The 12h column represents the difference in time between Greenwich noon and the Sun's real position overhead.

So on the 10th of June 2005, we see that Greenwich's Local Noon is 11:59, and that the 00h difference is 40 seconds, and the 12h difference is 34 seconds. The sun is moving fast, making it directly overhead early in Greenwich, at 11:59 (34 seconds ahead of schedule, like the table says). To make time equal again at Greenwich (hence Equation of Time), we'd have to add 34 seconds to Greenwich's clocks, and to our sight time as well. To make time equal again if we were shooting noon on the other half of the world (closer to the International Date Line), we'd have to add 40 seconds.

*Helpful Hint: Numbers in grey boxes represent negative numbers. Numbers with no shading are positive numbers. This is usually the case for any greyed area you find in the Almanac. Any equation of time in grey, subtract. Any without grey, add.*

Since these corrections will not increase or decrease more than a second or two in a given half-day, the easiest way to figure your correction is to base it off your current time or uncorrected Longitude (are you closer to the Prime Meridian, or the International Date Line?). Since your sight was taken at 4:55am, you are closer to 00h than 12h GMT, so take the 00h correction and add it (if it's not grey!) to your Longitude. If it was shaded grey, you should subtract that amount from your Longitude.

There are 2 ways of figuring in the Equation of Time. The easiest is to sum it with your sight time, and calculate it all down through the worksheet. One can also figure it into the end of the sight, by converting the minutes and seconds of time into minutes and seconds of longitude. We'll do it the easy way, of course.

## Breaking it Down:

Time: 04:55:30.
How many minutes away is Greenwich noon?
7 hours = 420 minutes
4 minutes = 4 minutes
30 seconds = .5 minutes.
**Total = 424.5 minutes until Greenwich Noon.**
  **+34 seconds or .56 minutes (Equation of Time correction)**
  **= 425.06 minutes until Greenwich Noon.** *For simplicy, strip the .06 for the following:*

**425** *minutes of time* **x 15** *minutes of arc per minute* = **6375** *minutes of arc from Greenwich.*
**6375** *minutes of arc* / **60** *(minutes/degree conversion)* = **106.25** *degrees of longitude from Greenwich.*
**.25** *degrees* **x 60** = **15** *minutes of longitude.*

*Your Longitude comes to* **106 degrees, 15 minutes.**

**Now, is that East or West Longitude?** If you don't know what half of the globe you are on, you need some serious help. But fortunately, you can still figure it out with simple logic. Your local noon was before Greenwich's noon. Since the sun rises from the East and sets to the West, this means you are in the Eastern Hemisphere, and naturally your Longitude is 106 degrees East, 15 minutes. Had your local noon been after Greenwich's noon, your Longitude would have been West.

## Review:
1. Take sights until you catch local noon.
2. Gather almanac information.
3. Determine local time difference from GMT.
4. Apply Equation of Time correction.
5. Convert time to distance.
6. Determine hemisphere.
7. Celebrate!

*Geek stuff for much later once you have mastered the book: There is a third way to determine the Equation of Time correction, and that is to calculate its value by 15 degrees arc per minute plus the Sun's GHA correction in the gray-tabbed "Increments and Corrections" tables, and add it to the end result. Why can't the Almanac Geeks just automatically calculate it for you in degrees, minutes, and seconds of arc in the first place??? The world may never know... Ponder this, young grasshopper.*

That wraps it up for Longitude by Noon Sight. Below is a worksheet that will make the work flow much more organized and sensible. Feel free to make copies.

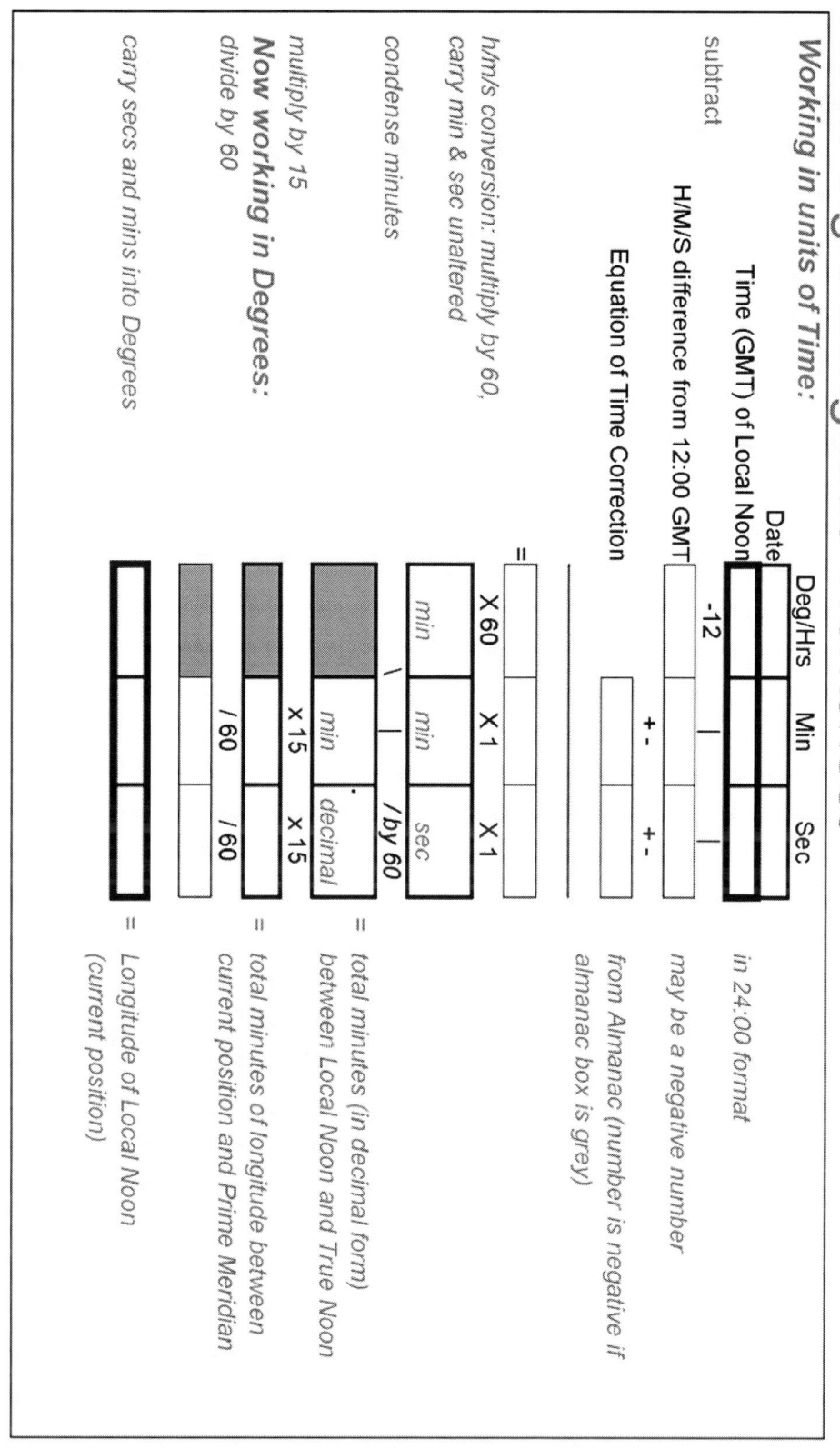

# Latitude by Noon Sight:

The Earth's axis is off-kilter in comparison to its orbit around the Sun, which explains why we have Summers and Winters. At the Summer and Winter Solstices, the Sun is at its most extreme angle, roughly 23.5 degrees from the Equator (these lines are also known as the Tropics). The rest of the year it is at a varying angle, going up or down to the Equator (on the Equinoxes) and on to the other side as the days pass.

Unless you are on the Equator or Tropics at noon during an Equinox or Solstice (during which you will not NEED to find your Latitude, because you know you are on the bloody Equator or Tropics!), you can use the Sun's "Declination" to find out what your Latitude is.

## What in the heck is Declination?

Declination is an angle measurement. Simply put, it is the angle drawn from the Equator, to the center of the Earth, to the object in the sky. This number is also the Latitude coordinate of the object's current Geographic Position (aka GP, the base of the flagpole).

Declination = Geographic Position Latitide = GP Latitude

It's no wonder why those OTHER books (you know who you are!) confuse us. Everything in Celestial Navigation has too many names to describe one thing.

Let's look back at our horribly wrong but easy-to-understand Geocentric model of the universe. The Sun is mounted at the top of our flagpole. Its base (or GP, as we discussed earlier), is just a set of coordinates (Latitude and Longitude) that tell us where the base is located on the Earth's surface.

We've already figured out where its Longitude is, by comparing our Local Noon to GMT Noon. Since the Great Geeks of History have marked down where the Sun will be on any day at any time, we can also now look up its Latitude (and therefore find ours) by comparing the angles.

# How to calculate the Sun's Declination:

Think back to the section on taking and correcting a sight. Yeah, you know the one. 10 pages ago in the part of the book that actually made sense. We're going to apply those same correction numbers to your Sun sight.

## Information from before:
- The date is the 10th of June 2005.
- We did our noon sights and determined that our local noon was 04:55:30 GMT, placing us on Longitude 106 degrees, 15 minutes.
- Just for example let's say that our sextant's noon sight reads, "55 degrees, 5.2 minutes."

We know our date, our local noon, and where the sun *appears to be* from our vantage point. But to figure out where we are, we need one more piece of information: Where is the base of that flagpole (The Sun's real Latitude/Declination)?

That piece of information is in your Nautical Almanac, which is probably starting to look dog-eared from all the attention it's been getting.

## Step 1: Find the Sun's Declination in the Almanac.

Open your Nautical Almanac to today's date, June 10, 2005. On the left, you see a column labeled "UT" for Universal Time, also known as Greenwich Mean Time or GMT (gotta love those many-named concepts!). Your sight was taken at 4:55:30.

Read down the column for the 10th, at 4 hours. Now slide sideways into the "Dec" (declination) column. You see the number 01.0. Unfortunately, this is not the full number we need-- there's more to it! Look up and down, and a space to the left, for the full degree number (labeled N or S appropriately). For some reason they do not print the full degree measurement on every line. **Make it a habit to check for that intermittently printed degree measurement.**

Read correctly, we should have N23 degrees, 1.0 minutes. Not far from the Tropics, not surprisingly, since it is only 11 days until the Solstice.

# Step 2: That little lowercase d, and the almanac's Increments and Corrections pages.

**Shortcut Alert: You can easily skip this correction for a Noon Sight by just using the Sun's dec on the Date Page for the hour your sight fell closest to.** However, do please read this, as the "d" number is very much needed for the moon and planets since they have their own orbits, which are not parallel with the Earth's spin.

At the very bottom of every sun column there are 2 numbers, "SD" and a lowercase "d" with a number. The SD is only for super-geeks and we'll never use it, so ignore that. The little "d" however is something we might want. You'll recognize that it matches the increments of declination for every hour in the Sun column.

We accounted for 4 hours of the Sun's passage, but the Sun never stops moving through the sky-- now we need to account for the remaining 55 minutes 30 seconds and find out how far it has gone in that time. It won't be significant but it can make your sight more accurate by a mile or two. You can save time and skip this step by grabbing the closest Dec measurement to your hour from the Date Page, or averaging the difference if you're in the middle of the hour.

Since declination moves so slowly, we can be even lazier and we don't even need to account for the 30 seconds, just the 55 minutes.

Flip to the back of the Nautical Almanac, into the gray-edged pages labeled "Increments and Corrections" at the top. These are separated into minutes and seconds, from 0 to 59, all the way through an entire hour of time. Turn through until you find the column for "55m".

Here's a place I got stumped before, because you'll notice that the "v or d" and "Corr" columns are lined up with the times and the sun/stars/planets information. *They are not related, other than to the whole minute of time on that page. These columns are independent of the second increments-- only pay attention to the v/d numbers (listed vertically) and its corresponding correction value (to the right, labeled "v or d corr")*

34

The way this works, is that there are 3 columns of "v or d" with "Corr" beside each. With the "d" number from before, we look down the columns until we find that number under "v or d". The number beside it, under "Corr" is how we adjust our declination for the minutes that have passed. It's rarely a large number, which is why it should be considered optional.

Now do we add or subtract this number? The answer depends on how the declination of the sun is progressing. Passing from winter to summer, the sun increases its declination, and from summer to winter decreases. It's easy to see what is going on by just reading the numbers down the almanac page. If the numbers are climbing, declination is increasing, so you will add the "d" correction. If the numbers are falling, then you subtract the "d".

Of course, this can all be scrapped, sanity saved, without a further thought if you just take the number closest to your current hour!!!

## A note on the "v or d" corrections:

You'll see a little "v" hiding to the left of the "d" at the bottom of your daily almanac pages. The "v" is under GHA, and the "d" is under Dec. Well, we know that "d" is related to Dec, so is "v" related to GHA? Yes! What is GHA? It stands for Greenwich Hour Angle, and we'll get to that in a few pages.

While "d" accounts for minor goofiness in objects' declinations, "v" accounts for minor goofiness in their GHA. These weird minor differences are here to account for the uneven, egg shaped orbit of the Earth. This doesn't have any effect on our Noon sight, but you may want to keep it in mind later for planet and moon sights.

There is no v correction for Sun sights, because it is included in its GHA and Equation of Time already (ever notice how GHA Sun at noon is never quite 0 or 360 degrees? It's the Bad Sun!).

## Step 3: Corrected Declination of the Sun

The table's declination of the sun for 4 hours is 23 degrees, 1.0 minutes. If we took the closest hour shortcut, we'd have a declination of 23 degrees, 1.2 minutes. If we used the optional "lowercase d" method, we'd still have arrived at 23 degrees, 1.2 minutes. As you can see, Dec changes very slowly, and you can probably figure out the "d" correction on your own just by looking at the Dec increments between the hours on the dated Almanac page.

## Step 4: Calculate the Height Observed of the Sun. (aka Corrected Altitude aka Adjusted Sextant Angle, blah!)

There are a million names for each concept in Celestial Navigation. It's tough! I'll try to use just one, and that will be Height Observed, because it appears so often in other Cel Nav stuff, and it is the only one that matches the HO abbreviation that is also so often used.

Lower limb observation: **55** degrees **5.2** minutes
Index correction: **+1** minute (suppose we dropped the sextant and it's been a minute off ever since!)
Dip correction: **-3** minutes

*Totaled, this gives us our lovely Apparent Altitude of **55** degrees, **3.2** minutes.*

***From this, we determine the following additional corrections:***

Refraction correction: **+0** (suppose 70 degrees F temperature) Note that since this particular sight is so high in the sky, there is a ZERO refraction correction.

Semi-Diameter correction, lower limb: **+15.6** minutes

*This gives us a final Height Observed (aka Corrected Altitude) of **55** degrees, **18.8** minutes.*

# Step 5: Grade School Math: What is the difference in our angles?

The altitude (sextant angle) of the sun at its GP (base) will always be 90 degrees—it's directly overhead there, I guarantee it. If you were standing at that base point and took a sight, you'd come up with 90 degrees every time.

90 degrees *(Sun's GP altitude, always 90 degrees)*
- 55 degrees, 18.8 minutes *(Height Observed)*
---
34 degrees, 40.2 minutes *(our distance from the Sun's GP/base)*

# Where is the Sun and Where are You?

If you don't know, you have major problems that I don't think I can help you with. Here it gets a little confusing, but trust me—I'll pull you through it. There are several ways, but this is the simplest way to do it. You don't need to understand the logic, just follow the rule and you'll do fine:

- If the Sun is in the same hemisphere as your boat, ADD the Declination. The result is your Latitude. Hint: Summer usually means same hemisphere.
- If the Sun is in the opposite hemisphere as your boat, SUBTRACT the Declination. The result is your Latitude. Hint: Winter usually means opposite hemisphere.

***FUNKY RULE:*** *There is sometimes a special case, when you are near the Equator and the Sun is between you and your current hemisphere's pole. This is rare, since the sun can be a maximum of 23.5 degrees North or South of the Equator, and only on Solstices at that! But if you find yourself in such a funky situation, follow this funky rule:*

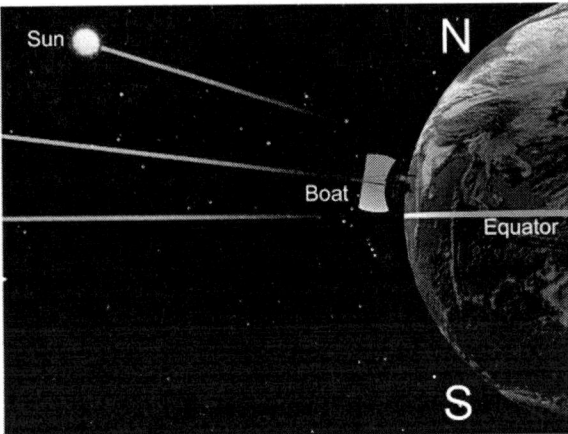

- If the Sun is North of the Equator and North of you, SUBTRACT the Declination. You will end up with a negative number. Pretend it is a positive number (use its absolute value). This is your North Latitude.

- If the Sun is South of the Equator, and South of you, SUBTRACT the Declination. You will end up with a negative number. Pretend it is a positive number (use its absolute value). This is your South Latitude.

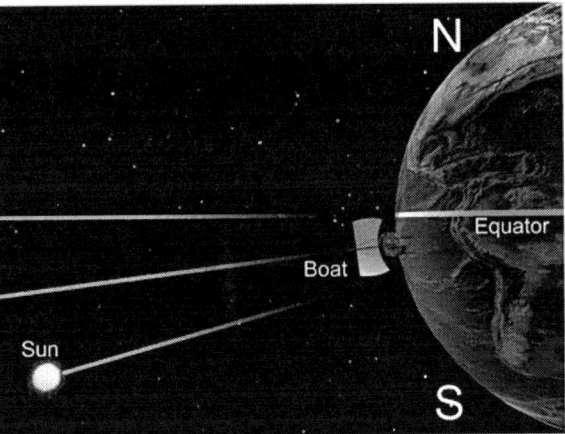

- If you ended up with a positive number for any of these "Funky Rule" calculations, you are not in the hemisphere you thought you were!!! The odds are against you being in that funky shallow equatorial zone where you will be doing funky math, so when in doubt, assume that the world is normal and go by the original rule.

| What Hemisphere? | | Sun's relation to you? | What do you do with the Sun's Declination? |
|---|---|---|---|
| You | Sun | | |
| N | N | N | Subtract & use abs. value |
| N | N | S | Add |
| N | S | S | Subtract |
| S | N | N | Subtract |
| S | S | N | Add |
| S | S | S | Subtract & use abs. value |

**Declination Math Table**

*So, now we know how to tackle this equation.*

34 degrees, 40.2 minutes *(our distance from the Sun's GP/base)*
+ N23 degrees, 1.2 minutes *(the Sun's Declination, North Hemisphere, was south of us = add!)*
---
N57 degrees, 41.4 minutes.

N 57 degrees, 41.4 minutes by E 106 degrees, 15 minutes puts us, uhm, smack dab in the mountains of Irkutsk, Russia, 180 miles northwest of Lake Baykal, the deepest lake in the world! But hey, for grabbing numbers out of thin air, at least we know where we landed!

Below is a worksheet that will make the workflow much more organized and sensible. You have my permission to make as many copies as you want.

# Noon Sight Latitude Worksheet

## Sight

|  | Date | Time (GMT) |  |  |
|---|---|---|---|---|
|  |  | Deg/Hrs | Min | Sec |
|  | Sextant reading |  |  |  |
| subtract | Index Error | - | - | - |
| add | Dip Correction | + | + | + |
| = | Apparent Altitude | = | = | = |

*use Apparent Altitude to find the following corrections...*

## Corrections

| | | Deg/Hrs | Min | Sec |
|---|---|---|---|---|
| add | Refraction | + | + | + |
| add | Alt/SD : Lower Limb | + | + | + |
| = | Height Observed (Ho) | = | = | = |

*use Adjusted Sextant Angle in the next stage....*

## Almanac Stuff

| | | Deg | Min | Sec |
|---|---|---|---|---|
| | Dec Sun | | | |
| *add or subtract? (according to almanac trend)* | d Corr | ? | ? | ? |
| | Corrected Dec Sun | = | = | = |

## Declination Math Table

| Hemisphere? | | Sun's relation to You? | What do you do with the Dec? |
|---|---|---|---|
| You | Sun | | |
| N | N | N | Subtract & use abs. value |
| N | N | S | Add |
| N | S | S | Subtract |
| S | S | S | Subtract & use abs. value |
| S | S | N | Add |
| S | N | N | Subtract |

## Calculations

| | | Deg/Hrs | Min | Sec |
|---|---|---|---|---|
| subtract | Sun's GP Altitude | 90 | 00 | 00 |
| | ...Height Observed (from above) | - | - | - |
| | = Distance from Sun's GP Latitude | = | = | = |
| *add or subtract? (See math table)* | Corrected Dec Sun | ? | ? | ? |
| *from top right* | Final Latitude of Observer | = | = | = |

# Using Calculators for Celestial Navigation:

Sure, using a calculator may save you a few valuable seconds during your month-long voyage across the ocean. My guess is that if you are out there, you are not exactly looking to save time doing much of anything. You'll probably want to drag out any simple task as long as it takes to keep your sanity. Good! Then you won't mind doing it on paper.

Calculators are evil in 2 ways—1: they die when exposed to salt water, and 2: they need electricity. And I'm not talking "jury-rig it with jumper cables to you ship's battery" electricity. I'm talking tiny little amounts that would be impossible to replicate if their internal battery died or their tiny solar panel got cracked. And then you'd be screwed, wishing you learned to do it with pencil and paper!

Old School may suck in your opinion, but it's good school nonetheless. I didn't get good at art because of computers. Computers only made me faster and cleaner. I got good at art by mashing charcoal into refined tree bark over and over until it looked like something recognizable and appealing (which is tough to do with charcoal and tree bark)! Only then, once I had the skill, did I move it into the computer realm, because that's just a lot less messy than mashing charcoal into tree bark. If my computer ever kicked the bucket, I could still get by with charcoal and tree bark.

And that's why you should learn to do your celestial navigation with charcoal and tree bark. It never fails! Old School forever! Old farts may not get stuff done fast, but we only have to get it done once.

# Intermediate Navigation: Perfecting your Polaris Sight

Remember earlier when I told you how to tighten the accuracy of your Polaris Latitude sight? Here's how, but it involves looking up what we call the LHA of Aries. It's a pain in the butt but it makes your readings much more accurate.

You're already familiar with taking a sight and correcting it; now we need to explain the difference between GHA (Greenwich Hour Angle) and LHA (Local Hour Angle) and learn some new table-hunting exercises. Is it really worth it? Maybe not, you decide. If you're comfortable with a potential *average* 55 mile error margin, then you're comfortable with it.

To make this easier on you, I recommend copying the Advanced Polaris worksheet in this chapter (also in the back of the book) and following along.

There is a table of corrections for Polaris's wobble, but it's all based on "LHA Aries" or the LHA of the constellation Aries. Do you have to actually sight Aries? NO! Kind of stupid, isn't it?

## What's the deal with Aries?

Aries is like the friend who can only speak in complete sentences when he's on a bender. We all have a friend like that, especially if we're boat people.

If Polaris is the Pole Star, Aries would be the "Equator Star". That is, if Aries were a star, if it were actually on the Equator, if Santa Claus was real, and if income tax laws made sense. Aries is not a star. It is a constellation. In other words, Aries rides near the equator 24 hours a day, 365 days a year, and it is as good as 90 degrees perpendicular to Polaris. Which provides an excellent point of reference for measuring the place of things in the sky.

Why don't we use a star? Because that would make too much sense! The brightest star in Orion's belt, Alnilam, is very close to the equator, with a declination averaging a mere 1.1 degrees South year round, and would make an excellent candidate. But no, we have to use Aries because the geeks say so and they have some strange master plan in mind for the workings of the universe. Feel the bitterness.

All other star positions are noted in relation to Aries (SHA in the Almanac means Sidereal Hour Angle, aka how many degrees West it is from Aries—no need to worry about that geek trivia just yet; we'll get to it much later when we talk about shooting the stars other than Polaris.)

Who knows why the Great Geeks of History declared Aries to be the origin of star measurement. They were probably all standing outside the Royal Observatory, completely stumped on how to measure the stars, "partaking in a tobacco product" until one of them said, while trying very hard not to laugh, "Dude, let's use Aries." And, of course, the rest laughed and said "Whoah, dude, you're so right!" Then they stayed up until daylight eating all the munchies in sight and drawing up charts and tables, all of which were surprisingly accurate.

Maybe they still get a laugh out of it today, pointing down on us and saying, "Look, they still use Aries! Hahahaha!". A constellation? Who decides what point in that constellation we throw our magical reference point? Nobody seems to know but the geeks who publish the almanac today, and nobody seems to care because their math is correct (so let them smoke all they want!), and as you'll see soon we have to measure Aries' position with a number we make up!!! How's that for craziness?

So the reason we need LHA Aries is that if you know its position in the sky (even if you can't see it), you therefore have a reference to where Polaris is in the sky, and the tables can tell you how much wobble is present in Polaris' position.

*As I later found out, the real (and less amusing) reason that Aries is used as a reference is because it contains (or contained) the intersection of the celestial equator and the ecliptic. However, since the heavens have drifted ever so slightly in the hundreds of years since those great geeks named Aries the origin of these measurements (a process called Procession), the real location is now more in the neighboring constellation Pisces than it is in Aries but nobody feels like changing the name to LHA Pisces. Nevertheless, the numbers in the Almanac are correct even if their names are funky.*

# Finding LHA Aries:

Now to get the LHA of Aries, we need a Longitude measurement of your current or assumed position. WHAT!? How am I supposed to know my Longitude when I'm trying to figure that all out in the first place???

The answer is to take an educated guess, using your last fix or a DR plot. If you really have absolutely no idea of your current Longitude, just pull numbers out of your butt until one sounds roughly reasonable.

Basically, the wobble of Polaris is enough to fudge your reading by a degree or so depending on what angle you shoot it at, and Aries lets us know that angle and how to compensate for the fudge. And we won't know where Aries is unless we have a vague number of Longitude.

Don't sweat it if your Assumed Longitude is off a bit. If you're sailing, chances are you won't make much more than 100 miles progress in 24 hours, your last noon fix was probably only 12 hours ago, which is only about .7 degrees of distance on the charts moving at a good clip, which won't account for a massive change in your readings.

Now—supposing we have some vague idea of our Longitude, we'll say it's 100 degrees West, we can plug it into the paper and pencil processor and figure out a cleaner Latitude from Polaris.

# Step 1: Take your sight of Polaris, mark the time, and correct your sight.

Suppose your sight gives an angle of 30 degrees, 5.8 minutes.

Correct your sight for Index Error, Dip, and Refraction as always.

Sight = 30 degrees 5.8 minutes
+ 0 Index Error (we re-zeroed our sextant after we dropped it again)
-2.4 minutes Dip

= 30 degrees 3.4 minutes Apparent Altitude
-1.7 minutes Altitude (or semidiameter) Correction
+ 0 Refraction (60 degrees F)

=30 degrees, 1.7 minutes Height Observed

# Step 2: Look up GHA Aries.

We need GHA Aries to determine LHA Aries. Easy enough. Look at your watch. What is the date and time of your sight? June 10, 2005, at 22:30:30 GMT.

Now check that date's page in the Nautical Almanac. Aries has its own column. You'll see at the top that it has its GHA listed next to the time. Run down the date and time column to Friday the 10th at 22 hours. You see 229 degrees, 21.1 minutes.

44

## Step 3: Increments and corrections.

22 hours of passage have occurred in Aries' "orbit" around the Earth, but there are 30 minutes and 30 seconds remaining. Flip to the Almanac's grey-edged pages, and find 30 minutes, 30 seconds. Aries has its own column here, and the additional passage is 7 degrees, 38.8 minutes

229 degrees, 21.1 minutes
+ 7 degrees, 38.8 minutes
= Corrected GHA Aries: 236 degrees, 59.9 minutes

## Step 4: Calculate LHA Aries.

LHA = GHA (+east or –west) Longitude
Let's just take a wild guess and say that our estimated Longitude is 100 degrees West

236 degrees 59.9 minutes
-100 degrees west longitude, our assumed position (add if east, subtract if west)
= LHA Aries: 136 degrees 59.9 minutes

## What happens if the number is greater than 360?

This is bound to happen to you 50% of the time. It's ok—don't panic. This simply means your measurement has looped around completely (like a clock striking twelve and then one), so we subtract 360 from the resulting number to get its true value.

## Is there a "v" correction for LHA Aries?

No. GHA and 'increments and corrections' makes this unnecessary.

# Step 5: Look up 3 more Polaris Sight Corrections based on LHA Aries.

There are 3 corrections we do to your Polaris sight, all based on LHA Aries, and we have to do them in order. They are listed as a0 (LHA Aries Correction), a1 (Lat Correction), and a2 (Month Correction).

After the calendar pages in your Nautical Almanac, after the section on more obscure stars, is a section titled "Polaris (Pole Star) Tables". These tables require LHA Aries in order to find your corrections.

a0 correction: Our LHA Aries is 136 degrees 59.9 minutes. Since this is so bloody close to 137 degrees, we'll consider it such in the tables.

We look across the tables at the top row (labeled, big surprise, LHA Aries!) and find "130-139 degrees" Scrolling down (according to the leftmost numbers) you will see that this top column contains all the numbers from 1-10 within a 10-number range. Thus the top number of this column is 130, the next one down is for 131, and our magic correction for LHA Aries 137 degrees is: 1 degree, 4.8 minutes. Be sure to watch for the missing degree numbers (to the left and up or down-- I think they omit them for 'readability').

We now add our a0 correction to our Height Observed to find our next correction.

30 degrees, 1.7 minutes (Height Observed)
+ 1 degree, 4.8 minutes (a0)
= 31 degrees, 6.5 minutes (this stage's official confusing name is called Latitude. Yes, stupid, considering we have another 2 corrections to make! Just be a good little robot and follow the others.)

We take this number and apply it to the next column down (marked "Lat." on that Polaris Tables page), find the closest number you can to our "Lat" number in the bold left side (in this case 30) and cross-reference it with our old LHA Aries column, to find a1's correction of 0.4 minutes.

31 degrees, 6.5 minutes (Lat)
+ 0.4 minutes (a1)
= 31 degrees, 6.9 minutes

46

The third stage is done by the month you took the sight in. Since it is June, we cross-reference June's table entry with our old 130-139 degree LHA Aries column, and find a 0.9 minute correction for a2.

31 degrees, 6.9 minutes
+0.9 minutes (a2)
=31 degrees, 7.8 minutes
-1 degree, always, with Polaris sights (Joy of joys, only the Great Dead Geeks know why!)
=30 degrees, 7.8 minutes (This IS your final answer! Good lord!)

What a pain in the neck! But considering our original reading would have been 30 degrees, 1.7 minutes, and our new reading is 30 degrees, 7.8 minutes, we would have been several miles off.

We're officially done with the complicated version of Latitude by Polaris! Time for an ice cold beer! You've earned it, and right now I could use 2 or 3... dozen!

*The Magical Mystery Degree explained:*
*Apparently the math to do the advanced Polaris corrections requires 1 degree to be added for the "a" terms to be positive, and make the math easier. Thus, you have to subtract 1 degree at the end to even it out.*

Here's another worksheet to help save your brain. Make as many copies as you like. Hand them out to confuse your friends! Why suffer alone?

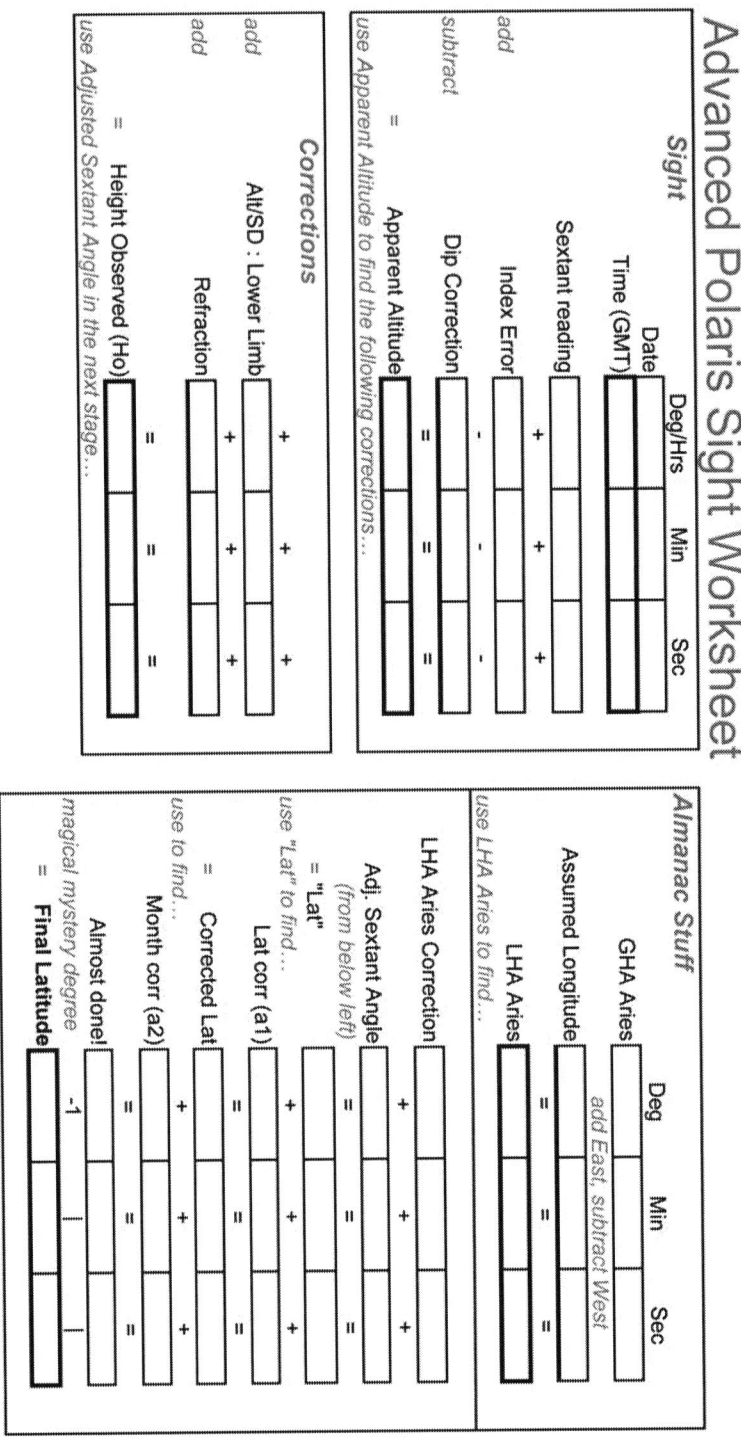

# LHA, GHA, and GMT: So what the heck did I just do?
## (Optional reading for hardcore geeks)

**GHA** and **LHA** are both meridian references, dealing with the passage of time. Meaning, they are imaginary lines drawn from the North to South pole, slicing the earth like an orange. Remember when we discussed GMT (Greenwich Mean Time)? The 3 are all related.

GHA stands for Greenwich Hour Angle, and it's defined for the purpose of telling what angle of Longitude an object lies on in relation to Greenwich's place on the Prime Meridian.

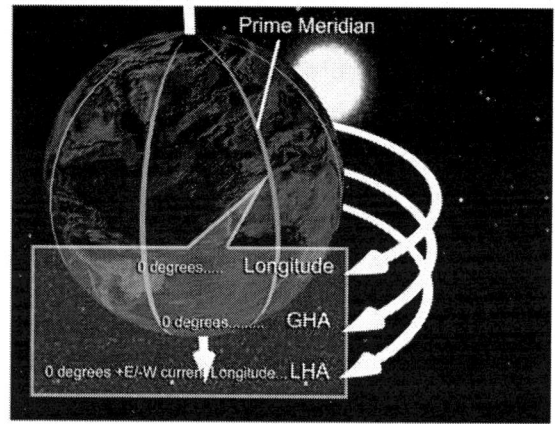

The passage of GMT time and GHA time are simultaneous. Where they deviate is how they are counted. GMT is counted in hours, minutes and seconds of time, its origin and end being at the International Date Line. GHA is counted in degrees, minutes, and seconds of Longitude.

BUT—here's where they try and lose you—GHA does not follow the rules of Longitude numbering like the Earth's meridians.

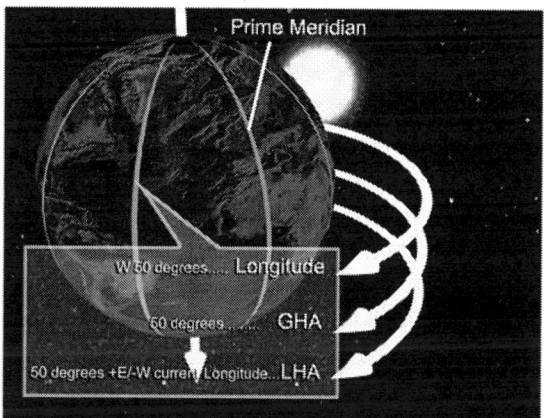

In a fit of weirdness, the great geeks of history decided that instead of originating GHA at the date line alongside Time, (which would be a quick logical 15x multiplication back and forth from time or longitude to figure out!!!), GHA starts at 0 on the Prime Meridian (12:00 hours GMT) and travels West, counting around to 180 degrees at the International Date Line, and continuing its complete circle, arriving at 360 or 0 degrees again back on the Prime Meridian.

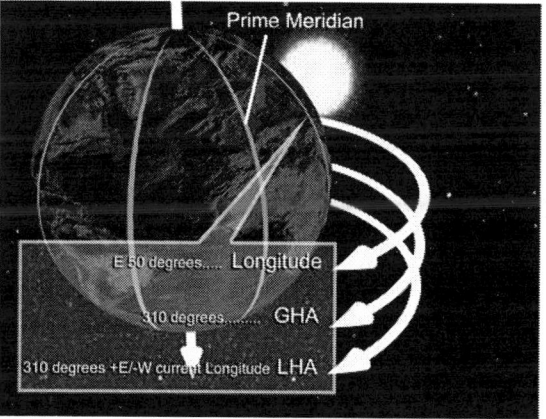

Geeks are technical, true, but nobody ever said they were logical.

Longitude starts at 180 degrees at the international date line and travels both directions around the Earth, counting down to 0 degrees when the two halves join back together at the Prime Meridian.

Now how stupid is that?!

Just try and remember: Greenwich Hour Angle "starts" at Greenwich.

LHA stands for Local Hour Angle. It follows the same method of counting as GHA, but LHA does not start at the Prime Meridian; rather, it starts at *your* Longitude (hence Local!). It is a differential measurement between your current Longitude and your selected celestial object's GHA position. So, in essence, LHA counting is GHA, 'displaced' by your current Longitude. The formula follows: LHA = GHA (+east or – west) Longitude.

But GHA stops when it reaches the Prime Meridian. What happens with LHA? Good you should ask. It keeps right on going. Think of it as GHA, but spinning freely with your location as its 0 degree origin.

If the math leading to your GHA or LHA is ever above 360, then simply subtract 360 to figure out what the real number is (because it has looped around the Earth).

If any of the LHA values ever exceed 360, it means they've looped the globe, so we then subtract 360 to get our real value. It can happen to GHA sometimes as well if your target is very close to passing the Prime Meridian and corrections fudge it just past 360. Either way, the rule is:

**If LHA or GHA > 360, then subtract 360.**

The concept may go way over your head right now, but that's ok. You don't need to know WHAT it is, just how to calculate it. And that's as easy as following step-by-step directions, right on the worksheets. So, now that you are thoroughly confused, let's move on shall we?

It's like trudging through mud!

# Using Universal Plotting Sheets

Plotting the many dots and lines involved with a Celestial Nav fix will take its toll on charts. Charts are expensive. Naturally, you don't want them turning to pulp under the torture of your pencil and eraser. This is why you should use Universal Plotting Sheets. Plotting sheets are typically sold in pads of 50, 13x14 inches, printed both sides, for about $6. This means you get 100 big caveman-sized pages at 6 cents per page. Not bad, considering it would cost about the same to copy them on 8.5x11 at any copy shop. The big preprinted sheets are very awkward to store, though. Unless your local boat supply folks are true hardcore salty pirate scalawags, you may have difficulty finding the big preprinted sheets through anything but mail order. Regardless of what sheets you use, there's a blank plotting sheet in the back of the book (along with all the other worksheets) for your copying pleasure.

Obviously, using plotting sheets requires learning how first. So here goes:

Let's look at the anatomy of the plotting sheet. Plotting sheets are set up with a compass rose in true degrees, 1 line of Longitude, a few lines of Latitude, and what looks like a segment of a globe in the corner.

None of the sheet's lines of Latitude or Longitude are numbered, because you will number them depending on the area you are plotting. Since the distance between lines of Latitude never changes, the lines of Latitude are marked on the sheet. A minute of Longitude is only a full nautical mile at the Equator. As you go further north or south, the distance between lines of Longitude shrinks until it's absolutely zero at the north and south poles.

That globe segment in the corner serves more to remind us of what Latitude we are on, but it is actually to scale with the rest of the plotting sheet. If we want, we can measure the width of our Longitude lines based on our Latitude.

The compass rose serves two purposes. First, it is used to mark our Azimuth angle (derived from your sight reduction further on), but as a secondary side effect of strange spherical geometry, it can also be used as a scale for marking lines of Longitude!

Check this out, it's really cool—

Suppose we're somewhere near Latitude N20 degrees by W11 degrees. Typical practice is to first mark the corner scale at the line of Latitude you are using as reference (circled small, red).

Next, mark the lines of Latitude on the chart, usually with your closest whole degree of Latitude at the center. In this case, it's 20 degrees. Mark the other 2 lines with their numbers, 19 and 21, as well.

Now comes the neat part— look at the right side of the compass rose. If you scan across it until you find the number of your Latitude, and draw a vertical line through that point (circled large, red), you've drawn a Longitude line that is for all intents and purposes 100% to proper scale with the area of the globe you are working in. Don't believe me? Check it with a pair of dividers, or use the scale in the corner!

The center line in this example would be your W11 mark, and the line you just drew would be your W10 mark. You can do the same on the other side of the compass rose but it will take some generic math, basically 270+current Latitude, to mark the proper intersecting spot on the rose.

When it's all said and done, you should have 3 lines of Latitude and 3 lines of Longitude, and a sheet covering roughly 180 nautical miles from the center point. Plenty of space to find out where you are!

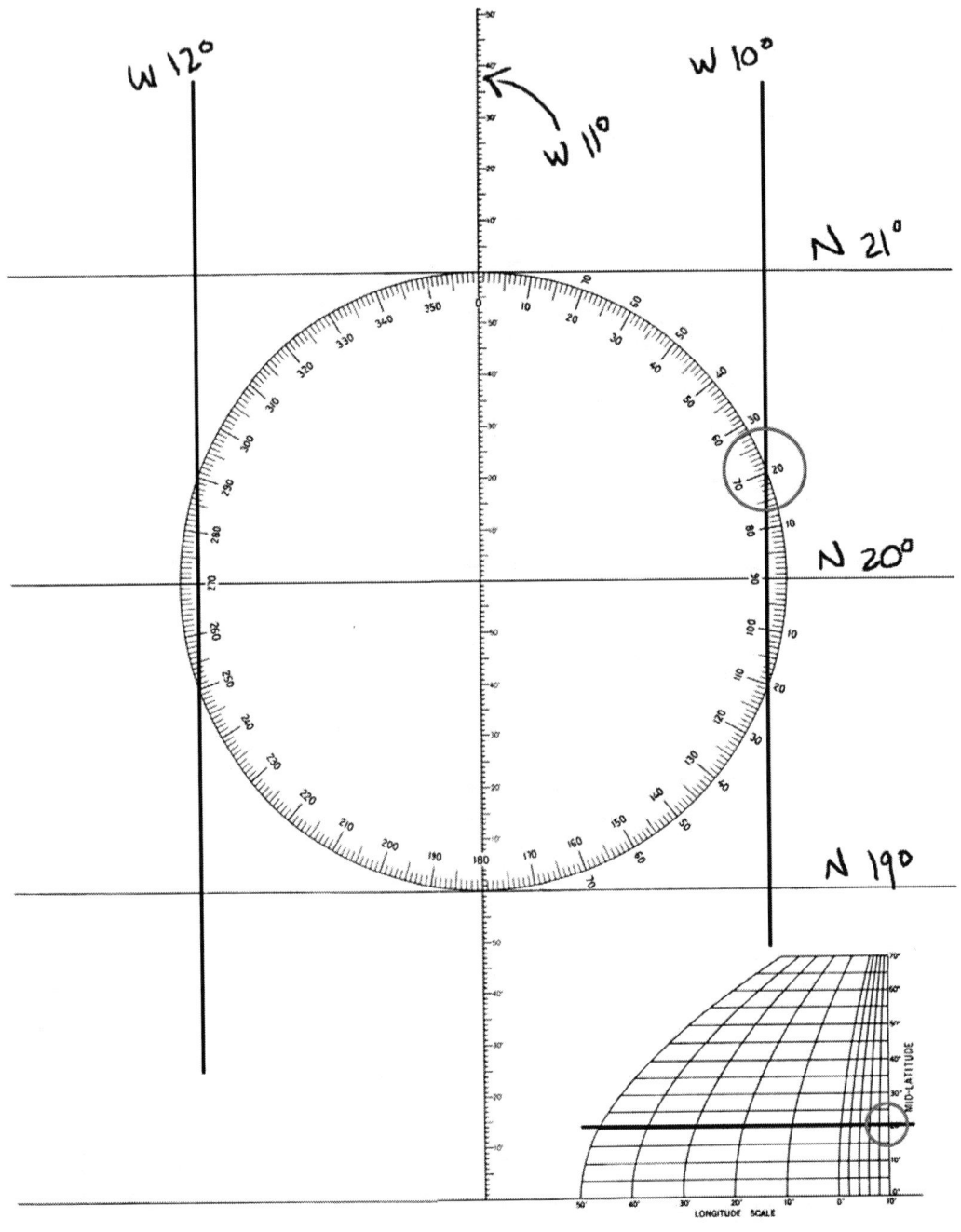

Now look at the second example below. Notice how the lines of Longitude are closer together, because we're marking off a section at a higher Latitude.

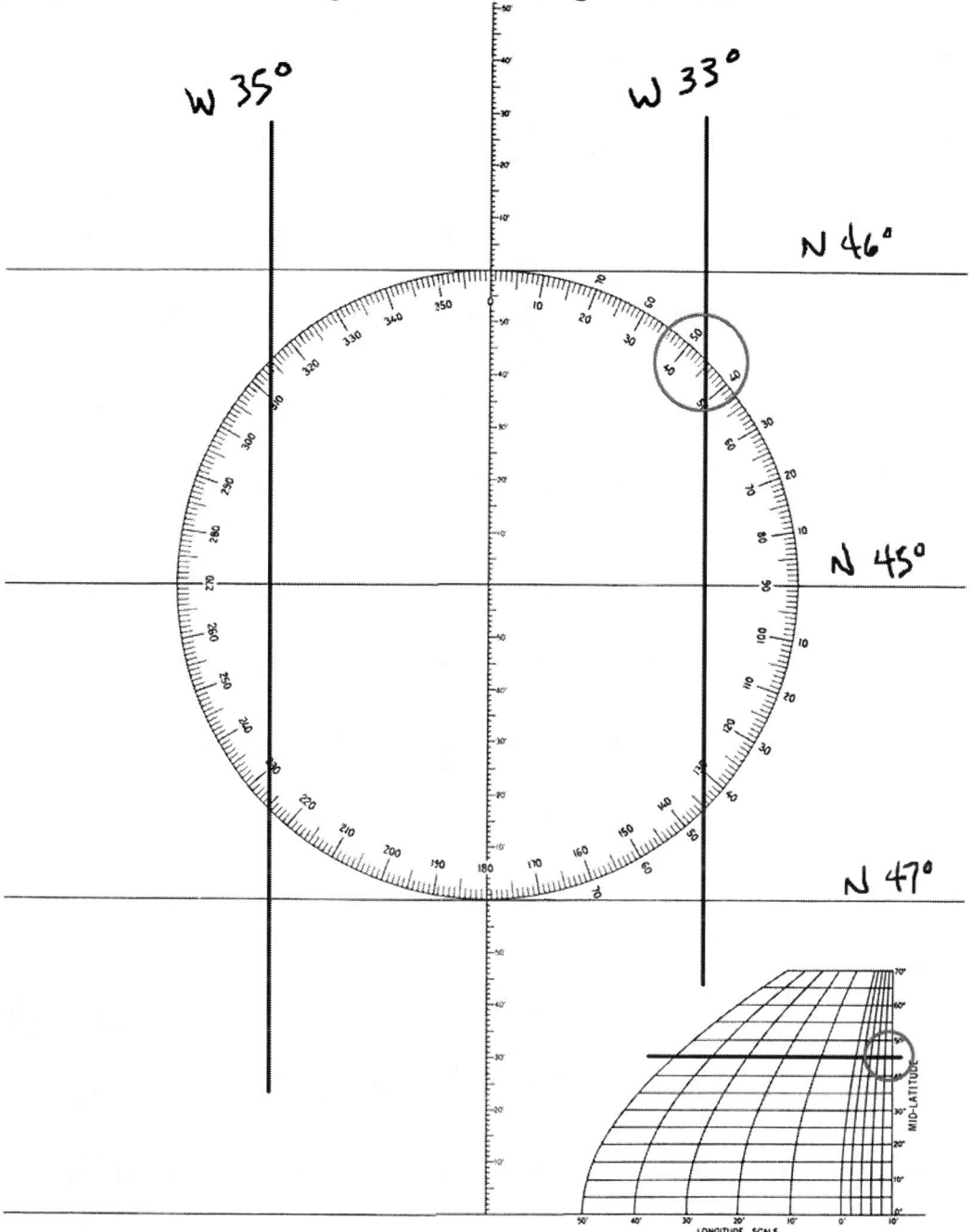

# Advanced Navigation: Sight Reductions and Plotting Great Circles

From here on in it's harder. We have to deal with sight reduction tables, thereby reducing our need to do heavy trigonometric math. The math crunching part is easy; it's the concepts that are hard to understand, and, in other books made *very* hard to understand because they explain it with a bazillion different names and their non-matching abbreviations.

I'll try to make it as easy as I can, but dust off the geek part of your brain because you'll need it.

The core concept of celestial navigation is deductive Sherlock Holmes math. 1: With the Almanac, you know where your target celestial object will be (its GP) in the sky. 2: You can calculate the distance between you and the GP by using the sextant.

With those clues to our mystery, an angle is formed. If the base of that angle is spun around with the GP as its center (around the flagpole), it creates a circle, on which you *must* be located.

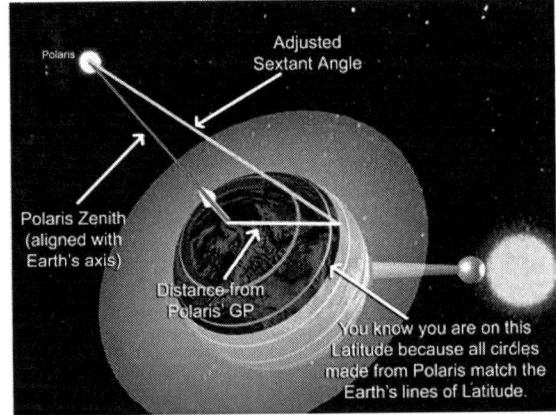

Think of it like drawing a circle with a compass (a pencil compass, not a magnetic one!). The pointy end of the compass would be the GP, the angle of the compass would be your celestial target, and as the pencil scribes a circle around, it's marking a line on which you would have to be to see the angle you are seeing with the sextant.

The reason that a basic Polaris Latitude sight is so easy is that since the Earth's Latitude lines match up with Polaris, we need only measure the angle, and we know then for a fact we are on that line of Latitude.

When you get a target that is not perfectly North or South, however, it gets more complicated. The circle will be at an angle to the poles, and not aligned to either Latitude or Longitude.

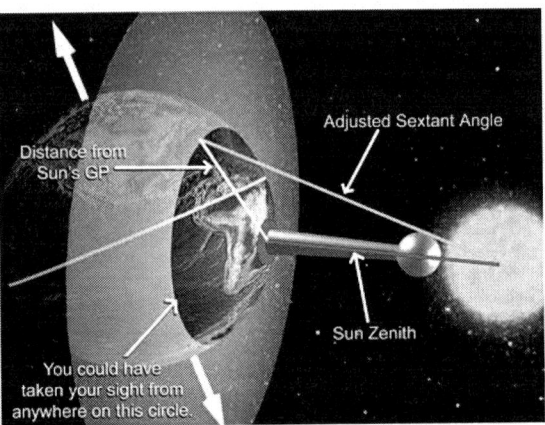

Yes, the sextant tells you how far you are from that object's GP (flagpole base). But that is only the first piece of information you need. You could be anywhere on that circle (and it's a VERY big circle!), so you need to find out what direction that object is in, so you know what part of that circle to plot on your chart.

And no, I know what you're thinking—you can't use a compass (a magnetic one)! Why? Because the magnetic pole of the Earth is not aligned with its rotational pole, and because of arcs and horrible spherical geometric math and other things that would make your brain catch on fire. Fortunately, though, the sight reduction tables give us the compass reading we need in True Degrees so it matches with the charts we use and makes navigation easy!

You need crossing lines to make a fix, so you need at least two reduced sights. Three is even better. Where they cross, is where you are located.

So how do we draw the Great Circle? We don't. We couldn't! You'd need a chart of the whole globe, and Great Circles, drawn on square grid charts of the globe, show up as egg shaped ellipses or s-curves. That would be of no help to us!

We draw only a small part of the Great Circle, the part that passes closest to where you are. When that big huge circle is drawn to scale next to you, it's such a small section of such a big circle, that it will show up as a straight line on your chart. And when you draw the second circle segment from a different celestial object, then your position is where those lines cross.

So you take your sights first, but you won't actually use their information until the VERY end of your sight reduction.

The Sight Reduction Tables require 3 things: Latitide, Dec, and LHA, all of which can only come from knowing where you are. How do we find out where we are if we have to know where we are first? Kind of dumb, no?

Sight reduction works like this: You run an Assumed Position (AP) through the tables. They will give you complete information on what Sextant Angle your celestial target would be in, *were you actually there*. This creates a "Great Circle" which is too large to plot on normal charts.

But which part of this great circle do we plot? Well, obviously the part where our assumed position is, but how do you tell what angle the circle segment is at to properly plot it?

This is where Azimuth comes in, and it's also a product of your Sight Reduction.

Where the Azimuth crosses the Great Circle, is the part of the line you will be plotting. This is where your Assumed Position crosses the Great Circle, and the Azimuth points towards the GP of your celestial target. But, once again, you're really not there at the AP. You are NEAR that area. But you have your real sextant reading, and you have the sextant reading you would have had at your Assumed Position (a product of the Sight Reduction Tables)…

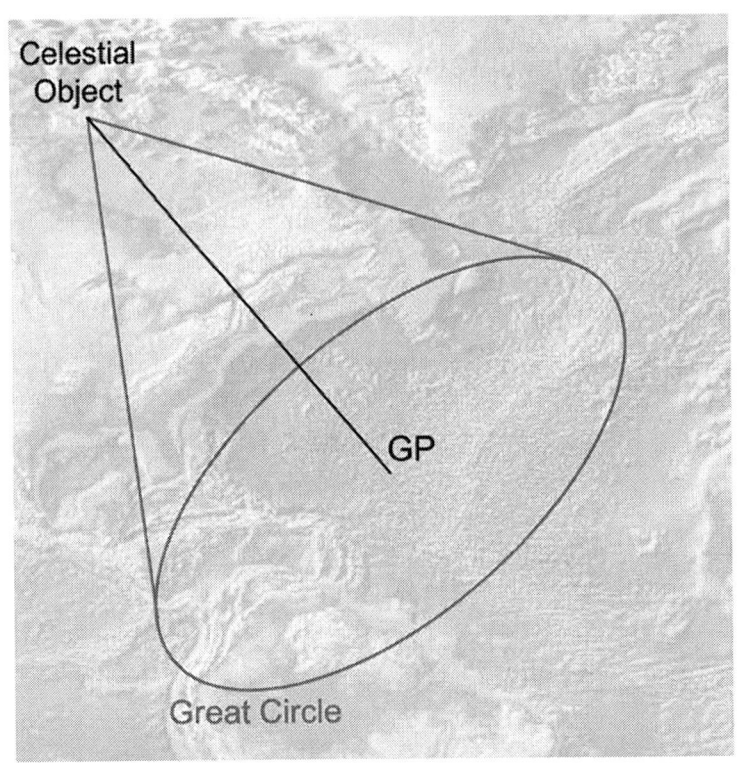

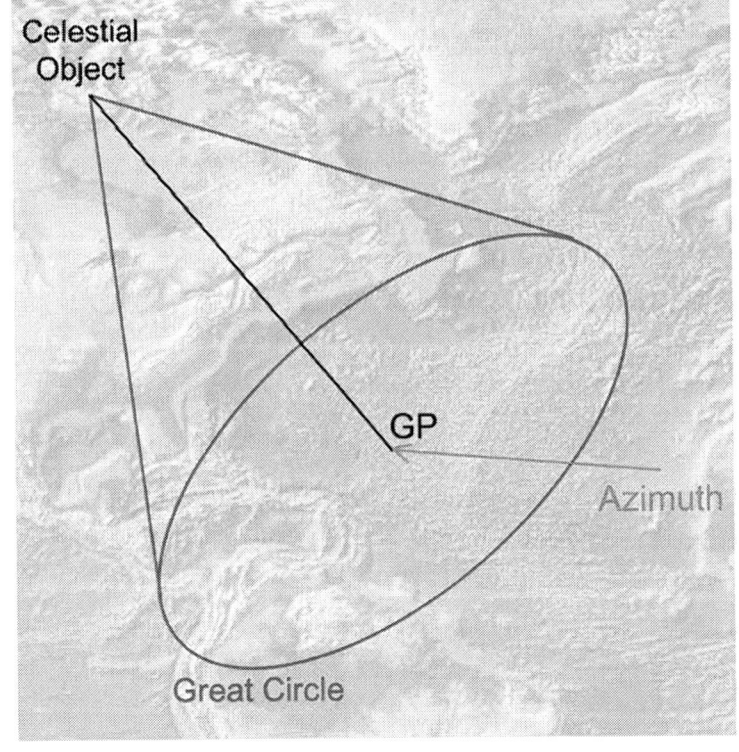

56

Well, then, all you have to do is compare the "would-be" sextant angle provided by the Sight Reduction Tables to your real sextant reading to find out how far from the AP's Great Circle you really are. Since you're spotting that same object along that same Azimuth bearing, you extend that Line Of Position (LOP) in or out the exact distance you calculated from the sextant angle comparison. And that, now, is the line that you are really located on.

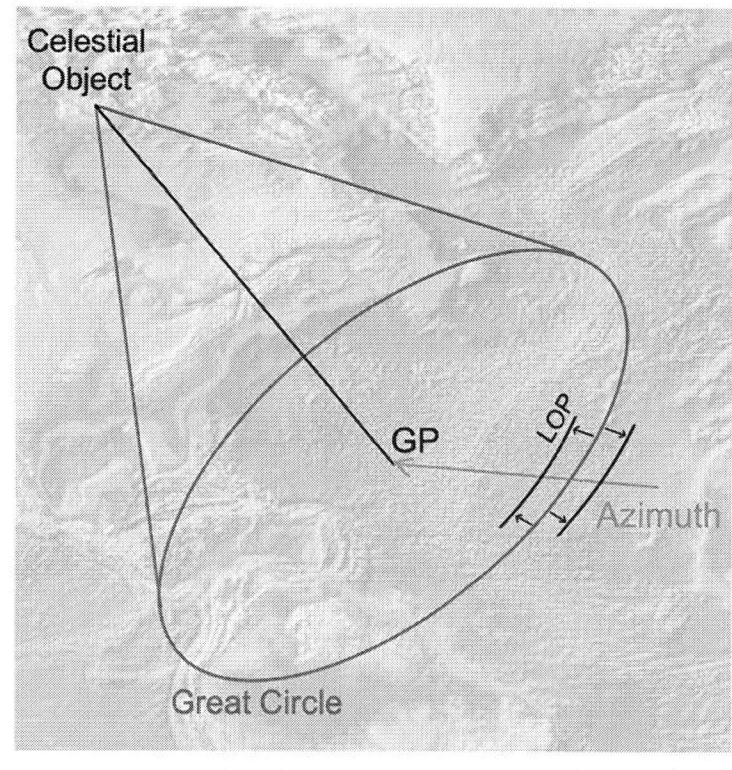

One way to think of it is that you are making your target celestial object into a free-floating Polaris, and the sight reduction tables give you its own crooked "line of Latitude" to reference from it, thereby finding your distance from the "pole".

The concept of the Assumed Position (AP) boggled me at first. What is it? How do you pick where it goes? Well, for starters, that's why Dead Reckoning is a skill you should use in conjunction with Cel Nav. It will give you a good general area to start. Your AP doesn't need to be somewhere you've been, or somewhere you're going. It doesn't need to be precise. You only need it to use as a basis of comparison, nothing more.

Ideally it should be somewhere within a hundred miles or so of where you think you might be, but it won't hurt you if it actually turns out to be 300 or even 1000 miles away. You'll find out just how far soon enough, and you can then modify your AP and recalculate for tighter, more accurate readings if you want.

Look at a chart, think about where you're going, point your finger, and say "We're somewhere around here."

As I've explained, AP doesn't have to be extremely close to you. It doesn't have to follow any other logic other than you think you're near it. In order to work the Sight Reduction Tables, you have to place your AP on a solid degree line of Latitude. In fact, we don't even calculate the seconds when we do sight reduction because the tables would take up a lot more room, and it's not worth it for a tenth of a mile when Cel Nav isn't that accurate and you'll travel three or more times that distance in the time it takes to run the tables and work the math.

So how do we prep for the tables? Let's begin. First, make a copy or two, or twelve, of this worksheet (full size can be found in the back of the book) so you can follow along. The NAO Concise Sight Reduction Form is actually one of the few government worksheets out there that does not suck. In earlier editions of this book I had included my own form but I eventually found that the NOA form kept me more accurate. It will remind you of tax form nightmares, but it works well.

### NAO CONCISE SIGHT REDUCTION FORM

| Date & UT of observation | h m s | Body | Estimated Latitude & Longitude ° ' ° ' |
|---|---|---|---|
| **Step** | **Calculate Altitude & Azimuth** | | **Summary of Rules & Notes** |
| Assumed latitude | $Lat =$ ° | | Nearest estimated latitude, integral number of degrees. |
| Assumed longitude | $Long =$ ° ' | | Choose $Long$ so that $LHA$ has integral number of degrees. |
| **1.** From the almanac: | $Dec =$ ° ' | | Record the $Dec$ for use in Step 3. |
| $GHA$ Aries h | $=$ ° ' | | Needed if using $SHA$. Tabular value. |
| Increment m s | $=$ ° ' | | for minutes and seconds of time. |
| $SHA$ | $SHA =$ ° ' | | |
| $GHA = GHA$ Aries $+ SHA$ | $GHA =$ ° ' | | Remove multiples of 360°. |
| Assumed longitude | $Long =$ ° ' | | West longitudes are negative. |
| $LHA = GHA + Long$ | $LHA =$ ° | | Remove multiples of 360°. |
| **2.** Reduction table, 1st entry $(Lat, LHA) = ($ °, °$)$ record $A$, $B$ and $Z_1$. | $A =$ ° ' $A° =$ ° $A' =$ ' | | nearest whole degree of $A$. minutes part of $A$. |
| | $B =$ ° ' $Z_1 =$ ? | | $B$ is minus if $90° < LHA < 270°$. $Z_1$ has the same sign as $B$. |
| **3.** From step 1 $F = B + Dec$ | $Dec =$ ° ' $F =$ ° ' $F° =$ ° $F' =$ ' | | $Dec$ is minus if contrary to $Lat$. Regard $F$ as positive until step 7. nearest whole degree of $F$. minutes part of $F$. |
| **4.** Reduction table, 2nd entry $(A°, F°) = ($ °, °$)$ record $H$, $P$ and $Z_2$. | $H =$ ° ' $P° =$ ° $Z_2 =$ ? | | nearest whole degree of $P$. |
| **5.** Auxiliary table, 1st entry $(F', P°) = ($ ', °$)$ record $corr_1$ | $corr_1 =$ ' | | $corr_1$ is minus if $F < 90°$ & $F' > 29'$, or if $F > 90°$ & $F' < 30'$. |
| **6.** Auxiliary table, 2nd entry $(A', Z_2°) = ($ ', °$)$ record $corr_2$ | $corr_2 =$ ' | | $Z_2°$ nearest whole degree of $Z_2$. $corr_2$ is minus if $A' < 30'$. |
| **7.** Calculated altitude $=$ $H_C = H + corr_1 + corr_2$ | $H_C =$ ° ' | | $H_C$ is minus if $F$ is negative, and object is below the horizon. |
| **8.** Azimuth, 1st component | $Z_1 =$ ° | | $Z_1$ has the same sign as $B$. |
| 2nd component | $Z_2 =$ ° | | $Z_2$ is minus if $F > 90°$. If $F$ is negative, $Z_2 = 180° - Z_2$ |
| $Z = Z_1 + Z_2$ | $Z =$ ° | | Ignore the sign of $Z$. N $Lat$: If $LHA > 180°$, $Z_n = Z$, or if $LHA < 180°$, $Z_n = 360° - Z$, S $Lat$: If $LHA > 180°$, $Z_n = 180° - Z$, or if $LHA < 180°$, $Z_n = 180° + Z$. |
| True azimuth | $Z_n =$ ° | | ©HMNAO |

For use with *The Nautical Almanac's* Concise Sight Reduction Tables pages 284-318.
*Copyright Council for the Central Laboratory of the Research Councils 2005*

# Sight Reduction: Gathering Information

## Simple Advice: Get used to Rounding numbers. In some places on the sight reduction form you will have to, or the amounts will not come out correct. Anywhere you see a decimal for minutes measurement, as we do below, save your brain by rounding it to the nearest whole number.

## Step 1: Take your sight.

For this tutorial, we are out in the Atlantic Ocean, on our way towards Jacksonville, Florida. We know we're somewhere in its general vicinity, so for simplicity's sake we'll use the lighthouse for an Assumed Position and see what information it gives us.

Our sight takes place on June 10, 2005, at 21:57:30 GMT. The sun is descending, it's approaching evening, and after all of our onerous corrections for dip, semidiameter, etc we have Height Observed of 29 degrees, 00 minutes.

## Step 2: Take a wild guess!

We need our AP (assumed position). Since we're bound for Jacksonville, we'll use the St. John's Lighthouse. Its coordinates are:

Latitude: N 30 degrees, 23.19 minutes
Longitude: W 81 degrees, 23.9 minutes (don't get too attached—the AP Longitude gets adjusted shortly…)

For ease of math, we'll strip our Latitude of its minutes and seconds, and round down to 30 degrees. It not only makes the math easier—we have to! The sight reduction tables only work in whole degree increments.

Take this moment to scribble your bearings down in the **margin** of your sight reduction sheet (you will need to adjust the Longitude in step 4):
N 30 degrees
W 81 degrees, 23.9 minutes (for simplicity's sake we round to 24 minutes)

## Step 3: Find LHA.

Gotta have GHA first to find LHA! Look in the almanac under June 10, 2005, at 21:00 UT (GMT)

GHA Sun = 135 degrees, 07.2' minutes. Round this to 7 minutes. Write it down in the sheet.

There are still 57 minutes 30 seconds remaining, so look in the Increments and Corrections pages (back of almanac, grey edges).

Increments and corrections for 57m 30s of sun is 14 degrees, 22.5 minutes (round to 23)

135 degrees, 07' minutes
+14 degrees, 23' minutes
=149 degrees, 30' minutes

Ye olde rule: LHA = GHA +East / –West Longitude.

Our AP Longitude is W 81 degrees, 23.9 (round to 24) minutes, so:
149 degrees, 30 minutes
- 81 degrees 24 mins (AP Longitude)
= 68 degrees 06 minutes

*Helpful hint:* Now is a time to check the reality of your LHA math. If your LHA is anything smaller than 30 and anything greater than 210, chances are it was behind the horizon. Which means it was impossible to see, and therefore you probably did something wrong.

# Step 4: Adjust the LHA to give a solid degree number, and adjust the AP Longitude in turn.

Since the tables need a solid degree number, our LHA needs to change. We can do this by nudging our AP's minutes slightly to compensate. This is simple as subtracting or adding minutes to the LHA until we arrive at a solid degree number, and applying the same to the AP's minutes. In this example, we subtract 6 minutes to make our LHA 68 degrees, and doing the same to our AP Longitude makes it now 81 degrees, 18 minutes.

Now, finally, you can write those numbers down at the top of your NAO sight reduction worksheet:

AP Latitude: N 30 degrees
AP Longitude: W 81 degrees, 18 minutes

# Step 5: Find Dec.

Right next to GHA in the almanac is Dec.

Dec Sun = N23 degrees, 4 minutes. Write it down in the margin somewhere. Note the lowercase "d" at bottom. (currently it's 0.2)
Look in the Increments and Corrections pages under '57 mintues'. Cross-reference the "v or d" of 0.2 with a Corr(ection) of 0.2 minutes.

Note that Dec is increasing as time goes on, so we ADD the "d" correction. Had it been falling, we'd have subtracted the "d" correction.

N23 degrees, 4 minutes
+ 0.2 minutes (d corr)
―――――――――――――――――――――――
=N23 degrees, 4.2 minutes (round back to a solid minutes number; this is your complete Dec Sun)
N23 degrees, 04 minutes -- *Write this down in the Dec section (section 1 of the NAO worksheet).*

*You should have something along these lines by now:*

| Step | Calculate Altitude & Azimuth | Summary of Rules & Notes |
|---|---|---|
| Assumed latitude | Lat = 30° N | Nearest estimated latitude, integral number of degrees. |
| Assumed longitude | Long = 81° ~~24~~ ' 18' | Choose *Long* so that *LHA* has integral number of degrees. |
| 1. From the almanac: | Dec = 23°04' | Record the *Dec* for use in Step 3. |
| GHA ~~Aries~~ sun     h | = 135°07' | Needed if using *SHA*. Tabular value. |
| Increment    m    s | = 14°23' | for minutes and seconds of time. |
| ~~SHA~~ final GHA | ~~SHA~~ = 149°30' |  |
| GHA = GHA Aries + SHA | GHA = 149°30' | Remove multiples of 360°. |
| Assumed longitude | Long = 81°24' | West longitudes are negative. |
| LHA = GHA + Long | LHA = 68°06' | Remove multiples of 360°. |

# Sight Reduction: Breaking it Down

## How to work the Almanac's Sight Reduction Tables

Now you have the 3 vital pieces of information you need to run the Sight Reduction Tables: AP Lat, Dec, and LHA.

There are a variety of sight reduction tables—various versions of HO (insert number here). HO229 is the marine version. These books are thick but easy to use—less math and writing involved. The problem, though, is that said ease of math requires 6 entire volumes, each of which contains about 400 pages. HO249 is the air version, which is only 3 volumes but is pretty much limited to measuring the Sun (and no other celestial objects). It should also be mentioned that each of these volumes costs $20 for the commercial edition, and much more for the swanky hardcover ones.

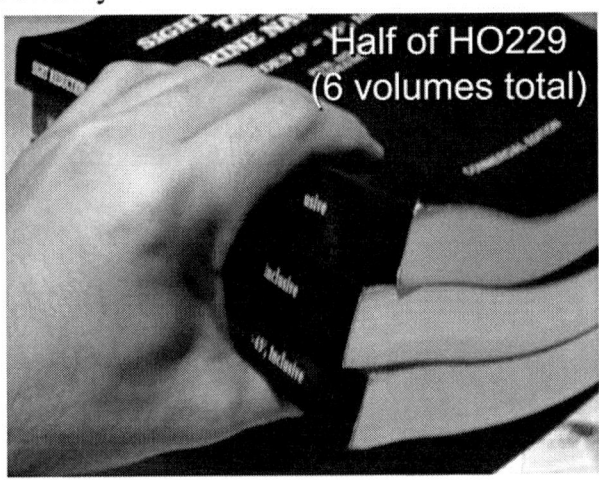

In this photo are 3 of the 6 HO229 books you'd need to cover the whole globe. Each volume is divided into 15 degree increments of Latitude. Considering you may not want to be in the Arctic or Antarctic circles, you might scrap the 6th or 5th volume, but at minimum for world cruising you'd probably want at least 4.

This is how thick these books are. I have big hands, and only 3 volumes are shown. So double this quantity for comparison…

…to the compact tables in the Nautical Almanac that achieve the same results.

The tables in the Nautical Almanac will achieve, number for number, the exact same information you get from HO229 or 249, with much less page count. Granted the compact tables require more basic grade school math and more steps in the process, but just think of the money and space you'll save.

The instructions for the compact sight reduction procedure provided in the Almanac are vague and hard to understand for someone learning, so please ignore them and follow me!

The Almanac's sight reduction tables are split into 2 parts: The actual reduction tables and a single page at the end called the Auxiliary Table. They each require 2 passes with various parts of your values above, so there will be 4 sets of numbers you run through the tables. If you follow along with the sight reduction worksheet provided in this book, you can see how it works step-by-step as we go along.

In fact, before you continue, please make a copy of the NAO form in the back of this book and start filling it out as we go, because otherwise you'll be completely lost.

## Step 1: Sight Reduction Tables: First Run

At first look you will notice the tables are printed sideways. Latitude is listed along the "top" of the pages in single degrees, and LHA is listed from 0 to 360 up and down the margins at both sides of the page. Each table spans 2 pages (you'll also notice that the LHA runs down into the second page and then back up).

Find your Lat in degrees in the top row, and its corresponding LHA in the margin. Where they cross, you find 3 numbers: A, B, and Z1. What these letters mean is insignificant—just know that the letters correspond to numbers in the table and on your sheet.

Lat = 30 degrees. LHA=68 degrees.

Our particular numbers we get from our first run are:
A: 53 degrees 25 minutes
B: 32 degrees 59 minutes

Z1: 38.9 degrees (Keep in mind that the Z numbers in these tables are representative of compass bearing degrees, and have decimals, not minutes. We do NOT round the Z numbers.)

***IMPORTANT ROUNDING:*** You will see rules and instructions in the margin of the NOA worksheet, with places to split the degrees and minutes up. When they say "Nearest whole degree of A" or "P" or any other letter, what they mean is to round the degree number up or down based on its minutes. In our case A is 53 degrees 25 minutes, so we do nothing to it. But if we had 53 degrees 40 minutes, we would put 54 degrees in the specific A degrees spot, and 40 minutes in the A minutes spot. The properly rounded degree amount is important, and can fudge your numbers in the end if you forget to do it. It won't be far, but it might damage your accuracy by 20-30 miles.

Now, as a special rule, B is negative if the LHA is between 90 and 270 degrees. This does not apply in our case. So we leave this value alone. This rule also applies to the value of $Z_1$.

## Step 2: Finding F

Add that new B number to your Dec to find the value F. As a rule, Dec is negative if the object sighted is in the opposite hemisphere of the observer. For our example, we're in the same hemisphere.

32 degrees 59 minutes (B)
+ 23 degrees 04 minutes (Dec)
---
F = 56 degrees, 03 minutes

Obviously, this is what goes into the "F" space in the worksheet. When we split the degrees and minutes on the form, don't forget to round!

*You should now have something in your worksheet that looks like this:*

| | | |
|---|---|---|
| 2. Reduction table, 1st entry (Lat, LHA) = (  °,   °) record A, B and $Z_1$. | A = 53° 25'  A° = 53°<br>A' = 25'<br>+ B = 32° 59'<br>$Z_1$ = 38.9 | nearest whole degree of A.<br>minutes part of A.<br>B is minus if 90° < LHA < 270°.<br>$Z_1$ has the same sign as B. |
| 3. From step 1<br>F = B + Dec | Dec = 23° 04'<br>F = 56° 03'<br>F° = 56°<br>F' = 03' | Dec is minus if contrary to *Lat*.<br>Regard F as positive until step 7.<br>nearest whole degree of F.<br>minutes part of F. |

# Step 3: Sight Reduction Tables: Second Run

The Lat/A row at the top of the pages works for both Lat and the degree portion of the A number you got. The LHA/F columns work for both LHA and the degrees of the F number you just calculated. These call for degree numbers, not minute numbers, so ignore the minutes and just use the degree values.

Running across the top of the table to 53 degrees (for A's degrees), with the 56 degree column for F degrees, you get:

H: 29 degrees 56 minutes

P: 23 degrees (We only use the rounded whole value of P which was 22 degrees 51 minutes. Notice there is no space for minutes in P's space, and the rule in the margin reminds us to round)

Z2: 40.2 degrees

Write these down in the worksheet.

| Lat./A | | 48° | | | 49° | | | 50° | | | 51° | | | 52° | | | 53° | | | Lat./A |
|---|---|---|---|---|---|---|---|---|---|---|---|---|---|---|---|---|---|---|---|---|
| LHA/F | | A/H | B/P | Z₁/Z₂ | A/H | B/P | Z₁/Z₂ | A/H | B/P | Z₁/Z₂ | A/H | B/P | Z₁/Z₂ | A/H | B/P | Z₁/Z₂ | A/H | B/P | Z₁/Z₂ | LHA |
| 45 | 135 | 28 14 | 32 29 | 53.4 | 27 38 | 31 35 | 53.0 | 27 02 | 30 41 | 52.5 | 26 25 | 29 48 | 52.1 | 25 48 | 28 55 | 51.8 | 25 11 | 28 03 | 51.4 | 225 | 315 |
| 46 | 134 | 28 46 | 32 01 | 52.4 | 28 10 | 31 08 | 52.0 | 27 32 | 30 14 | 51.6 | 26 55 | 29 22 | 51.2 | 26 17 | 28 29 | 50.8 | 25 39 | 27 38 | 50.4 | 226 | 314 |
| 47 | 133 | 29 18 | 31 33 | 51.4 | 28 40 | 30 40 | 51.0 | 28 02 | 29 47 | 50.6 | 27 24 | 28 55 | 50.2 | 26 46 | 28 03 | 49.8 | 26 07 | 27 12 | 49.4 | 227 | 313 |
| 48 | 132 | 29 49 | 31 04 | 50.5 | 29 11 | 30 11 | 50.0 | 28 32 | 29 19 | 49.6 | 27 53 | 28 27 | 49.2 | 27 14 | 27 36 | 48.8 | 26 34 | 26 46 | 48.4 | 228 | 312 |
| 49 | 131 | 30 20 | 30 34 | 49.5 | 29 41 | 29 42 | 49.0 | 29 01 | 28 50 | 48.6 | 28 21 | 27 59 | 48.2 | 27 41 | 27 08 | 47.8 | 27 01 | 26 18 | 47.4 | 229 | 311 |
| 50 | 130 | 30 50 | 30 04 | 48.5 | 30 10 | 29 12 | 48.0 | 29 30 | 28 20 | 47.6 | 28 49 | 27 30 | 47.2 | 28 08 | 26 40 | 46.8 | 27 27 | 25 51 | 46.4 | 230 | 310 |
| 51 | 129 | 31 20 | 29 32 | 47.5 | 30 39 | 28 41 | 47.0 | 29 58 | 27 50 | 46.6 | 29 17 | 27 00 | 46.2 | 28 35 | 26 11 | 45.8 | 27 53 | 25 22 | 45.4 | 231 | 309 |
| 52 | 128 | 31 49 | 29 00 | 46.4 | 31 08 | 28 09 | 46.0 | 30 26 | 27 19 | 45.6 | 29 44 | 26 30 | 45.2 | 29 01 | 25 41 | 44.8 | 28 19 | 24 53 | 44.4 | 232 | 308 |
| 53 | 127 | 32 18 | 28 27 | 45.4 | 31 36 | 27 37 | 45.0 | 30 53 | 26 48 | 44.5 | 30 10 | 25 59 | 44.1 | 29 27 | 25 11 | 43.7 | 28 44 | 24 24 | 43.3 | 233 | 307 |
| 54 | 126 | 32 46 | 27 53 | 44.4 | 32 03 | 27 04 | 43.9 | 31 20 | 26 15 | 43.5 | 30 36 | 25 27 | 43.1 | 29 52 | 24 40 | 42.7 | 29 08 | 23 53 | 42.3 | 234 | 306 |
| 55 | 125 | 33 14 | 27 19 | 43.3 | 32 30 | 26 30 | 42.9 | 31 46 | 25 42 | 42.4 | 31 02 | 24 55 | 42.0 | 30 17 | 24 08 | 41.6 | 29 32 | 23 22 | 41.2 | 235 | 305 |
| 56 | 124 | 33 42 | 26 44 | 42.2 | 32 57 | 25 55 | 41.8 | 32 12 | 25 08 | 41.4 | 31 27 | 24 22 | 41.0 | 30 41 | 23 36 | 40.6 | 29 56 | 22 51 | 40.2 | 236 | 304 |
| 57 | 123 | 34 08 | 26 07 | 41.1 | 33 23 | 25 20 | 40.7 | 32 37 | 24 34 | 40.3 | 31 51 | 23 48 | 39.9 | 31 05 | 23 03 | 39.5 | 30 19 | 22 19 | 39.1 | 237 | 303 |
| 58 | 122 | 34 34 | 25 30 | 40.1 | 33 48 | 24 44 | 39.6 | 33 02 | 23 58 | 39.2 | 32 15 | 23 14 | 38.8 | 31 28 | 22 29 | 38.4 | 30 41 | 21 46 | 38.0 | 238 | 302 |
| 59 | 121 | 35 00 | 24 53 | 39.0 | 34 13 | 24 07 | 38.5 | 33 26 | 23 22 | 38.1 | 32 39 | 22 38 | 37.7 | 31 51 | 21 55 | 37.3 | 31 03 | 21 13 | 37.0 | 239 | 301 |
| 60 | 120 | 35 25 | 24 14 | 37.8 | 34 37 | 23 30 | 37.4 | 33 50 | 22 46 | 37.0 | 33 02 | 22 03 | 36.6 | 32 13 | 21 20 | 36.2 | 31 25 | 20 39 | 35.9 | 240 | 300 |
| 61 | 119 | 35 49 | 23 35 | 36.7 | 35 01 | 22 51 | 36.3 | 34 12 | 22 08 | 35.9 | 33 24 | 21 26 | 35.5 | 32 35 | 20 45 | 35.1 | 31 46 | 20 04 | 34.8 | 241 | 299 |
| 62 | 118 | 36 13 | 22 55 | 35.6 | 35 24 | 22 12 | 35.2 | 34 35 | 21 30 | 34.8 | 33 45 | 20 49 | 34.4 | 32 56 | 20 09 | 34.0 | 32 06 | 19 29 | 33.7 | 242 | 298 |
| 63 | 117 | 36 36 | 22 14 | 34.4 | 35 46 | 21 32 | 34.0 | 34 56 | 20 51 | 33.6 | 34 06 | 20 11 | 33.3 | 33 16 | 19 32 | 32.9 | 32 26 | 18 53 | 32.5 | 243 | 297 |
| 64 | 116 | 36 58 | 21 32 | 33.3 | 36 08 | 20 52 | 32.9 | 35 17 | 20 12 | 32.5 | 34 27 | 19 33 | 32.1 | 33 36 | 18 54 | 31.8 | 32 45 | 18 17 | 31.4 | 244 | 296 |
| 65 | 115 | 37 20 | 20 50 | 32.1 | 36 29 | 20 10 | 31.7 | 35 38 | 19 32 | 31.3 | 34 47 | 18 54 | 31.0 | 33 55 | 18 16 | 30.6 | 33 03 | 17 40 | 30.3 | 245 | 295 |
| 66 | 114 | 37 41 | 20 07 | 30.9 | 36 49 | 19 28 | 30.5 | 35 58 | 18 51 | 30.2 | 35 06 | 18 14 | 29.8 | 34 13 | 17 38 | 29.5 | 33 21 | 17 02 | 29.1 | 246 | 294 |
| 67 | 113 | 38 01 | 19 23 | 29.7 | 37 09 | 18 46 | 29.4 | 36 17 | 18 09 | 29.0 | 35 24 | 17 33 | 28.6 | 34 31 | 16 59 | 28.3 | 33 38 | 16 24 | 28.0 | 247 | 293 |
| 68 | 112 | 38 21 | 18 38 | 28.5 | 37 28 | 18 02 | 28.2 | 36 35 | 17 27 | 27.8 | 35 42 | 16 53 | 27.5 | 34 48 | 16 19 | 27.1 | 33 55 | 15 46 | 26.8 | 248 | 292 |
| 69 | 111 | 38 40 | 17 53 | 27.3 | 37 46 | 17 18 | 27.0 | 36 53 | 16 44 | 26.6 | 35 59 | 16 11 | 26.3 | 35 05 | 15 38 | 26.0 | 34 11 | 15 07 | 25.7 | 249 | 291 |
| 70 | 110 | 38 58 | 17 07 | 26.1 | 38 04 | 16 33 | 25.7 | 37 10 | 16 01 | 25.4 | 36 15 | 15 29 | 25.1 | 35 21 | 14 58 | 24.8 | 34 26 | 14 27 | 24.5 | 250 | 290 |
| 71 | 109 | 39 15 | 16 20 | 24.9 | 38 20 | 15 48 | 24.5 | 37 26 | 15 17 | 24.2 | 36 31 | 14 46 | 23.9 | 35 36 | 14 16 | 23.6 | 34 41 | 13 47 | 23.3 | 251 | 289 |
| 72 | 108 | 39 31 | 15 33 | 23.6 | 38 36 | 15 02 | 23.3 | 37 41 | 14 32 | 23.0 | 36 46 | 14 03 | 22.7 | 35 50 | 13 34 | 22.4 | 34 55 | 13 07 | 22.1 | 252 | 288 |
| 73 | 107 | 39 47 | 14 45 | 22.4 | 38 51 | 14 16 | 22.1 | 37 56 | 13 47 | 21.8 | 37 00 | 13 19 | 21.5 | 36 04 | 12 52 | 21.2 | 35 08 | 12 25 | 20.9 | 253 | 287 |
| 74 | 106 | 40 02 | 13 56 | 21.1 | 39 06 | 13 28 | 20.8 | 38 10 | 13 01 | 20.5 | 37 13 | 12 35 | 20.3 | 36 17 | 12 09 | 20.0 | 35 21 | 11 44 | 19.8 | 254 | 286 |
| 75 | 105 | 40 16 | 13 07 | 19.8 | 39 19 | 12 41 | 19.5 | 38 23 | 12 15 | 19.3 | 37 26 | 11 50 | 19.0 | 36 29 | 11 26 | 18.8 | 35 33 | 11 02 | 18.5 | 255 | 285 |
| 76 | 104 | 40 29 | 12 17 | 18.5 | 39 32 | 11 53 | 18.3 | 38 35 | 11 28 | 18.0 | 37 38 | 11 05 | 17.8 | 36 41 | 10 42 | 17.6 | 35 44 | 10 20 | 17.3 | 256 | 284 |
| 77 | 103 | 40 41 | 11 27 | 17.3 | 39 44 | 11 04 | 17.0 | 38 47 | 10 41 | 16.8 | 37 49 | 10 19 | 16.5 | 36 52 | 9 58 | 16.3 | 35 54 | 9 37 | 16.1 | 257 | 283 |
| 78 | 102 | 40 53 | 10 36 | 16.0 | 39 55 | 10 15 | 15.7 | 38 57 | 9 54 | 15.5 | 38 00 | 9 33 | 15.3 | 37 02 | 9 14 | 15.1 | 36 04 | 8 54 | 14.9 | 258 | 282 |
| 79 | 101 | 41 04 | 9 45 | 14.7 | 40 05 | 9 25 | 14.4 | 39 07 | 9 06 | 14.2 | 38 09 | 8 47 | 14.0 | 37 11 | 8 29 | 13.9 | 36 13 | 8 11 | 13.7 | 259 | 281 |
| 80 | 100 | 41 13 | 8 53 | 13.3 | 40 15 | 8 35 | 13.2 | 39 16 | 8 17 | 13.0 | 38 18 | 8 00 | 12.8 | 37 19 | 7 44 | 12.6 | 36 21 | 7 27 | 12.5 | 260 | 280 |
| 81 | 99 | 41 22 | 8 01 | 12.0 | 40 23 | 7 45 | 11.9 | 39 25 | 7 29 | 11.7 | 38 26 | 7 13 | 11.5 | 37 27 | 6 58 | 11.4 | 36 28 | 6 43 | 11.2 | 261 | 279 |
| 82 | 98 | 41 30 | 7 09 | 10.7 | 40 31 | 6 54 | 10.5 | 39 32 | 6 40 | 10.4 | 38 33 | 6 26 | 10.3 | 37 34 | 6 12 | 10.1 | 36 35 | 5 59 | 10.0 | 262 | 278 |
| 83 | 97 | 41 37 | 6 16 | 9.4 | 40 38 | 6 03 | 9.2 | 39 39 | 5 50 | 9.1 | 38 39 | 5 38 | 9.0 | 37 40 | 5 26 | 8.9 | 36 41 | 5 15 | 8.7 | 263 | 277 |
| 84 | 96 | 41 43 | 5 23 | 8.1 | 40 44 | 5 12 | 7.9 | 39 44 | 5 01 | 7.8 | 38 45 | 4 50 | 7.7 | 37 45 | 4 40 | 7.6 | 36 46 | 4 30 | 7.5 | 264 | 276 |
| 85 | 95 | 41 48 | 4 29 | 6.7 | 40 49 | 4 20 | 6.6 | 39 49 | 4 11 | 6.5 | 38 49 | 4 02 | 6.4 | 37 50 | 3 54 | 6.3 | 36 50 | 3 45 | 6.3 | 265 | 275 |
| 86 | 94 | 41 52 | 3 36 | 5.4 | 40 53 | 3 28 | 5.3 | 39 53 | 3 21 | 5.2 | 38 53 | 3 14 | 5.1 | 37 53 | 3 07 | 5.1 | 36 54 | 3 01 | 5.0 | 266 | 274 |
| 87 | 93 | 41 56 | 2 42 | 4.0 | 40 56 | 2 36 | 4.0 | 39 56 | 2 31 | 3.9 | 38 56 | 2 26 | 3.9 | 37 56 | 2 20 | 3.8 | 36 56 | 2 16 | 3.8 | 267 | 273 |
| 88 | 92 | 41 58 | 1 48 | 2.7 | 40 58 | 1 44 | 2.6 | 39 58 | 1 41 | 2.6 | 38 58 | 1 37 | 2.6 | 37 58 | 1 34 | 2.5 | 36 58 | 1 30 | 2.5 | 268 | 272 |
| 89 | 91 | 42 00 | 0 54 | 1.3 | 41 00 | 0 52 | 1.3 | 40 00 | 0 50 | 1.3 | 39 00 | 0 49 | 1.3 | 38 00 | 0 47 | 1.3 | 37 00 | 0 45 | 1.3 | 269 | 271 |
| 90 | 90 | 42 00 | 0 00 | 0.0 | 41 00 | 0 00 | 0.0 | 40 00 | 0 00 | 0.0 | 39 00 | 0 00 | 0.0 | 38 00 | 0 00 | 0.0 | 37 00 | 0 00 | 0.0 | 270 | 270 |

N. Lat: for LHA > 180°... $Z_n = Z$
        for LHA < 180°... $Z_n = 360° - Z$

S. Lat.: for LHA > 180°... $Z_n = 180° - Z$
        for LHA < 180°... $Z_n = 180° + Z$

# Step 4: Auxiliary Table: First Run

The Auxiliary Table, like the Reduction Tables, is sideways and spans 2 pages. Its top row works for both F minutes and A minutes and its columns on the left and right, respectively, work for both P degrees and Z2 degrees.

DO NOT confuse the columns on the left and right as being for the same numbers. They are not. Each is labeled separately, for F and for P.

The first number we need to arrive at is "corr1" and we use the minutes from F and the degrees from P to find it. Crossing the top row to 03 minutes (from F) and down the margin on the LEFT to 23 degrees (from P), we find a 1 minute value.

As a rule, corr1 is negative if F's degrees are less than 90 and its minutes are greater than 29. It is also negative if F's degrees are greater than 90 and its minutes are less than 30.

corr1 is − if F(deg)<90 and F(min)>29
corr1 is − if F(def)>90 and F(min)<30

F's degrees in our case were less than 90, but its minutes were not greater than 29. So corr1 remains positive.

corr1 = +1 minutes (Write this down in your worksheet.)

# Step 5: Auxiliary Table: Second Run

Now we use the table, cruising the top for A's minutes (25) and Z2's degrees (40) down the RIGHT side, and crossing them we find a value of 19. Normally, as a rule, corr2 is negative if A's minutes are less than 30.

corr2 is − if A(mins)<30

Since A's minutes are indeed less than 30, then our corr2 is now labeled negative. Write down "-19" in corr2's space.

**Now we're done with tables, hooray! Time for some more grade school math!**

# Step 6: Grade School Math: Finding Hc

On the right side of your worksheet, you will see now our trusty H value (from before, on the left—you got that from the tables. It's the same H). Copy the number from the left to the right. Below it are our friends corr1 and corr2, also from before.

Add corr1 and corr2 (or subtract, if they are negative numbers) to H, and this gives us our Sextant Angle, otherwise called the Hc for you master trivia geeks. Had we actually been there at the Assumed Position, this is what our corrected sextant sight would have read. Who knows how the tables got the numbers right—but it works! Pretty cool. Praise be to the geeks!

29 degrees, 56 minutes (H)
+ 1 minutes (corr1)
- 19 minutes (corr2)
---
29 degrees, 38 minutes (Hc)

As a rule, HC is negative if F is negative, which in this case it is not.

*Our next reality check:*

| | | |
|---|---|---|
| 4. Reduction table, $2^{nd}$ entry $(A°, F°) = (53°, 56°)$ record H, P and $Z_2$. | $H = 29°56'$   $P° = 23°$  $Z_2 = 40°2$ | nearest whole degree of P. |
| 5. Auxiliary table, $1^{st}$ entry $(F', P°) = (03', 23°)$ record $corr_1$ | $corr_1 = +1'$ | $corr_1$ is minus if $F < 90°$ & $F' > 29'$, or if $F > 90°$ & $F' < 30'$. |
| 6. Auxiliary table, $2^{nd}$ entry $(A', Z_2°) = (25', 40°)$ record $corr_2$ | $corr_2 = -19'$ | $Z_2°$ nearest whole degree of $Z_2$. $corr_2$ is minus if $A' < 30'$. |
| 7. Calculated altitude = $H_c = H + corr_1 + corr_2$ | $H_c = 29°38'$ | $H_c$ is minus if F is negative, and object is below the horizon. |

## Step 7: Grade School Math: Finding Zenith

Lots of Z's! I'd be snoring now too if I were you. Our friends Z1 and Z2 from before have come back on the right side of the page to be calculated.

There's a funny rule regarding Z2, which is on the worksheet so you remember. Z2 is negative if F's degrees (F from the left side of the sheet) are greater than 90 degrees. And, if F is a negative number, replace Z2 with 180 degrees – Z2's previous value.

Add (or subtract if negative) their values, to arrive at plain old Z. If Z ever happens to be a negative number, use its absolute value (erase the – sign and consider it positive).

Z is the Zenith Angle of our object, which helps for geeks but is hard to understand for we the slow people. You don't need to know—it's ok. We'll plug Z into the next box which will force it to make sense to us.

Since our F is neither greater than 90 nor a negative number, then we add both Z1 and Z2 together.

$$\begin{array}{r} 38.9 \text{ degrees (Z1)} \\ + 40.2 \text{ degrees (Z2)} \\ \hline Z = 79.1 \text{ degrees} \end{array}$$

## Step 8: Finding True Azimuth.

What is Azimuth? It is the angle, in true degrees (similar to magnetic degrees, but measured by earth's polar axis, not its magnetic field) in which the object you sighted is floating in the sky. Azimuth is labeled by the value Zn. There is not much math in this part; it is merely applying logic. The logic stuff is printed there on the reduction sheet so it's easier to use.

Ye onerous logic rules:

For North Latitudes:
    If your LHA is greater than 180 degrees, then Zn = Z
    If your LHA is less than 180 degrees, then Zn = 360 – Z
For South Latitudes:
    If your LHA is greater than 180, then Zn = 180 –Z
    If your LHA is less than 180, then Zn = 180 + Z

Our LHA was 68, and we're in North Latitudes, so Zn = 360 – Z.
360 – 79.1 (Z) = 280.9 degrees (Zn), round to 281 degrees.

# Step 9: Plotting and finding your real Line of Position

Mark your AP on the chart. It should be simple to do. Now use your parallel ruler to draw a line from your AP in the direction of your Azimuth angle, which we determined was 279.9 degrees. Mark the end of your Azimuth line with an arrow head. Now, if you drew a line perpendicular to that Azimuth, through your AP (either by using a protractor, or by running a parallel ruler 90 degrees off the Azimuth), that line would be your AP's Line of Position (a segment of that great circle!).

If we were actually there, we'd be somewhere on that line, but we're not—we're still lost somewhere in the ocean. But we know what direction we're looking in at the object we sighted, we know what the sextant angle would have shown if we were at our AP, and we know what the sextant shows now.

This means we can figure out our distance from the AP's line of position to our real line of position.

Our AP's sextant angle (Hc) was 29 degrees, 38 minutes. The sextant sight we actually took showed 29 degrees, 00 minutes. Find the difference between the two (subtract the lesser value from the larger one)

29 deg 38 mins (Ho)
-29 deg 00 mins (Hc)
―――――――――――――――――――――――
0 degrees 38 mins

We are 38 minutes distance from our AP. This means we're 38 nautical miles from our AP. But are we closer or farther from the GP (flagpole base) of our object?

There is an old rhyme/acronym thingie to help you remember-- associative memory techniques perfected by the Navy and coasties to make sure the slow ones could remember it:

**CGA** = **C**oast **G**uard **A**cademy = **C**alculated (**c**orrected) **G**reater, **A**way.

If the corrected (calculated) sextant angle (Hc) is greater, that means the AP is closer to the GP than you are. Basically, geometric laws state that someone taking a sight at the AP would have to look higher in the sky to see your object. So if your calculated Hc is greater than your actual Ho, you will plot your line AWAY from the GP.

In our case, our calculated angle is indeed greater than our observed angle. So we move our Line of Position 38 miles away from the target's GP, along that Azimuth line, and drop it down there. This Line of Position is the one we're actually on! Cool!

Now we just need a second object to shoot to give us another Line of Position, and we'll have an "X" on the chart showing where we really are.

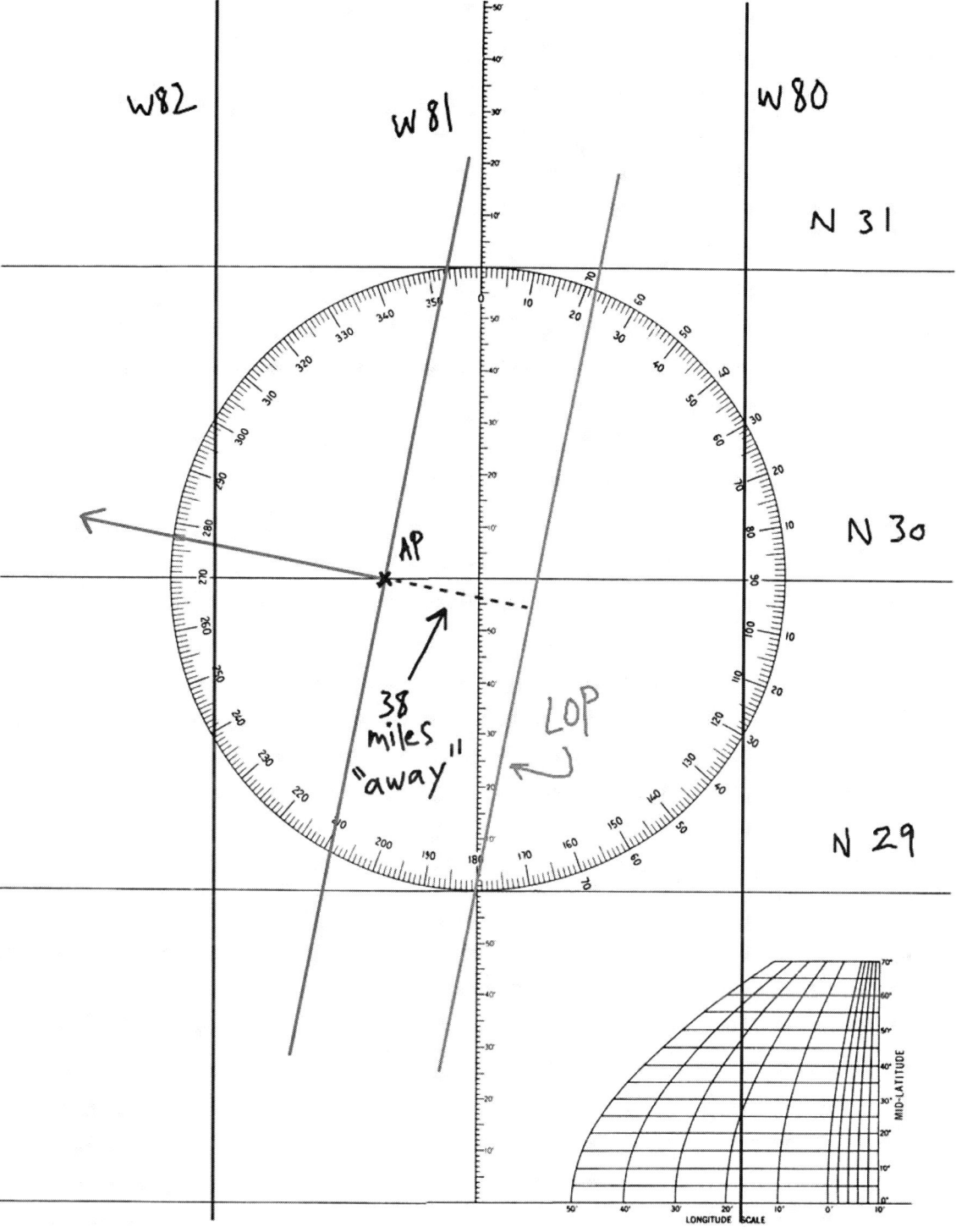

*This is what our Sight Reduction sheet would look like:*

## NAO CONCISE SIGHT REDUCTION FORM 319

| Date & UT of observation | | Body | Estimated Latitude & Longitude |
|---|---|---|---|
| 6-10-05 | 21:57:30 | | |

| Step | Calculate Altitude & Azimuth | Summary of Rules & Notes |
|---|---|---|
| Assumed latitude | Lat = 30° N | Nearest estimated latitude, integral number of degrees. |
| Assumed longitude | Long = 81° ~~24~~ 18' | Choose Long so that LHA has integral number of degrees. |
| 1. From the almanac: Dec | Dec = 23° 04' | Record the Dec for use in Step 3. |
| GHA ~~Aries~~ sun  h | = 135° 07' | Needed if using SHA. Tabular value. |
| Increment  m  s | = 14' 23" | for minutes and seconds of time. |
| ~~SHA~~ final GHA | SHA = 149° 30' | |
| GHA = GHA Aries + SHA | GHA = 149° 30' | Remove multiples of 360°. |
| Assumed longitude | Long = 81° 24' | West longitudes are negative. |
| LHA = GHA + Long | LHA = 68° 06' | Remove multiples of 360°. |
| 2. Reduction table, 1st entry (Lat, LHA) = (  °,  °) record A, B and $Z_1$. | A = 53° 25'   A° = 53° | nearest whole degree of A. |
| | A' = 25' | minutes part of A. |
| | + B = 32° 59' | B is minus if 90° < LHA < 270°. |
| | $Z_1$ = 38.9 | $Z_1$ has the same sign as B. |
| 3. From step 1 | Dec = 23° 04' | Dec is minus if contrary to Lat. |
| F = B + Dec | F = 56° 03' | Regard F as positive until step 7. |
| | F° = 56° | nearest whole degree of F. |
| | F' = 03' | minutes part of F. |
| 4. Reduction table, 2nd entry (A°, F°) = (53°, 56°) record H, P and $Z_2$. | H = 29° 56'   P° = 23° | nearest whole degree of P. |
| | $Z_2$ = 40.2 | |
| 5. Auxiliary table, 1st entry (F', P°) = (03', 23°) record $corr_1$ | $corr_1$ = + 1' | $corr_1$ is minus if F < 90° & F' > 29', or if F > 90° & F' < 30'. |
| 6. Auxiliary table, 2nd entry (A', $Z_2$°) = (25', 40°) record $corr_2$ | $corr_2$ = − 19' | $Z_2$° nearest whole degree of $Z_2$. *$corr_2$ is minus if A' < 30'.* |
| 7. Calculated altitude = $H_c$ = H + $corr_1$ + $corr_2$ | $H_c$ = 29° 38' | $H_c$ is minus if F is negative, and object is below the horizon. |
| 8. Azimuth, 1st component | $Z_1$ = 38.9 | $Z_1$ has the same sign as B. |
| 2nd component | $Z_2$ = 40.2 | $Z_2$ is minus if F > 90°. If F is negative, $Z_2$ = 180° − $Z_2$ |
| Z = $Z_1$ + $Z_2$ | Z = 79.1 | Ignore the sign of Z. |
| | | N Lat: If LHA > 180°, $Z_n$ = Z, or *if LHA < 180°, $Z_n$ = 360° − Z.* |
| | | S Lat: If LHA > 180°, $Z_n$ = 180° − Z, or if LHA < 180°, $Z_n$ = 180° + Z. |
| True azimuth | $Z_n$ = 280.9  (281°) | ©HMNAO |

For use with *The Nautical Almanac's* Concise Sight Reduction Tables pages 284-318.

Copyright Council for the Central Laboratory of the Research Councils 2005

# How to use HO229 for sight reduction:

There are indeed virtues to be found in the huge volumes of the HO229 tables. Now that you've learned how to do sight reductions the hard way, it will take all of one page to teach you how to use HO229. Yes, I am a heartless bastard, but you cannot know the sweet until you have tasted the bitter.

HO229 is set up in pages numbered by LHA.

1. Flip to the page with your LHA number.
2. At the top and bottom of the pages are statements declaring whether or not the numbers are for Latitude Same or Contrary to Declination (is your target in the same or opposite hemisphere?). The pages that contain both contrary and same hemisphere information are divided by a line, with the halves properly labeled.
3. Finding your LHA page, and your pertinent Same/Contrary section, run your finger across the top/bottom bar of Latitude degrees until you find the proper one.
4. Now steer your finger up/down the column until you find your target's Dec (declination) number.
5. There will be 3 values listed. Hc, d, and Z. Write these down.

If you take our old numbers (LHA 68, Lat 30, Dec 23), using the sample page, we find:

Hc = 29 degrees, 36.2 min     d = +22.8     Z = 79.0

You will notice that Dec was only listed in whole numbers. There are increments and correction tables in the inside front and back covers of the volume, and these pertain to the d value. The d value is summed with the Hc value to achieve our end result. If d was negative, you will be subtracting the correction. If d is positive, you will be adding the correction.

1. Find your Dec Increment (d value) in the bold margin numbers of the increment tables. 1-30 is on the front inside cover, 30-60 is on the back inside cover.
2. You will see values for tens on the left side of the columns, and individual units on the right side of the columns. If you have, say, 15 minutes of Dec to account for, you'd first grab the 10s value, then the 5 units value, and add them together for the total correction.

Our d value was +22.8. Scroll down the bold Dec. Inc. column to 22.8. Our Dec is 23 degrees, 4 minutes. We're only correcting for minutes here so 4 minutes gives us a correction of +1.8. Our Hc is 29 degrees 36.2 minutes. Add 1.8 minutes, for a total of 29 degrees, 38 minutes. Notice that it's the exact same result the hard way gave us). Z is also the same.

Don't bother with any further increments, as they will not be large enough to affect the accuracy of your plot.   Now we have a finished Hc and Z, which we can use to plot our Azimuth and LOP. **That's all there is to it!**

68°, 292° L.H.A. LATITUDE SAME NAME AS DECLINATION

N. Lat. {L.H.A. greater than 180° .....Zn=Z; L.H.A. less than 180° ..........Zn=360°−Z}

| Dec. | 30° Hc | 30° d | 30° Z | 31° Hc | 31° d | 31° Z | 32° Hc | 32° d | 32° Z | 33° Hc | 33° d | 33° Z | 34° Hc | 34° d | 34° Z | 35° Hc | 35° d | 35° Z | 36° Hc | 36° d | 36° Z | 37° Hc | 37° d | 37° Z | Dec. |
|---|---|---|---|---|---|---|---|---|---|---|---|---|---|---|---|---|---|---|---|---|---|---|---|---|---|
| ° | ° ′ | ′ | ° | ° ′ | ′ | ° | ° ′ | ′ | ° | ° ′ | ′ | ° | ° ′ | ′ | ° | ° ′ | ′ | ° | ° ′ | ′ | ° | ° ′ | ′ | ° | ° |
| 0 | 18 55.8 | +31.6 | 101.4 | 18 43.8 | +32.5 | 101.8 | 18 31.4 | +33.4 | 102.1 | 18 18.6 | +34.4 | 102.4 | 18 05.6 | +35.2 | 102.7 | 17 52.2 | +36.1 | 103.0 | 17 38.5 | +36.9 | 103.4 | 17 24.5 | +37.7 | 103.7 | 0 |
| 1 | 19 27.4 | +31.3 | 100.5 | 19 16.3 | +32.2 | 100.9 | 19 04.8 | +33.1 | 101.2 | 18 53.0 | +34.0 | 101.5 | 18 40.8 | +34.9 | 101.9 | 18 28.3 | +35.8 | 102.2 | 18 15.4 | +36.7 | 102.5 | 18 02.2 | +37.6 | 102.9 | 1 |
| 2 | 19 58.7 | +31.1 | 99.6 | 19 48.5 | +32.0 | 100.0 | 19 37.9 | +32.9 | 100.3 | 19 27.0 | +33.8 | 100.7 | 19 15.7 | +34.7 | 101.0 | 19 04.1 | +35.6 | 101.4 | 18 52.1 | +36.5 | 101.7 | 18 39.8 | +37.3 | 102.0 | 2 |
| 3 | 20 29.8 | +30.7 | 98.7 | 20 20.5 | +31.7 | 99.1 | 20 10.8 | +32.7 | 99.4 | 20 00.8 | +33.6 | 99.8 | 19 50.4 | +34.5 | 100.2 | 19 39.7 | +35.3 | 100.5 | 19 28.6 | +36.2 | 100.9 | 19 17.1 | +37.1 | 101.2 | 3 |
| 4 | 21 00.5 | +30.5 | 97.8 | 20 52.2 | +31.4 | 98.2 | 20 43.5 | +32.3 | 98.5 | 20 34.4 | +33.2 | 98.9 | 20 24.9 | +34.2 | 99.3 | 20 15.0 | +35.1 | 99.6 | 20 04.8 | +36.0 | 100.0 | 19 54.2 | +36.8 | 100.4 | 4 |
| 5 | 21 31.0 | +30.1 | 96.9 | 21 23.6 | +31.1 | 97.2 | 21 15.8 | +32.1 | 97.6 | 21 07.6 | +33.0 | 98.0 | 20 59.1 | +33.9 | 98.4 | 20 50.1 | +34.8 | 98.8 | 20 40.8 | +35.7 | 99.2 | 20 31.0 | +36.6 | 99.5 | 5 |
| 6 | 22 01.1 | +29.8 | 95.9 | 21 54.7 | +30.8 | 96.3 | 21 47.9 | +31.7 | 96.7 | 21 40.6 | +32.8 | 97.1 | 21 33.0 | +33.6 | 97.5 | 21 24.9 | +34.6 | 97.9 | 21 16.5 | +35.5 | 98.3 | 21 07.6 | +36.4 | 98.7 | 6 |
| 7 | 22 30.9 | +29.5 | 95.0 | 22 25.5 | +30.5 | 95.4 | 22 19.6 | +31.5 | 95.8 | 22 13.4 | +32.4 | 96.2 | 22 06.6 | +33.4 | 96.6 | 21 59.5 | +34.3 | 97.0 | 21 52.0 | +35.2 | 97.4 | 21 44.0 | +36.1 | 97.8 | 7 |
| 8 | 23 00.4 | +29.2 | 94.0 | 22 56.0 | +30.1 | 94.5 | 22 51.1 | +31.1 | 94.9 | 22 45.8 | +32.0 | 95.3 | 22 40.0 | +33.0 | 95.7 | 22 33.8 | +34.0 | 96.1 | 22 27.2 | +34.9 | 96.6 | 22 20.1 | +35.8 | 97.0 | 8 |
| 9 | 23 29.6 | +28.8 | 93.1 | 23 26.1 | +29.8 | 93.5 | 23 22.2 | +30.8 | 94.0 | 23 17.8 | +31.8 | 94.4 | 23 13.0 | +32.8 | 94.8 | 23 07.8 | +33.6 | 95.2 | 23 02.1 | +34.6 | 95.7 | 22 55.9 | +35.5 | 96.1 | 9 |
| 10 | 23 58.4 | +28.5 | 92.1 | 23 55.9 | +29.5 | 92.6 | 23 53.0 | +30.5 | 93.0 | 23 49.6 | +31.4 | 93.5 | 23 45.8 | +32.4 | 93.9 | 23 41.4 | +33.4 | 94.3 | 23 36.7 | +34.3 | 94.8 | 23 31.4 | +35.3 | 95.2 | 10 |
| 11 | 24 26.9 | +28.0 | 91.2 | 24 25.4 | +29.1 | 91.6 | 24 23.5 | +30.1 | 92.1 | 24 21.0 | +31.1 | 92.5 | 24 18.2 | +32.0 | 93.0 | 24 14.8 | +33.0 | 93.4 | 24 11.0 | +34.0 | 93.9 | 24 06.7 | +34.9 | 94.3 | 11 |
| 12 | 24 54.9 | +27.7 | 90.2 | 24 54.5 | +28.7 | 90.7 | 24 53.6 | +29.7 | 91.1 | 24 52.1 | +30.8 | 91.6 | 24 50.2 | +31.7 | 92.1 | 24 47.8 | +32.7 | 92.5 | 24 45.0 | +33.6 | 93.0 | 24 41.6 | +34.6 | 93.4 | 12 |
| 13 | 25 22.6 | +27.4 | 89.2 | 25 23.2 | +28.4 | 89.7 | 25 23.3 | +29.3 | 90.2 | 25 22.9 | +30.3 | 90.6 | 25 21.9 | +31.4 | 91.1 | 25 20.5 | +32.4 | 91.6 | 25 18.6 | +33.3 | 92.1 | 25 16.2 | +34.3 | 92.5 | 13 |
| 14 | 25 50.0 | +26.9 | 88.2 | 25 51.6 | +27.9 | 88.7 | 25 52.6 | +29.0 | 89.2 | 25 53.2 | +30.0 | 89.7 | 25 53.3 | +31.0 | 90.2 | 25 52.9 | +31.9 | 90.7 | 25 51.9 | +33.0 | 91.1 | 25 50.5 | +33.9 | 91.6 | 14 |
| 15 | 26 16.9 | +26.5 | 87.2 | 26 19.5 | +27.5 | 87.7 | 26 21.6 | +28.6 | 88.2 | 26 23.2 | +29.6 | 88.7 | 26 24.3 | +30.6 | 89.2 | 26 24.8 | +31.7 | 89.7 | 26 24.9 | +32.6 | 90.2 | 26 24.4 | +33.6 | 90.7 | 15 |
| 16 | 26 43.4 | +26.0 | 86.2 | 26 47.0 | +27.1 | 86.7 | 26 50.2 | +28.1 | 87.2 | 26 52.8 | +29.2 | 87.7 | 26 54.9 | +30.2 | 88.3 | 26 56.5 | +31.2 | 88.8 | 26 57.5 | +32.2 | 89.3 | 26 58.0 | +33.2 | 89.8 | 16 |
| 17 | 27 09.4 | +25.6 | 85.2 | 27 14.1 | +26.7 | 85.7 | 27 18.3 | +27.8 | 86.3 | 27 22.0 | +28.8 | 86.8 | 27 25.1 | +29.8 | 87.3 | 27 27.7 | +30.8 | 87.8 | 27 29.7 | +31.8 | 88.3 | 27 31.2 | +32.8 | 88.8 | 17 |
| 18 | 27 35.0 | +25.2 | 84.2 | 27 40.8 | +26.3 | 84.7 | 27 46.1 | +27.3 | 85.3 | 27 50.8 | +28.3 | 85.8 | 27 54.9 | +29.4 | 86.3 | 27 58.5 | +30.4 | 86.8 | 28 01.5 | +31.5 | 87.4 | 28 04.0 | +32.4 | 87.9 | 18 |
| 19 | 28 00.2 | +24.7 | 83.2 | 28 07.1 | +25.8 | 83.7 | 28 13.4 | +26.8 | 84.2 | 28 19.1 | +27.9 | 84.8 | 28 24.3 | +28.9 | 85.3 | 28 28.9 | +30.0 | 85.9 | 28 33.0 | +31.0 | 86.4 | 28 36.4 | +32.1 | 86.9 | 19 |
| 20 | 28 24.9 | +24.3 | 82.1 | 28 32.9 | +25.3 | 82.7 | 28 40.2 | +26.4 | 83.2 | 28 47.0 | +27.5 | 83.8 | 28 53.2 | +28.5 | 84.3 | 28 58.9 | +29.5 | 84.9 | 29 04.0 | +30.6 | 85.4 | 29 08.5 | +31.6 | 86.0 | 20 |
| 21 | 28 49.2 | +23.7 | 81.1 | 28 58.2 | +24.8 | 81.6 | 29 06.6 | +25.9 | 82.2 | 29 14.5 | +27.0 | 82.8 | 29 21.7 | +28.1 | 83.3 | 29 28.4 | +29.1 | 83.9 | 29 34.6 | +30.1 | 84.4 | 29 40.1 | +31.2 | 85.0 | 21 |
| 22 | [illegible] | [illegible] | [illegible] | 29 23.0 | +24.4 | 80.6 | 29 32.5 | +25.5 | 81.2 | 29 41.5 | +26.5 | 81.7 | 29 49.8 | +27.6 | 82.3 | 29 57.5 | +28.7 | 82.9 | 30 04.7 | +29.7 | 83.4 | 30 11.3 | +30.7 | 84.0 | 22 |
| 23 | 29 36.2 | +22.8 | 79.0 | 29 47.4 | +23.8 | 79.6 | 29 58.0 | +24.9 | 80.1 | 30 08.0 | +26.0 | 80.7 | 30 17.4 | +27.1 | 81.3 | 30 26.2 | +28.1 | 81.8 | 30 34.4 | +29.2 | 82.4 | 30 42.0 | +30.3 | 83.0 | 23 |
| 24 | [illegible] | [illegible] | [illegible] | 30 11.2 | +23.4 | 78.5 | 30 22.9 | +24.4 | 79.1 | 30 34.0 | +25.5 | 79.6 | 30 44.5 | +26.6 | 80.2 | 30 54.3 | +27.7 | 80.8 | 31 03.6 | +28.7 | 81.4 | 31 12.3 | +29.7 | 82.0 | 24 |
| 25 | 30 21.2 | +21.7 | 76.9 | 30 34.6 | +22.8 | 77.4 | 30 47.3 | +23.9 | 78.0 | 30 59.5 | +25.0 | 78.6 | 31 11.1 | +26.0 | 79.2 | 31 22.0 | +27.2 | 79.8 | 31 32.3 | +28.3 | 80.4 | 31 42.0 | +29.3 | 81.0 | 25 |
| 26 | 30 42.9 | +21.2 | 75.8 | 30 57.4 | +22.2 | 76.4 | 31 11.2 | +23.4 | 76.9 | 31 24.5 | +24.4 | 77.5 | 31 37.1 | +25.6 | 78.1 | 31 49.2 | +26.6 | 78.7 | 32 00.6 | +27.7 | 79.3 | 32 11.3 | +28.8 | 80.0 | 26 |
| 27 | 31 04.1 | +20.6 | 74.7 | 31 19.6 | +21.7 | 75.3 | 31 34.6 | +22.8 | 75.9 | 31 48.9 | +24.0 | 76.5 | 32 02.7 | +25.0 | 77.1 | 32 15.8 | +26.1 | 77.7 | 32 28.3 | +27.2 | 78.3 | 32 40.1 | +28.3 | 78.9 | 27 |
| 28 | 31 24.7 | +20.0 | 73.6 | 31 41.3 | +21.2 | 74.2 | 31 57.4 | +22.3 | 74.8 | 32 12.9 | +23.3 | 75.4 | 32 27.7 | +24.5 | 76.0 | 32 41.9 | +25.6 | 76.6 | 32 55.5 | +26.6 | 77.2 | 33 08.4 | +27.8 | 77.9 | 28 |
| 29 | 31 44.7 | +19.5 | 72.5 | 32 02.5 | +20.6 | 73.1 | 32 19.7 | +21.7 | 73.7 | 32 36.2 | +22.8 | 74.3 | 32 52.2 | +23.9 | 74.9 | 33 07.5 | +25.0 | 75.5 | 33 22.1 | +26.1 | 76.2 | 33 36.2 | +27.1 | 76.8 | 29 |
| 30 | 32 04.2 | +18.9 | 71.4 | 32 23.1 | +20.0 | 72.0 | 32 41.4 | +21.1 | 72.6 | 32 59.0 | +22.2 | 73.2 | 33 16.1 | +23.3 | 73.8 | 33 32.5 | +24.4 | 74.4 | 33 48.2 | +25.6 | 75.1 | 34 03.3 | +26.7 | 75.7 | 30 |
| 31 | 32 23.1 | +18.3 | 70.2 | 32 43.1 | +19.4 | 70.8 | 33 02.5 | +20.5 | 71.5 | 33 21.2 | +21.6 | 72.1 | 33 39.4 | +22.7 | 72.7 | 33 56.9 | +23.8 | 73.3 | 34 13.8 | +24.9 | 74.0 | 34 30.0 | +26.0 | 74.7 | 31 |
| 32 | 32 41.4 | +17.6 | 69.1 | 33 02.5 | +18.7 | 69.7 | 33 23.0 | +19.8 | 70.3 | 33 42.8 | +21.0 | 71.0 | 34 02.1 | +22.1 | 71.6 | 34 20.7 | +23.3 | 72.2 | 34 38.7 | +24.3 | 72.9 | 34 56.0 | +25.5 | 73.6 | 32 |
| 33 | 32 59.0 | +17.1 | 68.0 | 33 21.2 | +18.2 | 68.6 | 33 42.8 | +19.3 | 69.2 | 34 03.8 | +20.4 | 69.8 | 34 24.2 | +21.5 | 70.5 | 34 44.0 | +22.6 | 71.1 | 35 03.0 | +23.8 | 71.8 | 35 21.5 | +24.8 | 72.5 | 33 |
| 34 | 33 16.1 | +16.4 | 66.8 | 33 39.4 | +17.5 | 67.4 | 34 02.1 | +18.6 | 68.1 | 34 24.2 | +19.8 | 68.7 | 34 45.7 | +20.9 | 69.3 | 35 06.6 | +21.9 | 70.0 | 35 26.8 | +23.1 | 70.7 | 35 46.3 | +24.2 | 71.3 | 34 |
| 35 | 33 32.5 | +15.7 | 65.7 | 33 56.9 | +16.9 | 66.3 | 34 20.7 | +18.0 | 66.9 | 34 44.0 | +19.0 | 67.5 | 35 06.6 | +20.2 | 68.2 | 35 28.5 | +21.4 | 68.8 | 35 49.9 | +22.4 | 69.5 | 36 10.5 | +23.6 | 70.2 | 35 |
| 36 | 33 48.2 | +15.1 | 64.5 | 34 13.8 | +16.2 | 65.1 | 34 38.7 | +17.3 | 65.8 | 35 03.0 | +18.5 | 66.4 | 35 26.8 | +19.5 | 67.0 | 35 49.9 | +20.6 | 67.7 | 36 12.3 | +21.8 | 68.4 | 36 34.1 | +22.9 | 69.1 | 36 |
| 37 | 34 03.3 | +14.5 | 63.4 | 34 30.0 | +15.5 | 64.0 | 34 56.0 | +16.7 | 64.6 | 35 21.5 | +17.7 | 65.2 | 35 46.3 | +18.9 | 65.9 | 36 10.5 | +20.0 | 66.5 | 36 34.1 | +21.1 | 67.2 | 36 57.0 | +22.2 | 67.9 | 37 |
| 38 | 34 17.8 | +13.8 | 62.2 | 34 45.5 | +14.9 | 62.8 | 35 12.7 | +15.9 | 63.4 | 35 39.2 | +17.1 | 64.1 | 36 05.2 | +18.1 | 64.7 | 36 30.5 | +19.3 | 65.4 | 36 55.2 | +20.4 | 66.0 | 37 19.2 | +21.5 | 66.7 | 38 |
| 39 | 34 31.6 | +13.0 | 61.0 | 35 00.4 | +14.1 | 61.6 | 35 28.6 | +15.3 | 62.2 | 35 56.3 | +16.3 | 62.9 | 36 23.3 | +17.5 | 63.5 | 36 49.8 | +18.6 | 64.2 | 37 15.6 | +19.7 | 64.9 | 37 40.7 | +20.9 | 65.6 | 39 |
| 40 | 34 44.6 | +12.4 | 59.8 | 35 14.5 | +13.5 | 60.4 | 35 43.9 | +14.5 | 61.0 | 36 12.6 | +15.7 | 61.7 | 36 40.8 | +16.8 | 62.3 | 37 08.4 | +17.8 | 63.0 | 37 35.3 | +19.0 | 63.7 | 38 01.6 | +20.1 | 64.4 | 40 |
| 41 | 34 57.0 | +11.7 | 58.6 | 35 28.0 | +12.8 | 59.2 | 35 58.4 | +13.9 | 59.8 | 36 28.3 | +14.9 | 60.5 | 36 57.6 | +16.0 | 61.1 | 37 26.2 | +17.2 | 61.8 | 37 54.3 | +18.2 | 62.5 | 38 21.7 | +19.3 | 63.2 | 41 |
| 42 | 35 08.7 | +11.0 | 57.4 | 35 40.8 | +12.0 | 58.0 | 36 12.3 | +13.1 | 58.6 | 36 43.2 | +14.2 | 59.3 | 37 13.6 | +15.3 | 59.9 | 37 43.4 | +16.3 | 60.6 | 38 12.5 | +17.5 | 61.3 | 38 41.0 | +18.6 | 62.0 | 42 |
| 43 | 35 19.7 | +10.3 | 56.2 | 35 52.8 | +11.3 | 56.8 | 36 25.4 | +12.4 | 57.4 | 36 57.4 | +13.5 | 58.1 | 37 28.9 | +14.5 | 58.7 | 37 59.7 | +15.7 | 59.4 | 38 30.0 | +16.7 | 60.0 | 38 59.6 | +17.9 | 60.7 | 43 |
| 44 | 35 30.0 | +9.5 | 55.0 | 36 04.1 | +10.6 | 55.6 | 36 37.8 | +11.6 | 56.2 | 37 10.9 | +12.6 | 56.8 | 37 43.4 | +13.8 | 57.5 | 38 15.4 | +14.8 | 58.1 | 38 46.7 | +16.0 | 58.8 | 39 17.5 | +17.0 | 59.5 | 44 |
| 45 | 35 39.5 | +8.8 | 53.8 | 36 14.7 | +9.8 | 54.4 | 36 49.4 | +10.9 | 55.0 | 37 23.5 | +12.0 | 55.6 | 37 57.2 | +12.9 | 56.2 | 38 30.2 | +14.1 | 56.9 | 39 02.7 | +15.1 | 57.6 | 39 34.5 | +16.3 | 58.3 | 45 |
| 46 | 35 48.3 | +8.1 | 52.6 | 36 24.5 | +9.1 | 53.2 | 37 00.3 | +10.1 | 53.8 | 37 35.5 | +11.1 | 54.4 | 38 10.1 | +12.2 | 55.0 | 38 44.3 | +13.2 | 55.7 | 39 17.8 | +14.4 | 56.3 | 39 50.8 | +15.4 | 57.0 | 46 |
| 47 | 35 56.4 | +7.3 | 51.4 | 36 33.6 | +8.3 | 51.9 | 37 10.4 | +9.3 | 52.5 | 37 46.6 | +10.4 | 53.1 | 38 22.3 | +11.5 | 53.8 | 38 57.5 | +12.5 | 54.4 | 39 32.2 | +13.5 | 55.1 | 40 06.2 | +14.7 | 55.8 | 47 |
| 48 | 36 03.7 | +6.5 | 50.1 | 36 41.9 | +7.6 | 50.7 | 37 19.7 | +8.5 | 51.3 | 37 57.0 | +9.5 | 51.9 | 38 33.8 | +10.5 | 52.5 | 39 10.0 | +11.6 | 53.1 | 39 45.7 | +12.7 | 53.8 | 40 20.9 | +13.7 | 54.5 | 48 |
| 49 | 36 10.2 | +5.8 | 48.9 | 36 49.5 | +6.7 | 49.5 | 37 28.2 | +7.8 | 50.0 | 38 06.5 | +8.8 | 50.6 | 38 44.3 | +9.8 | 51.2 | 39 21.6 | +10.9 | 51.9 | 39 58.4 | +11.9 | 52.5 | 40 34.6 | +13.0 | 53.2 | 49 |
| 50 | 36 16.0 | +5.1 | 47.7 | 36 56.2 | +6.0 | 48.2 | 37 36.0 | +7.0 | 48.8 | 38 15.3 | +8.0 | 49.4 | 38 54.1 | +9.0 | 50.0 | 39 32.5 | +9.9 | 50.6 | 40 10.3 | +11.0 | 51.3 | 40 47.6 | +12.0 | 51.9 | 50 |
| 51 | 36 21.1 | +4.3 | 46.4 | 37 02.2 | +5.3 | 47.0 | 37 43.0 | +6.1 | 47.5 | 38 23.3 | +7.1 | 48.1 | 39 03.1 | +8.1 | 48.7 | 39 42.4 | +9.2 | 49.3 | 40 21.3 | +10.1 | 50.0 | 40 59.6 | +11.2 | 50.6 | 51 |
| 52 | 36 25.4 | +3.5 | 45.2 | 37 07.5 | +4.4 | 45.7 | 37 49.1 | +5.4 | 46.3 | 38 30.4 | +6.3 | 46.8 | 39 11.2 | +7.3 | 47.4 | 39 51.6 | +8.2 | 48.0 | 40 31.4 | +9.3 | 48.7 | 41 10.8 | +10.3 | 49.3 | 52 |
| 53 | 36 28.9 | +2.7 | 43.9 | 37 11.9 | +3.6 | 44.5 | 37 54.5 | +4.6 | 45.0 | 38 36.7 | +5.5 | 45.6 | 39 18.5 | +6.4 | 46.1 | 39 59.8 | +7.4 | 46.8 | 40 40.7 | +8.4 | 47.4 | 41 21.1 | +9.4 | 48.0 | 53 |
| 54 | 36 31.6 | +2.0 | 42.7 | 37 15.5 | +2.9 | 43.2 | 37 59.1 | +3.7 | 43.7 | 38 42.2 | +4.7 | 44.3 | 39 24.9 | +5.6 | 44.9 | 40 07.2 | +6.6 | 45.5 | 40 49.1 | +7.5 | 46.1 | 41 30.5 | +8.5 | 46.7 | 54 |
| 55 | 36 33.6 | +1.1 | 41.5 | 37 18.4 | +2.0 | 42.0 | 38 02.8 | +2.9 | 42.5 | 38 46.9 | +3.8 | 43.0 | 39 30.5 | +4.8 | 43.6 | 40 13.8 | +5.6 | 44.2 | 40 56.6 | +6.6 | 44.8 | 41 39.0 | +7.6 | 45.4 | 55 |
| 56 | 36 34.7 | +0.5 | 40.2 | 37 20.4 | +1.2 | 40.7 | 38 05.7 | +2.1 | 41.2 | 38 50.7 | +2.9 | 41.7 | 39 35.3 | +3.8 | 42.3 | 40 19.4 | +4.8 | 42.8 | 41 03.2 | +5.7 | 43.4 | 41 46.6 | +6.6 | 44.0 | 56 |
| 57 | 36 35.2 | −0.4 | 39.0 | 37 21.6 | +0.5 | 39.4 | 38 07.8 | +1.3 | 39.9 | 38 53.6 | +2.2 | 40.5 | 39 39.1 | +3.0 | 41.0 | 40 24.2 | +3.9 | 41.5 | 41 08.9 | +4.8 | 42.1 | 41 53.2 | +5.8 | 42.7 | 57 |
| 58 | 36 34.8 | −1.2 | 37.7 | 37 22.1 | −0.4 | 38.2 | 38 09.1 | +0.5 | 38.7 | 38 55.8 | +1.3 | 39.2 | 39 42.1 | +2.2 | 39.7 | 40 28.1 | +3.0 | 40.2 | 41 13.7 | +3.9 | 40.8 | 41 59.0 | +4.8 | 41.4 | 58 |
| 59 | 36 33.6 | −1.9 | 36.5 | 37 21.7 | −1.1 | 36.9 | 38 09.6 | −0.4 | 37.4 | 38 57.1 | +0.4 | 37.9 | 39 44.3 | +1.2 | 38.4 | 40 31.1 | +2.1 | 38.9 | 41 17.6 | +3.0 | 39.5 | 42 03.8 | +3.8 | 40.0 | 59 |
| 60 | 36 31.7 | −2.7 | 35.2 | 37 20.6 | −2.0 | 35.7 | 38 09.2 | −1.2 | 36.1 | 38 57.5 | −0.4 | 36.6 | 39 45.5 | +0.4 | 37.1 | 40 33.2 | +1.2 | 37.6 | 41 20.6 | +2.0 | 38.1 | 42 07.6 | +2.9 | 38.7 | 60 |
| 61 | 36 29.0 | −3.5 | 34.0 | 37 18.6 | −2.7 | 34.4 | 38 08.0 | −2.0 | 34.9 | 38 57.1 | −1.2 | 35.3 | 39 45.9 | −0.5 | 35.8 | 40 34.4 | +0.4 | 36.3 | 41 22.6 | +1.2 | 36.8 | 42 10.5 | +2.0 | 37.3 | 61 |
| 62 | 36 25.5 | −4.2 | 32.8 | 37 15.9 | −3.6 | 33.2 | 38 06.0 | −2.8 | 33.6 | 38 55.9 | −2.1 | 34.0 | 39 45.4 | −1.3 | 34.5 | 40 34.8 | −0.6 | 35.0 | 41 23.8 | +0.2 | 35.5 | 42 12.5 | +1.0 | 36.0 | 62 |
| 63 | 36 21.3 | −5.0 | 31.5 | 37 12.3 | −4.3 | 31.9 | 38 03.2 | −3.7 | 32.3 | 38 53.8 | −3.0 | 32.7 | 39 44.1 | −2.2 | 33.2 | 40 34.2 | −1.5 | 33.7 | 41 24.0 | −0.7 | 34.1 | 42 13.5 | +0.1 | 34.6 | 63 |
| 64 | 36 16.3 | −5.8 | 30.3 | 37 08.0 | −5.1 | 30.7 | 37 59.5 | −4.4 | 31.0 | 38 50.8 | −3.8 | 31.5 | 39 41.9 | −3.1 | 31.9 | 40 32.7 | −2.4 | 32.3 | 41 23.3 | −1.7 | 32.8 | 42 13.6 | −0.9 | 33.3 | 64 |
| 65 | 36 10.5 | −6.5 | 29.0 | 37 02.9 | −5.9 | 29.4 | 37 55.1 | −5.3 | 29.8 | 38 47.0 | −4.6 | 30.2 | 39 38.8 | −4.0 | 30.6 | 40 30.3 | −3.2 | 31.0 | 41 21.6 | −2.5 | 31.5 | 42 12.7 | −1.9 | 31.9 | 65 |
| 66 | 36 04.0 | −7.3 | 27.8 | 36 57.0 | −6.7 | 28.2 | 37 49.8 | −6.1 | 28.5 | 38 42.4 | −5.4 | 28.9 | 39 34.8 | −4.8 | 29.3 | 40 27.1 | −4.2 | 29.7 | 41 19.1 | −3.5 | 30.1 | 42 10.8 | −2.7 | 30.6 | 66 |
| 67 | 35 56.7 | −8.0 | 26.6 | 36 50.3 | −7.5 | 26.9 | 37 43.7 | −6.9 | 27.3 | 38 37.0 | −6.3 | 27.6 | 39 30.0 | −5.6 | 28.0 | 40 22.9 | −5.0 | 28.4 | 41 15.6 | −4.4 | 28.8 | 42 08.1 | −3.8 | 29.2 | 67 |
| 68 | 35 48.7 | −8.8 | 25.4 | 36 42.8 | −8.2 | 25.7 | 37 36.8 | −7.6 | 26.0 | 38 30.7 | −7.1 | 26.4 | 39 24.4 | −6.5 | 26.7 | 40 17.9 | −5.9 | 27.1 | 41 11.2 | −5.3 | 27.5 | 42 04.3 | −4.6 | 27.9 | 68 |
| 69 | 35 39.9 | −9.5 | 24.1 | 36 34.6 | −9.0 | 24.4 | 37 29.2 | −8.5 | 24.8 | 38 23.6 | −7.9 | 25.1 | 39 17.9 | −7.4 | 25.4 | 40 12.0 | −6.8 | 25.8 | 41 05.9 | −6.2 | 26.2 | 41 59.7 | −5.6 | 26.6 | 69 |
| 70 | 35 30.4 | −10.2 | 22.9 | 36 25.6 | −9.7 | 23.2 | 37 20.7 | −9.2 | 23.5 | 38 15.7 | −8.8 | 23.8 | 39 10.5 | −8.2 | 24.1 | 40 05.2 | −7.7 | 24.5 | 40 59.7 | −7.1 | 24.8 | 41 54.1 | −6.6 | 25.2 | 70 |
| 71 | 35 20.2 | −10.9 | 21.7 | 36 15.9 | −10.5 | 22.0 | 37 11.5 | −10.0 | 22.3 | 38 06.9 | −9.5 | 22.6 | 39 02.3 | −9.0 | 22.9 | 39 57.5 | −8.5 | 23.2 | 40 52.6 | −8.0 | 23.5 | 41 47.5 | −7.4 | 23.9 | 71 |
| 72 | 35 09.3 | −11.7 | 20.5 | 36 05.4 | −11.2 | 20.8 | 37 01.5 | −10.8 | 21.0 | 37 57.4 | −10.3 | 21.3 | 38 53.3 | −9.9 | 21.6 | 39 49.0 | −9.4 | 21.9 | 40 44.6 | −8.9 | 22.2 | 41 40.1 | −8.4 | 22.6 | 72 |
| 73 | 34 57.6 | −12.4 | 19.3 | 35 54.2 | −12.0 | 19.6 | 36 50.7 | −11.6 | 19.8 | 37 47.1 | −11.1 | 20.1 | 38 43.4 | −10.7 | 20.3 | 39 39.6 | −10.2 | 20.6 | 40 35.7 | −9.8 | 20.9 | 41 31.7 | −9.3 | 21.2 | 73 |
| 74 | 34 45.2 | −13.0 | 18.1 | 35 42.2 | −12.7 | 18.3 | 36 39.1 | −12.3 | 18.6 | 37 36.0 | −11.9 | 18.8 | 38 32.7 | −11.5 | 19.1 | 39 29.4 | −11.1 | 19.3 | 40 25.9 | −10.6 | 19.6 | 41 22.4 | −10.2 | 19.9 | 74 |
| 75 | 34 32.2 | −13.8 | 16.9 | 35 29.5 | −13.3 | 17.1 | 36 26.8 | −13.0 | 17.4 | 37 24.1 | −12.7 | 17.6 | 38 21.2 | −12.2 | 17.8 | 39 18.3 | −11.9 | 18.1 | 40 15.3 | −11.5 | 18.3 | 41 12.2 | −11.0 | 18.6 | 75 |
| 76 | 34 18.4 | −14.4 | 15.8 | 35 16.2 | −14.1 | 15.9 | 36 13.8 | −13.7 | 16.1 | 37 11.4 | −13.4 | 16.4 | 38 09.0 | −13.1 | 16.6 | 39 06.4 | −12.7 | 16.8 | 40 03.8 | −12.3 | 17.0 | 41 01.2 | −12.0 | 17.3 | 76 |
| 77 | 34 04.0 | −15.1 | 14.6 | 35 02.1 | −14.8 | 14.8 | 36 00.1 | −14.5 | 14.9 | 36 58.0 | −14.1 | 15.1 | 37 55.9 | −13.8 | 15.3 | 38 53.7 | −13.5 | 15.5 | 39 51.5 | −13.1 | 15.8 | 40 49.2 | −12.8 | 16.0 | 77 |
| 78 | 33 48.9 | −15.7 | 13.4 | 34 47.3 | −15.5 | 13.6 | 35 45.6 | −15.2 | 13.7 | 36 43.9 | −14.9 | 13.9 | 37 42.1 | −14.6 | 14.1 | 38 40.2 | −14.3 | 14.3 | 39 38.4 | −14.0 | 14.5 | 40 36.4 | −13.6 | 14.7 | 78 |
| 79 | 33 33.2 | −16.4 | 12.3 | 34 31.8 | −16.1 | 12.4 | 35 30.4 | −15.9 | 12.6 | 36 29.0 | −15.7 | 12.7 | 37 27.5 | −15.4 | 12.9 | 38 25.9 | −15.0 | 13.1 | 39 24.4 | −14.8 | 13.2 | 40 22.8 | −14.6 | 13.4 | 79 |
| 80 | 33 16.8 | −17.0 | 11.1 | 34 15.7 | −16.8 | 11.2 | 35 14.5 | −16.5 | 11.4 | 36 13.3 | −16.3 | 11.5 | 37 12.1 | −16.1 | 11.7 | 38 10.9 | −15.9 | 11.8 | 39 09.6 | −15.6 | 12.0 | 40 08.2 | −15.3 | 12.2 | 80 |
| 81 | 32 59.8 | −17.6 | 10.0 | 33 58.9 | −17.4 | 10.1 | 34 58.0 | −17.3 | 10.2 | 35 57.0 | −17.0 | 10.3 | 36 56.0 | −16.8 | 10.5 | 37 55.0 | −16.6 | 10.6 | 38 54.0 | −16.4 | 10.7 | 39 52.9 | −16.1 | 10.9 | 81 |
| 82 | 32 42.2 | −18.3 | 8.8 | 33 41.5 | −18.1 | 8.9 | 34 40.7 | −17.9 | 9.0 | 35 40.0 | −17.7 | 9.1 | 36 39.2 | −17.5 | 9.3 | 37 38.4 | −17.3 | 9.4 | 38 37.6 | −17.2 | 9.5 | 39 36.8 | −17.0 | 9.6 | 82 |
| 83 | 32 23.9 | −18.8 | 7.7 | 33 23.4 | −18.7 | 7.8 | 34 22.8 | −18.5 | 7.9 | 35 22.3 | −18.4 | 8.0 | 36 21.7 | −18.3 | 8.1 | 37 21.1 | −18.1 | 8.2 | 38 20.4 | −17.9 | 8.3 | 39 19.8 | −17.7 | 8.4 | 83 |
| 84 | 32 05.1 | −19.5 | 6.6 | 33 04.7 | −19.3 | 6.6 | 34 04.3 | −19.2 | 6.7 | 35 03.9 | −19.1 | 6.8 | 36 03.4 | −18.9 | 6.9 | 37 03.0 | −18.8 | 7.0 | 38 02.5 | −18.6 | 7.1 | 39 02.1 | −18.5 | 7.2 | 84 |
| 85 | 31 45.6 | −20.0 | 5.5 | 32 45.4 | −20.0 | 5.5 | 33 45.1 | −19.8 | 5.6 | 34 44.8 | −19.7 | 5.6 | 35 44.5 | −19.6 | 5.7 | 36 44.2 | −19.5 | 5.8 | 37 43.9 | −19.4 | 5.9 | 38 43.6 | −19.3 | 5.9 | 85 |
| 86 | 31 25.6 | −20.6 | 4.3 | 32 25.4 | −20.5 | 4.4 | 33 25.3 | −20.5 | 4.4 | 34 25.1 | −20.4 | 4.5 | 35 24.9 | −20.3 | 4.6 | 36 24.7 | −20.2 | 4.6 | 37 24.5 | −20.1 | 4.7 | 38 24.3 | −20.0 | 4.7 | 86 |
| 87 | 31 05.0 | −21.1 | 3.2 | 32 04.9 | −21.0 | 3.3 | 33 04.8 | −21.0 | 3.3 | 34 04.7 | −20.9 | 3.4 | 35 04.6 | −20.9 | 3.4 | 36 04.5 | −20.8 | 3.4 | 37 04.4 | −20.8 | 3.5 | 38 04.3 | −20.7 | 3.5 | 87 |
| 88 | 30 43.9 | −21.7 | 2.2 | 31 43.9 | −21.7 | 2.2 | 32 43.8 | −21.6 | 2.2 | 33 43.8 | −21.6 | 2.2 | 34 43.7 | −21.5 | 2.3 | 35 43.7 | −21.5 | 2.3 | 36 43.6 | −21.5 | 2.3 | 37 43.6 | −21.5 | 2.3 | 88 |
| 89 | 30 22.2 | −22.2 | 1.1 | 31 22.2 | −22.2 | 1.1 | 32 22.2 | −22.2 | 1.1 | 33 22.2 | −22.2 | 1.1 | 34 22.2 | −22.2 | 1.1 | 35 22.2 | −22.2 | 1.1 | 36 22.1 | −22.1 | 1.2 | 37 22.1 | −22.1 | 1.2 | 89 |
| 90 | 30 00.0 | −22.7 | 0.0 | 31 00.0 | −22.7 | 0.0 | 32 00.0 | −22.8 | 0.0 | 33 00.0 | −22.8 | 0.0 | 34 00.0 | −22.8 | 0.0 | 35 00.0 | −22.8 | 0.0 | 36 00.0 | −22.8 | 0.0 | 37 00.0 | −22.8 | 0.0 | 90 |
| | 30° | | | 31° | | | 32° | | | 33° | | | 34° | | | 35° | | | 36° | | | 37° | | | |

68°, 292° L.H.A. LATITUDE SAME NAME AS DECLINATION

74

## INTERPOLATION TABLE

| Dec. Inc. | Tens 10′ | 20′ | 30′ | 40′ | 50′ | Decimals | Units 0′ | 1′ | 2′ | 3′ | 4′ | 5′ | 6′ | 7′ | 8′ | 9′ |
|---|---|---|---|---|---|---|---|---|---|---|---|---|---|---|---|---|
| ° | ′ | ′ | ′ | ′ | ′ | ′ | ′ | ′ | ′ | ′ | ′ | ′ | ′ | ′ | ′ | ′ |
| **16.0** | 2.6 | 5.3 | 8.0 | 10.6 | 13.3 | .0 | 0.0 | 0.3 | 0.5 | 0.8 | 1.1 | 1.4 | 1.6 | 1.9 | 2.2 | 2.5 |
| **16.1** | 2.7 | 5.3 | 8.0 | 10.7 | 13.4 | .1 | 0.0 | 0.3 | 0.6 | 0.9 | 1.1 | 1.4 | 1.7 | 2.0 | 2.2 | 2.5 |
| **16.2** | 2.7 | 5.4 | 8.1 | 10.8 | 13.5 | .2 | 0.1 | 0.3 | 0.6 | 0.9 | 1.2 | 1.4 | 1.7 | 2.0 | 2.3 | 2.5 |
| **16.3** | 2.7 | 5.4 | 8.1 | 10.9 | 13.6 | .3 | 0.1 | 0.4 | 0.6 | 0.9 | 1.2 | 1.5 | 1.7 | 2.0 | 2.3 | 2.6 |
| **16.4** | 2.7 | 5.5 | 8.2 | 10.9 | 13.7 | .4 | 0.1 | 0.4 | 0.7 | 0.9 | 1.2 | 1.5 | 1.8 | 2.0 | 2.3 | 2.6 |
| **16.5** | 2.8 | 5.5 | 8.3 | 11.0 | 13.8 | .5 | 0.1 | 0.4 | 0.7 | 1.0 | 1.2 | 1.5 | 1.8 | 2.1 | 2.3 | 2.6 |
| **16.6** | 2.8 | 5.5 | 8.3 | 11.1 | 13.8 | .6 | 0.2 | 0.4 | 0.7 | 1.0 | 1.3 | 1.5 | 1.8 | 2.1 | 2.4 | 2.6 |
| **16.7** | 2.8 | 5.6 | 8.4 | 11.2 | 13.9 | .7 | 0.2 | 0.5 | 0.7 | 1.0 | 1.3 | 1.6 | 1.8 | 2.1 | 2.4 | 2.7 |
| **16.8** | 2.8 | 5.6 | 8.4 | 11.2 | 14.0 | .8 | 0.2 | 0.5 | 0.8 | 1.0 | 1.3 | 1.6 | 1.9 | 2.1 | 2.4 | 2.7 |
| **16.9** | 2.9 | 5.7 | 8.5 | 11.3 | 14.1 | .9 | 0.2 | 0.5 | 0.8 | 1.1 | 1.3 | 1.6 | 1.9 | 2.2 | 2.4 | 2.7 |
| **17.0** | 2.8 | 5.6 | 8.5 | 11.3 | 14.1 | .0 | 0.0 | 0.3 | 0.6 | 0.9 | 1.2 | 1.5 | 1.7 | 2.0 | 2.3 | 2.6 |
| **17.1** | 2.8 | 5.7 | 8.5 | 11.4 | 14.2 | .1 | 0.0 | 0.3 | 0.6 | 0.9 | 1.2 | 1.5 | 1.8 | 2.1 | 2.4 | 2.7 |
| **17.2** | 2.8 | 5.7 | 8.6 | 11.4 | 14.3 | .2 | 0.1 | 0.3 | 0.6 | 0.9 | 1.2 | 1.5 | 1.8 | 2.1 | 2.4 | 2.7 |
| **17.3** | 2.9 | 5.8 | 8.6 | 11.5 | 14.4 | .3 | 0.1 | 0.4 | 0.7 | 1.0 | 1.3 | 1.5 | 1.8 | 2.1 | 2.4 | 2.7 |
| **17.4** | 2.9 | 5.8 | 8.7 | 11.6 | 14.5 | .4 | 0.1 | 0.4 | 0.7 | 1.0 | 1.3 | 1.6 | 1.9 | 2.2 | 2.4 | 2.7 |
| **17.5** | 2.9 | 5.8 | 8.8 | 11.7 | 14.6 | .5 | 0.1 | 0.4 | 0.7 | 1.0 | 1.3 | 1.6 | 1.9 | 2.2 | 2.5 | 2.8 |
| **17.6** | 2.9 | 5.9 | 8.8 | 11.7 | 14.7 | .6 | 0.2 | 0.5 | 0.8 | 1.0 | 1.3 | 1.6 | 1.9 | 2.2 | 2.5 | 2.8 |
| **17.7** | 3.0 | 5.9 | 8.9 | 11.8 | 14.8 | .7 | 0.2 | 0.5 | 0.8 | 1.1 | 1.4 | 1.7 | 2.0 | 2.2 | 2.5 | 2.8 |
| **17.8** | 3.0 | 6.0 | 8.9 | 11.9 | 14.9 | .8 | 0.2 | 0.5 | 0.8 | 1.1 | 1.4 | 1.7 | 2.0 | 2.3 | 2.6 | 2.9 |
| **17.9** | 3.0 | 6.0 | 9.0 | 12.0 | 15.0 | .9 | 0.3 | 0.6 | 0.8 | 1.1 | 1.4 | 1.7 | 2.0 | 2.3 | 2.6 | 2.9 |
| **18.0** | 3.0 | 6.0 | 9.0 | 12.0 | 15.0 | .0 | 0.0 | 0.3 | 0.6 | 0.9 | 1.2 | 1.5 | 1.8 | 2.2 | 2.5 | 2.8 |
| **18.1** | 3.0 | 6.0 | 9.0 | 12.0 | 15.1 | .1 | 0.0 | 0.3 | 0.6 | 1.0 | 1.3 | 1.6 | 1.9 | 2.2 | 2.5 | 2.8 |
| **18.2** | 3.0 | 6.0 | 9.1 | 12.1 | 15.1 | .2 | 0.1 | 0.4 | 0.7 | 1.0 | 1.3 | 1.6 | 1.9 | 2.2 | 2.5 | 2.8 |
| **18.3** | 3.0 | 6.1 | 9.1 | 12.2 | 15.2 | .3 | 0.1 | 0.4 | 0.7 | 1.0 | 1.3 | 1.6 | 1.9 | 2.3 | 2.6 | 2.9 |
| **18.4** | 3.1 | 6.1 | 9.2 | 12.3 | 15.3 | .4 | 0.1 | 0.4 | 0.7 | 1.0 | 1.4 | 1.7 | 2.0 | 2.3 | 2.6 | 2.9 |
| **18.5** | 3.1 | 6.2 | 9.3 | 12.3 | 15.4 | .5 | 0.2 | 0.5 | 0.8 | 1.1 | 1.4 | 1.7 | 2.0 | 2.3 | 2.6 | 2.9 |
| **18.6** | 3.1 | 6.2 | 9.3 | 12.4 | 15.5 | .6 | 0.2 | 0.5 | 0.8 | 1.1 | 1.4 | 1.7 | 2.0 | 2.3 | 2.7 | 3.0 |
| **18.7** | 3.1 | 6.3 | 9.4 | 12.5 | 15.6 | .7 | 0.2 | 0.5 | 0.8 | 1.1 | 1.4 | 1.8 | 2.1 | 2.4 | 2.7 | 3.0 |
| **18.8** | 3.2 | 6.3 | 9.4 | 12.6 | 15.7 | .8 | 0.2 | 0.6 | 0.9 | 1.2 | 1.5 | 1.8 | 2.1 | 2.4 | 2.7 | 3.0 |
| **18.9** | 3.2 | 6.3 | 9.5 | 12.6 | 15.8 | .9 | 0.3 | 0.6 | 0.9 | 1.2 | 1.5 | 1.8 | 2.1 | 2.4 | 2.7 | 3.1 |
| **19.0** | 3.1 | 6.3 | 9.5 | 12.6 | 15.8 | .0 | 0.0 | 0.3 | 0.6 | 1.0 | 1.3 | 1.6 | 1.9 | 2.3 | 2.6 | 2.9 |
| **19.1** | 3.2 | 6.3 | 9.5 | 12.7 | 15.9 | .1 | 0.0 | 0.4 | 0.7 | 1.0 | 1.3 | 1.7 | 2.0 | 2.3 | 2.6 | 3.0 |
| **19.2** | 3.2 | 6.4 | 9.6 | 12.8 | 16.0 | .2 | 0.1 | 0.4 | 0.7 | 1.0 | 1.4 | 1.7 | 2.0 | 2.3 | 2.7 | 3.0 |
| **19.3** | 3.2 | 6.4 | 9.6 | 12.9 | 16.1 | .3 | 0.1 | 0.4 | 0.7 | 1.1 | 1.4 | 1.7 | 2.0 | 2.4 | 2.7 | 3.0 |
| **19.4** | 3.2 | 6.5 | 9.7 | 12.9 | 16.2 | .4 | 0.1 | 0.5 | 0.8 | 1.1 | 1.4 | 1.8 | 2.1 | 2.4 | 2.7 | 3.1 |
| **19.5** | 3.3 | 6.5 | 9.8 | 13.0 | 16.3 | .5 | 0.2 | 0.5 | 0.8 | 1.1 | 1.5 | 1.8 | 2.1 | 2.4 | 2.8 | 3.1 |
| **19.6** | 3.3 | 6.5 | 9.8 | 13.1 | 16.3 | .6 | 0.2 | 0.5 | 0.8 | 1.2 | 1.5 | 1.8 | 2.1 | 2.5 | 2.8 | 3.1 |
| **19.7** | 3.3 | 6.6 | 9.9 | 13.2 | 16.4 | .7 | 0.2 | 0.6 | 0.9 | 1.2 | 1.5 | 1.9 | 2.2 | 2.5 | 2.8 | 3.2 |
| **19.8** | 3.3 | 6.6 | 9.9 | 13.2 | 16.5 | .8 | 0.3 | 0.6 | 0.9 | 1.2 | 1.6 | 1.9 | 2.2 | 2.5 | 2.9 | 3.2 |
| **19.9** | 3.4 | 6.7 | 10.0 | 13.3 | 16.6 | .9 | 0.3 | 0.6 | 0.9 | 1.3 | 1.6 | 1.9 | 2.2 | 2.6 | 2.9 | 3.2 |
| **20.0** | 3.3 | 6.6 | 10.0 | 13.3 | 16.6 | .0 | 0.0 | 0.3 | 0.7 | 1.0 | 1.4 | 1.7 | 2.0 | 2.4 | 2.7 | 3.1 |
| **20.1** | 3.3 | 6.7 | 10.0 | 13.4 | 16.7 | .1 | 0.0 | 0.4 | 0.7 | 1.1 | 1.4 | 1.7 | 2.1 | 2.4 | 2.8 | 3.1 |
| **20.2** | 3.3 | 6.7 | 10.1 | 13.4 | 16.8 | .2 | 0.1 | 0.4 | 0.8 | 1.1 | 1.4 | 1.8 | 2.1 | 2.5 | 2.8 | 3.1 |
| **20.3** | 3.4 | 6.8 | 10.1 | 13.5 | 16.9 | .3 | 0.1 | 0.4 | 0.8 | 1.1 | 1.5 | 1.8 | 2.2 | 2.5 | 2.8 | 3.2 |
| **20.4** | 3.4 | 6.8 | 10.2 | 13.6 | 17.0 | .4 | 0.1 | 0.5 | 0.8 | 1.2 | 1.5 | 1.8 | 2.2 | 2.5 | 2.9 | 3.2 |
| **20.5** | 3.4 | 6.8 | 10.3 | 13.7 | 17.1 | .5 | 0.2 | 0.5 | 0.9 | 1.2 | 1.5 | 1.9 | 2.2 | 2.6 | 2.9 | 3.2 |
| **20.6** | 3.4 | 6.9 | 10.3 | 13.7 | 17.2 | .6 | 0.2 | 0.5 | 0.9 | 1.2 | 1.6 | 1.9 | 2.3 | 2.6 | 2.9 | 3.3 |
| **20.7** | 3.5 | 6.9 | 10.4 | 13.8 | 17.3 | .7 | 0.2 | 0.6 | 0.9 | 1.3 | 1.6 | 1.9 | 2.3 | 2.6 | 3.0 | 3.3 |
| **20.8** | 3.5 | 7.0 | 10.4 | 13.9 | 17.4 | .8 | 0.3 | 0.6 | 1.0 | 1.3 | 1.6 | 2.0 | 2.3 | 2.7 | 3.0 | 3.3 |
| **20.9** | 3.5 | 7.0 | 10.5 | 14.0 | 17.5 | .9 | 0.3 | 0.6 | 1.0 | 1.3 | 1.7 | 2.0 | 2.4 | 2.7 | 3.0 | 3.4 |
| **21.0** | 3.5 | 7.0 | 10.5 | 14.0 | 17.5 | .0 | 0.0 | 0.4 | 0.7 | 1.1 | 1.4 | 1.8 | 2.1 | 2.5 | 2.9 | 3.2 |
| **21.1** | 3.5 | 7.0 | 10.5 | 14.0 | 17.6 | .1 | 0.0 | 0.4 | 0.8 | 1.1 | 1.5 | 1.8 | 2.2 | 2.5 | 2.9 | 3.3 |
| **21.2** | 3.5 | 7.0 | 10.6 | 14.1 | 17.6 | .2 | 0.1 | 0.4 | 0.8 | 1.1 | 1.5 | 1.9 | 2.2 | 2.6 | 2.9 | 3.3 |
| **21.3** | 3.5 | 7.1 | 10.6 | 14.2 | 17.7 | .3 | 0.1 | 0.5 | 0.8 | 1.2 | 1.5 | 1.9 | 2.3 | 2.6 | 3.0 | 3.3 |
| **21.4** | 3.6 | 7.1 | 10.7 | 14.3 | 17.8 | .4 | 0.1 | 0.5 | 0.9 | 1.2 | 1.6 | 1.9 | 2.3 | 2.7 | 3.0 | 3.4 |
| **21.5** | 3.6 | 7.2 | 10.8 | 14.3 | 17.9 | .5 | 0.2 | 0.5 | 0.9 | 1.3 | 1.6 | 2.0 | 2.3 | 2.7 | 3.0 | 3.4 |
| **21.6** | 3.6 | 7.2 | 10.8 | 14.4 | 18.0 | .6 | 0.2 | 0.6 | 0.9 | 1.3 | 1.6 | 2.0 | 2.4 | 2.7 | 3.1 | 3.4 |
| **21.7** | 3.6 | 7.3 | 10.9 | 14.5 | 18.1 | .7 | 0.3 | 0.6 | 1.0 | 1.3 | 1.7 | 2.0 | 2.4 | 2.8 | 3.1 | 3.5 |
| **21.8** | 3.7 | 7.3 | 10.9 | 14.6 | 18.2 | .8 | 0.3 | 0.6 | 1.0 | 1.4 | 1.7 | 2.1 | 2.4 | 2.8 | 3.2 | 3.5 |
| **21.9** | 3.7 | 7.3 | 11.0 | 14.6 | 18.3 | .9 | 0.3 | 0.7 | 1.0 | 1.4 | 1.8 | 2.1 | 2.5 | 2.8 | 3.2 | 3.5 |
| **22.0** | 3.6 | 7.3 | 11.0 | 14.6 | 18.3 | .0 | 0.0 | 0.4 | 0.7 | 1.1 | 1.5 | 1.9 | 2.2 | 2.6 | 3.0 | 3.4 |
| **22.1** | 3.7 | 7.3 | 11.0 | 14.7 | 18.4 | .1 | 0.0 | 0.4 | 0.8 | 1.2 | 1.5 | 1.9 | 2.3 | 2.7 | 3.0 | 3.4 |
| **22.2** | 3.7 | 7.4 | 11.1 | 14.8 | 18.5 | .2 | 0.1 | 0.4 | 0.8 | 1.2 | 1.6 | 1.9 | 2.3 | 2.7 | 3.1 | 3.4 |
| **22.3** | 3.7 | 7.4 | 11.1 | 14.9 | 18.6 | .3 | 0.1 | 0.5 | 0.9 | 1.2 | 1.6 | 2.0 | 2.4 | 2.7 | 3.1 | 3.5 |
| **22.4** | 3.7 | 7.5 | 11.2 | 14.9 | 18.7 | .4 | 0.1 | 0.5 | 0.9 | 1.3 | 1.6 | 2.0 | 2.4 | 2.8 | 3.1 | 3.5 |
| **22.5** | 3.8 | 7.5 | 11.3 | 15.0 | 18.8 | .5 | 0.2 | 0.6 | 0.9 | 1.3 | 1.7 | 2.1 | 2.4 | 2.8 | 3.2 | 3.6 |
| **22.6** | 3.8 | 7.5 | 11.3 | 15.1 | 18.8 | .6 | 0.2 | 0.6 | 1.0 | 1.3 | 1.7 | 2.1 | 2.5 | 2.8 | 3.2 | 3.6 |
| **22.7** | 3.8 | 7.6 | 11.4 | 15.2 | 18.9 | .7 | 0.3 | 0.6 | 1.0 | 1.4 | 1.8 | 2.1 | 2.5 | 2.9 | 3.3 | 3.6 |
| **22.8** | 3.8 | 7.6 | 11.4 | 15.2 | 19.0 | .8 | 0.3 | 0.7 | 1.0 | 1.4 | 1.8 | 2.2 | 2.5 | 2.9 | 3.3 | 3.7 |
| **22.9** | 3.9 | 7.7 | 11.5 | 15.3 | 19.1 | .9 | 0.3 | 0.7 | 1.1 | 1.5 | 1.8 | 2.2 | 2.6 | 3.0 | 3.3 | 3.7 |
| **23.0** | 3.8 | 7.6 | 11.5 | 15.3 | 19.1 | .0 | 0.0 | 0.4 | 0.8 | 1.2 | 1.6 | 2.0 | 2.3 | 2.7 | 3.1 | 3.5 |
| **23.1** | 3.8 | 7.7 | 11.5 | 15.4 | 19.2 | .1 | 0.0 | 0.4 | 0.8 | 1.2 | 1.6 | 2.0 | 2.4 | 2.8 | 3.2 | 3.6 |
| **23.2** | 3.8 | 7.7 | 11.6 | 15.4 | 19.3 | .2 | 0.1 | 0.5 | 0.9 | 1.3 | 1.6 | 2.0 | 2.4 | 2.8 | 3.2 | 3.6 |
| **23.3** | 3.9 | 7.8 | 11.6 | 15.5 | 19.4 | .3 | 0.1 | 0.5 | 0.9 | 1.3 | 1.7 | 2.1 | 2.5 | 2.9 | 3.3 | 3.6 |
| **23.4** | 3.9 | 7.8 | 11.7 | 15.6 | 19.5 | .4 | 0.2 | 0.5 | 0.9 | 1.3 | 1.7 | 2.1 | 2.5 | 2.9 | 3.3 | 3.7 |
| **23.5** | 3.9 | 7.8 | 11.8 | 15.7 | 19.6 | .5 | 0.2 | 0.6 | 1.0 | 1.4 | 1.8 | 2.2 | 2.5 | 2.9 | 3.3 | 3.7 |
| **23.6** | 3.9 | 7.9 | 11.8 | 15.7 | 19.7 | .6 | 0.2 | 0.6 | 1.0 | 1.4 | 1.8 | 2.2 | 2.6 | 3.0 | 3.4 | 3.8 |
| **23.7** | 4.0 | 7.9 | 11.9 | 15.8 | 19.8 | .7 | 0.3 | 0.7 | 1.1 | 1.4 | 1.8 | 2.2 | 2.6 | 3.0 | 3.4 | 3.8 |
| **23.8** | 4.0 | 8.0 | 11.9 | 15.9 | 19.9 | .8 | 0.3 | 0.7 | 1.1 | 1.5 | 1.9 | 2.3 | 2.7 | 3.1 | 3.4 | 3.8 |
| **23.9** | 4.0 | 8.0 | 12.0 | 16.0 | 20.0 | .9 | 0.4 | 0.7 | 1.1 | 1.5 | 1.9 | 2.3 | 2.7 | 3.1 | 3.5 | 3.9 |
| | 10′ | 20′ | 30′ | 40′ | 50′ | | 0′ | 1′ | 2′ | 3′ | 4′ | 5′ | 6′ | 7′ | 8′ | 9′ |

Double Second Diff. and Corr. (16.0–17.9)

| Diff. | Corr. |
|---|---|
| 1.0 | 0.1 |
| 3.0 | 0.2 |
| 4.9 | 0.3 |
| 6.9 | 0.4 |
| 8.9 | 0.5 |
| 10.8 | 0.6 |
| 12.8 | 0.7 |
| 14.8 | 0.8 |
| 16.7 | 0.9 |
| 18.7 | 1.0 |
| 20.7 | 1.1 |
| 22.7 | 1.2 |
| 24.6 | 1.3 |
| 26.6 | 1.4 |
| 28.6 | 1.5 |
| 30.5 | 1.6 |
| 32.5 | 1.7 |
| 34.5 | |

Double Second Diff. and Corr. (18.0–19.9)

| Diff. | Corr. |
|---|---|
| 0.9 | 0.1 |
| 2.8 | 0.2 |
| 4.6 | 0.3 |
| 6.5 | 0.4 |
| 8.3 | 0.5 |
| 10.2 | 0.6 |
| 12.0 | 0.7 |
| 13.9 | 0.8 |
| 15.7 | 0.9 |
| 17.6 | 1.0 |
| 19.4 | 1.1 |
| 21.3 | 1.2 |
| 23.1 | 1.3 |
| 25.0 | 1.4 |
| 26.8 | 1.5 |
| 28.7 | 1.6 |
| 30.5 | 1.7 |
| 32.3 | 1.8 |
| 34.2 | |

Double Second Diff. and Corr. (20.0–21.9)

| Diff. | Corr. |
|---|---|
| 0.9 | 0.1 |
| 2.6 | 0.2 |
| 4.4 | 0.3 |
| 6.2 | 0.4 |
| 7.9 | 0.5 |
| 9.7 | 0.6 |
| 11.4 | 0.7 |
| 13.2 | 0.8 |
| 14.9 | 0.9 |
| 16.7 | 1.0 |
| 18.5 | 1.1 |
| 20.2 | 1.2 |
| 22.0 | 1.3 |
| 23.7 | 1.4 |
| 25.5 | 1.5 |
| 27.3 | 1.6 |
| 29.0 | 1.7 |
| 30.8 | 1.8 |
| 32.5 | 1.9 |
| 34.3 | |

Double Second Diff. and Corr. (22.0–23.9)

| Diff. | Corr. |
|---|---|
| 0.8 | 0.1 |
| 2.5 | 0.2 |
| 4.2 | 0.3 |
| 5.9 | 0.4 |
| 7.6 | 0.5 |
| 9.3 | 0.6 |
| 11.0 | 0.7 |
| 12.7 | 0.8 |
| 14.4 | 0.9 |
| 16.1 | 1.0 |
| 17.8 | 1.1 |
| 19.5 | 1.2 |
| 21.2 | 1.3 |
| 22.8 | 1.4 |
| 24.5 | 1.5 |
| 26.2 | 1.6 |
| 27.9 | 1.7 |
| 29.6 | 1.8 |
| 31.3 | 1.9 |
| 33.0 | 2.0 |
| 34.7 | |

| Dec. Inc. | Tens 10′ | 20′ | 30′ | 40′ | 50′ | Decimals | Units 0′ | 1′ | 2′ | 3′ | 4′ | 5′ | 6′ | 7′ | 8′ | 9′ |
|---|---|---|---|---|---|---|---|---|---|---|---|---|---|---|---|---|
| ° | ′ | ′ | ′ | ′ | ′ | ′ | ′ | ′ | ′ | ′ | ′ | ′ | ′ | ′ | ′ | ′ |
| **24.0** | 4.0 | 8.0 | 12.0 | 16.0 | 20.0 | .0 | 0.0 | 0.4 | 0.8 | 1.2 | 1.6 | 2.0 | 2.4 | 2.9 | 3.3 | 3.7 |
| **24.1** | 4.0 | 8.0 | 12.0 | 16.0 | 20.1 | .1 | 0.0 | 0.4 | 0.9 | 1.3 | 1.7 | 2.1 | 2.5 | 2.9 | 3.3 | 3.7 |
| **24.2** | 4.0 | 8.0 | 12.1 | 16.1 | 20.1 | .2 | 0.1 | 0.5 | 0.9 | 1.3 | 1.7 | 2.1 | 2.5 | 2.9 | 3.3 | 3.8 |
| **24.3** | 4.0 | 8.1 | 12.1 | 16.2 | 20.2 | .3 | 0.1 | 0.5 | 0.9 | 1.3 | 1.8 | 2.2 | 2.6 | 3.0 | 3.4 | 3.8 |
| **24.4** | 4.1 | 8.1 | 12.2 | 16.3 | 20.3 | .4 | 0.2 | 0.6 | 1.0 | 1.4 | 1.8 | 2.2 | 2.6 | 3.0 | 3.4 | 3.8 |
| **24.5** | 4.1 | 8.2 | 12.3 | 16.3 | 20.4 | .5 | 0.2 | 0.6 | 1.0 | 1.4 | 1.8 | 2.2 | 2.7 | 3.1 | 3.5 | 3.9 |
| **24.6** | 4.1 | 8.2 | 12.3 | 16.4 | 20.5 | .6 | 0.2 | 0.7 | 1.1 | 1.5 | 1.9 | 2.3 | 2.7 | 3.1 | 3.5 | 3.9 |
| **24.7** | 4.1 | 8.3 | 12.4 | 16.5 | 20.6 | .7 | 0.3 | 0.7 | 1.1 | 1.5 | 1.9 | 2.3 | 2.7 | 3.1 | 3.6 | 4.0 |
| **24.8** | 4.2 | 8.3 | 12.4 | 16.6 | 20.7 | .8 | 0.3 | 0.7 | 1.1 | 1.6 | 2.0 | 2.4 | 2.8 | 3.2 | 3.6 | 4.0 |
| **24.9** | 4.2 | 8.3 | 12.5 | 16.6 | 20.8 | .9 | 0.4 | 0.8 | 1.2 | 1.6 | 2.0 | 2.4 | 2.8 | 3.2 | 3.6 | 4.0 |
| **25.0** | 4.1 | 8.3 | 12.5 | 16.6 | 20.8 | .0 | 0.0 | 0.4 | 0.8 | 1.3 | 1.7 | 2.1 | 2.5 | 3.0 | 3.4 | 3.8 |
| **25.1** | 4.2 | 8.3 | 12.5 | 16.7 | 20.9 | .1 | 0.0 | 0.5 | 0.9 | 1.3 | 1.7 | 2.2 | 2.6 | 3.0 | 3.4 | 3.9 |
| **25.2** | 4.2 | 8.4 | 12.6 | 16.8 | 21.0 | .2 | 0.1 | 0.5 | 0.9 | 1.4 | 1.8 | 2.2 | 2.6 | 3.1 | 3.5 | 3.9 |
| **25.3** | 4.2 | 8.4 | 12.6 | 16.9 | 21.1 | .3 | 0.1 | 0.6 | 1.0 | 1.4 | 1.8 | 2.3 | 2.7 | 3.1 | 3.5 | 4.0 |
| **25.4** | 4.2 | 8.5 | 12.7 | 16.9 | 21.2 | .4 | 0.2 | 0.6 | 1.0 | 1.4 | 1.9 | 2.3 | 2.7 | 3.1 | 3.6 | 4.0 |
| **25.5** | 4.3 | 8.5 | 12.8 | 17.0 | 21.3 | .5 | 0.2 | 0.6 | 1.1 | 1.5 | 1.9 | 2.3 | 2.8 | 3.2 | 3.6 | 4.0 |
| **25.6** | 4.3 | 8.5 | 12.8 | 17.1 | 21.3 | .6 | 0.3 | 0.7 | 1.1 | 1.5 | 2.0 | 2.4 | 2.8 | 3.2 | 3.7 | 4.1 |
| **25.7** | 4.3 | 8.6 | 12.9 | 17.2 | 21.4 | .7 | 0.3 | 0.7 | 1.1 | 1.6 | 2.0 | 2.4 | 2.8 | 3.3 | 3.7 | 4.1 |
| **25.8** | 4.3 | 8.6 | 12.9 | 17.2 | 21.5 | .8 | 0.3 | 0.8 | 1.2 | 1.6 | 2.0 | 2.5 | 2.9 | 3.3 | 3.7 | 4.2 |
| **25.9** | 4.4 | 8.7 | 13.0 | 17.3 | 21.6 | .9 | 0.4 | 0.8 | 1.2 | 1.7 | 2.1 | 2.5 | 2.9 | 3.4 | 3.8 | 4.2 |
| **26.0** | 4.3 | 8.6 | 13.0 | 17.3 | 21.6 | .0 | 0.0 | 0.4 | 0.9 | 1.3 | 1.8 | 2.2 | 2.6 | 3.1 | 3.5 | 4.0 |
| **26.1** | 4.3 | 8.7 | 13.0 | 17.4 | 21.7 | .1 | 0.0 | 0.5 | 0.9 | 1.4 | 1.8 | 2.3 | 2.7 | 3.1 | 3.6 | 4.0 |
| **26.2** | 4.3 | 8.7 | 13.1 | 17.4 | 21.8 | .2 | 0.1 | 0.5 | 1.0 | 1.4 | 1.9 | 2.3 | 2.7 | 3.2 | 3.6 | 4.1 |
| **26.3** | 4.4 | 8.8 | 13.1 | 17.5 | 21.9 | .3 | 0.1 | 0.6 | 1.0 | 1.5 | 1.9 | 2.3 | 2.8 | 3.2 | 3.7 | 4.1 |
| **26.4** | 4.4 | 8.8 | 13.2 | 17.6 | 22.0 | .4 | 0.2 | 0.6 | 1.1 | 1.5 | 1.9 | 2.4 | 2.8 | 3.3 | 3.7 | 4.2 |
| **26.5** | 4.4 | 8.8 | 13.3 | 17.7 | 22.1 | .5 | 0.2 | 0.7 | 1.1 | 1.5 | 2.0 | 2.4 | 2.9 | 3.3 | 3.8 | 4.2 |
| **26.6** | 4.4 | 8.9 | 13.3 | 17.7 | 22.2 | .6 | 0.3 | 0.7 | 1.1 | 1.6 | 2.0 | 2.5 | 2.9 | 3.4 | 3.8 | 4.2 |
| **26.7** | 4.5 | 8.9 | 13.4 | 17.8 | 22.3 | .7 | 0.3 | 0.8 | 1.2 | 1.6 | 2.1 | 2.5 | 3.0 | 3.4 | 3.8 | 4.3 |
| **26.8** | 4.5 | 9.0 | 13.4 | 17.9 | 22.4 | .8 | 0.4 | 0.8 | 1.2 | 1.7 | 2.1 | 2.6 | 3.0 | 3.4 | 3.9 | 4.3 |
| **26.9** | 4.5 | 9.0 | 13.5 | 18.0 | 22.5 | .9 | 0.4 | 0.8 | 1.3 | 1.7 | 2.2 | 2.6 | 3.0 | 3.5 | 3.9 | 4.4 |
| **27.0** | 4.5 | 9.0 | 13.5 | 18.0 | 22.5 | .0 | 0.0 | 0.5 | 0.9 | 1.4 | 1.8 | 2.3 | 2.7 | 3.2 | 3.7 | 4.1 |
| **27.1** | 4.5 | 9.0 | 13.5 | 18.0 | 22.6 | .1 | 0.0 | 0.5 | 1.0 | 1.4 | 1.9 | 2.3 | 2.8 | 3.3 | 3.7 | 4.2 |
| **27.2** | 4.5 | 9.0 | 13.6 | 18.1 | 22.6 | .2 | 0.1 | 0.5 | 1.0 | 1.5 | 1.9 | 2.4 | 2.8 | 3.3 | 3.8 | 4.2 |
| **27.3** | 4.5 | 9.1 | 13.6 | 18.2 | 22.7 | .3 | 0.1 | 0.6 | 1.1 | 1.5 | 2.0 | 2.4 | 2.9 | 3.3 | 3.8 | 4.3 |
| **27.4** | 4.6 | 9.1 | 13.7 | 18.3 | 22.8 | .4 | 0.2 | 0.6 | 1.1 | 1.6 | 2.0 | 2.5 | 2.9 | 3.4 | 3.8 | 4.3 |
| **27.5** | 4.6 | 9.2 | 13.8 | 18.3 | 22.9 | .5 | 0.2 | 0.7 | 1.1 | 1.6 | 2.1 | 2.5 | 3.0 | 3.4 | 3.9 | 4.4 |
| **27.6** | 4.6 | 9.2 | 13.8 | 18.4 | 23.0 | .6 | 0.3 | 0.7 | 1.2 | 1.6 | 2.1 | 2.6 | 3.0 | 3.5 | 3.9 | 4.4 |
| **27.7** | 4.6 | 9.3 | 13.9 | 18.5 | 23.1 | .7 | 0.3 | 0.8 | 1.2 | 1.7 | 2.2 | 2.6 | 3.1 | 3.5 | 4.0 | 4.4 |
| **27.8** | 4.7 | 9.3 | 13.9 | 18.6 | 23.2 | .8 | 0.4 | 0.8 | 1.3 | 1.7 | 2.2 | 2.7 | 3.1 | 3.6 | 4.0 | 4.5 |
| **27.9** | 4.7 | 9.3 | 14.0 | 18.6 | 23.3 | .9 | 0.4 | 0.9 | 1.3 | 1.8 | 2.2 | 2.7 | 3.2 | 3.6 | 4.1 | 4.5 |
| **28.0** | 4.6 | 9.3 | 14.0 | 18.6 | 23.3 | .0 | 0.0 | 0.5 | 0.9 | 1.4 | 1.9 | 2.4 | 2.8 | 3.3 | 3.8 | 4.3 |
| **28.1** | 4.7 | 9.3 | 14.0 | 18.7 | 23.4 | .1 | 0.0 | 0.5 | 1.0 | 1.5 | 1.9 | 2.4 | 2.9 | 3.4 | 3.8 | 4.3 |
| **28.2** | 4.7 | 9.4 | 14.1 | 18.8 | 23.5 | .2 | 0.1 | 0.6 | 1.0 | 1.5 | 2.0 | 2.5 | 2.9 | 3.4 | 3.9 | 4.4 |
| **28.3** | 4.7 | 9.4 | 14.1 | 18.9 | 23.6 | .3 | 0.1 | 0.6 | 1.1 | 1.6 | 2.0 | 2.5 | 3.0 | 3.5 | 3.9 | 4.4 |
| **28.4** | 4.7 | 9.5 | 14.2 | 18.9 | 23.7 | .4 | 0.2 | 0.7 | 1.1 | 1.6 | 2.1 | 2.6 | 3.0 | 3.5 | 4.0 | 4.5 |
| **28.5** | 4.8 | 9.5 | 14.3 | 19.0 | 23.8 | .5 | 0.2 | 0.7 | 1.2 | 1.7 | 2.1 | 2.6 | 3.1 | 3.6 | 4.0 | 4.5 |
| **28.6** | 4.8 | 9.5 | 14.3 | 19.1 | 23.8 | .6 | 0.3 | 0.8 | 1.2 | 1.7 | 2.2 | 2.7 | 3.1 | 3.6 | 4.1 | 4.6 |
| **28.7** | 4.8 | 9.6 | 14.4 | 19.2 | 23.9 | .7 | 0.3 | 0.8 | 1.3 | 1.8 | 2.2 | 2.7 | 3.2 | 3.7 | 4.1 | 4.6 |
| **28.8** | 4.8 | 9.6 | 14.4 | 19.2 | 24.0 | .8 | 0.4 | 0.9 | 1.3 | 1.8 | 2.3 | 2.8 | 3.2 | 3.7 | 4.2 | 4.7 |
| **28.9** | 4.9 | 9.7 | 14.5 | 19.3 | 24.1 | .9 | 0.4 | 0.9 | 1.4 | 1.9 | 2.3 | 2.8 | 3.3 | 3.8 | 4.2 | 4.7 |
| **29.0** | 4.8 | 9.6 | 14.5 | 19.3 | 24.1 | .0 | 0.0 | 0.5 | 1.0 | 1.5 | 2.0 | 2.5 | 2.9 | 3.4 | 3.9 | 4.4 |
| **29.1** | 4.8 | 9.7 | 14.5 | 19.4 | 24.2 | .1 | 0.0 | 0.5 | 1.0 | 1.5 | 2.0 | 2.5 | 3.0 | 3.5 | 4.0 | 4.5 |
| **29.2** | 4.8 | 9.7 | 14.6 | 19.4 | 24.3 | .2 | 0.1 | 0.6 | 1.1 | 1.6 | 2.1 | 2.6 | 3.0 | 3.5 | 4.0 | 4.5 |
| **29.3** | 4.9 | 9.8 | 14.6 | 19.5 | 24.4 | .3 | 0.1 | 0.6 | 1.1 | 1.6 | 2.1 | 2.6 | 3.1 | 3.6 | 4.1 | 4.6 |
| **29.4** | 4.9 | 9.8 | 14.7 | 19.6 | 24.5 | .4 | 0.2 | 0.7 | 1.2 | 1.7 | 2.2 | 2.7 | 3.1 | 3.6 | 4.1 | 4.6 |
| **29.5** | 4.9 | 9.8 | 14.8 | 19.7 | 24.6 | .5 | 0.2 | 0.7 | 1.2 | 1.7 | 2.2 | 2.7 | 3.2 | 3.7 | 4.2 | 4.7 |
| **29.6** | 4.9 | 9.9 | 14.8 | 19.7 | 24.7 | .6 | 0.3 | 0.8 | 1.3 | 1.8 | 2.3 | 2.8 | 3.2 | 3.7 | 4.2 | 4.7 |
| **29.7** | 5.0 | 9.9 | 14.9 | 19.8 | 24.8 | .7 | 0.3 | 0.8 | 1.3 | 1.8 | 2.3 | 2.8 | 3.3 | 3.8 | 4.3 | 4.8 |
| **29.8** | 5.0 | 10.0 | 14.9 | 19.9 | 24.9 | .8 | 0.4 | 0.9 | 1.4 | 1.9 | 2.4 | 2.9 | 3.3 | 3.8 | 4.3 | 4.8 |
| **29.9** | 5.0 | 10.0 | 15.0 | 20.0 | 25.0 | .9 | 0.4 | 0.9 | 1.4 | 1.9 | 2.4 | 2.9 | 3.4 | 3.9 | 4.4 | 4.9 |
| **30.0** | 5.0 | 10.0 | 15.0 | 20.0 | 25.0 | .0 | 0.0 | 0.5 | 1.0 | 1.5 | 2.0 | 2.5 | 3.0 | 3.6 | 4.1 | 4.6 |
| **30.1** | 5.0 | 10.0 | 15.0 | 20.0 | 25.1 | .1 | 0.1 | 0.6 | 1.1 | 1.6 | 2.1 | 2.6 | 3.1 | 3.6 | 4.1 | 4.6 |
| **30.2** | 5.0 | 10.0 | 15.1 | 20.1 | 25.1 | .2 | 0.1 | 0.6 | 1.1 | 1.6 | 2.1 | 2.6 | 3.2 | 3.7 | 4.2 | 4.7 |
| **30.3** | 5.0 | 10.1 | 15.1 | 20.2 | 25.2 | .3 | 0.2 | 0.7 | 1.2 | 1.7 | 2.2 | 2.7 | 3.2 | 3.7 | 4.2 | 4.7 |
| **30.4** | 5.1 | 10.1 | 15.2 | 20.3 | 25.3 | .4 | 0.2 | 0.7 | 1.2 | 1.7 | 2.2 | 2.7 | 3.3 | 3.8 | 4.3 | 4.8 |
| **30.5** | 5.1 | 10.2 | 15.3 | 20.3 | 25.4 | .5 | 0.3 | 0.8 | 1.3 | 1.8 | 2.3 | 2.8 | 3.3 | 3.8 | 4.3 | 4.8 |
| **30.6** | 5.1 | 10.2 | 15.3 | 20.4 | 25.5 | .6 | 0.3 | 0.8 | 1.3 | 1.8 | 2.3 | 2.8 | 3.4 | 3.9 | 4.4 | 4.9 |
| **30.7** | 5.1 | 10.3 | 15.4 | 20.5 | 25.6 | .7 | 0.4 | 0.9 | 1.4 | 1.9 | 2.4 | 2.9 | 3.4 | 3.9 | 4.4 | 4.9 |
| **30.8** | 5.2 | 10.3 | 15.4 | 20.6 | 25.7 | .8 | 0.4 | 0.9 | 1.4 | 1.9 | 2.4 | 2.9 | 3.5 | 4.0 | 4.5 | 5.0 |
| **30.9** | 5.2 | 10.3 | 15.5 | 20.6 | 25.8 | .9 | 0.5 | 1.0 | 1.5 | 2.0 | 2.5 | 3.0 | 3.5 | 4.0 | 4.5 | 5.0 |
| **31.0** | 5.1 | 10.3 | 15.5 | 20.6 | 25.8 | .0 | 0.0 | 0.5 | 1.0 | 1.6 | 2.1 | 2.6 | 3.1 | 3.7 | 4.2 | 4.7 |
| **31.1** | 5.2 | 10.3 | 15.5 | 20.7 | 25.9 | .1 | 0.1 | 0.6 | 1.1 | 1.6 | 2.2 | 2.7 | 3.2 | 3.7 | 4.3 | 4.8 |
| **31.2** | 5.2 | 10.4 | 15.6 | 20.8 | 26.0 | .2 | 0.1 | 0.6 | 1.2 | 1.7 | 2.2 | 2.7 | 3.3 | 3.8 | 4.3 | 4.8 |
| **31.3** | 5.2 | 10.4 | 15.6 | 20.9 | 26.1 | .3 | 0.2 | 0.7 | 1.2 | 1.7 | 2.3 | 2.8 | 3.3 | 3.8 | 4.4 | 4.9 |
| **31.4** | 5.2 | 10.5 | 15.7 | 20.9 | 26.2 | .4 | 0.2 | 0.7 | 1.3 | 1.8 | 2.3 | 2.8 | 3.4 | 3.9 | 4.4 | 4.9 |
| **31.5** | 5.3 | 10.5 | 15.8 | 21.0 | 26.3 | .5 | 0.3 | 0.8 | 1.3 | 1.8 | 2.4 | 2.9 | 3.4 | 3.9 | 4.5 | 5.0 |
| **31.6** | 5.3 | 10.5 | 15.8 | 21.1 | 26.3 | .6 | 0.3 | 0.8 | 1.4 | 1.9 | 2.4 | 2.9 | 3.5 | 4.0 | 4.5 | 5.0 |
| **31.7** | 5.3 | 10.6 | 15.9 | 21.2 | 26.4 | .7 | 0.4 | 0.9 | 1.4 | 1.9 | 2.5 | 3.0 | 3.5 | 4.0 | 4.6 | 5.1 |
| **31.8** | 5.3 | 10.6 | 15.9 | 21.2 | 26.5 | .8 | 0.4 | 0.9 | 1.5 | 2.0 | 2.5 | 3.0 | 3.6 | 4.1 | 4.6 | 5.1 |
| **31.9** | 5.4 | 10.7 | 16.0 | 21.3 | 26.6 | .9 | 0.5 | 1.0 | 1.5 | 2.0 | 2.6 | 3.1 | 3.6 | 4.1 | 4.7 | 5.2 |
| | 10′ | 20′ | 30′ | 40′ | 50′ | | 0′ | 1′ | 2′ | 3′ | 4′ | 5′ | 6′ | 7′ | 8′ | 9′ |

Double Second Diff. and Corr. (24.0–25.9)

| Diff. | Corr. |
|---|---|
| 0.8 | 0.1 |
| 2.5 | 0.2 |
| 4.1 | 0.3 |
| 5.8 | 0.4 |
| 7.4 | 0.5 |
| 9.1 | 0.6 |
| 10.7 | 0.7 |
| 12.3 | 0.8 |
| 14.0 | 0.9 |
| 15.6 | 1.0 |
| 17.3 | 1.1 |
| 18.9 | 1.2 |
| 20.6 | 1.3 |
| 22.2 | 1.4 |
| 23.9 | 1.5 |
| 25.5 | 1.6 |
| 27.2 | 1.7 |
| 28.8 | 1.8 |
| 30.4 | 1.9 |
| 32.1 | 2.0 |
| 33.7 | 2.1 |
| 35.4 | |

Double Second Diff. and Corr. (26.0–27.9)

| Diff. | Corr. |
|---|---|
| 0.8 | 0.1 |
| 2.4 | 0.2 |
| 4.0 | 0.3 |
| 5.7 | 0.4 |
| 7.3 | 0.5 |
| 8.9 | 0.6 |
| 10.5 | 0.7 |
| 12.1 | 0.8 |
| 13.7 | 0.9 |
| 15.4 | 1.0 |
| 17.0 | 1.1 |
| 18.6 | 1.2 |
| 20.2 | 1.3 |
| 21.8 | 1.4 |
| 23.4 | 1.5 |
| 25.1 | 1.6 |
| 26.7 | 1.7 |
| 28.3 | 1.8 |
| 29.9 | 1.9 |
| 31.5 | 2.0 |
| 33.1 | 2.1 |
| 34.7 | |

Double Second Diff. and Corr. (28.0–29.9)

| Diff. | Corr. |
|---|---|
| 0.8 | 0.1 |
| 2.4 | 0.2 |
| 4.0 | 0.3 |
| 5.6 | 0.4 |
| 7.2 | 0.5 |
| 8.8 | 0.6 |
| 10.4 | 0.7 |
| 12.0 | 0.8 |
| 13.6 | 0.9 |
| 15.2 | 1.0 |
| 16.8 | 1.1 |
| 18.4 | 1.2 |
| 20.0 | 1.3 |
| 21.6 | 1.4 |
| 23.2 | 1.5 |
| 24.8 | 1.6 |
| 26.4 | 1.7 |
| 28.0 | 1.8 |
| 29.6 | 1.9 |
| 31.2 | 2.0 |
| 32.8 | 2.1 |
| 34.4 | |

Double Second Diff. and Corr. (30.0–31.9)

| Diff. | Corr. |
|---|---|
| 0.8 | 0.1 |
| 2.4 | 0.2 |
| 4.0 | 0.3 |
| 5.6 | 0.4 |
| 7.2 | 0.5 |
| 8.8 | 0.6 |
| 10.4 | 0.7 |
| 12.0 | 0.8 |
| 13.6 | 0.9 |
| 15.2 | 1.0 |
| 16.8 | 1.1 |
| 18.4 | 1.2 |
| 20.0 | 1.3 |
| 21.6 | 1.4 |
| 23.2 | 1.5 |
| 24.8 | 1.6 |
| 26.4 | 1.7 |
| 28.0 | 1.8 |
| 29.6 | 1.9 |
| 31.2 | 2.0 |
| 32.8 | 2.1 |
| 34.4 | |

The Double-Second-Difference correction (Corr.) is always to be added to the tabulated altitude.

# Reality Check: Common Mistakes

There are many places where you can go wrong in this procedure. Here is a list of potential snags that I ran into, so hopefully emphasizing them here will help you avoid them:

1. Your LHA should usually be between 30 and 210. Anything different than that means that you shot something beyond the horizon, which is certainly *possible*, but not *probable*. If you end up with an LHA less than 30 or more than 210, especially if you are shooting something nowhere near the horizon, then it is imperative that you double-check your math.

2. Increments and corrections-- Unless your sight falls on an exact hour of GMT, don't forget to check your increments and corrections tables to make up for the minutes and seconds of time that have passed. Not so important with a declination amount, but very important for the v corrections on GHA.

3. Is the declination of your target increasing or decreasing as time goes on? Check its trend in the almanac, as it determines whether you add or subtract your dec corrections.

4. Always mark down the N/S/E/W designations of your AP and Dec! Are you shooting an object in the same or opposite hemisphere? Better be sure-- it can ruin your math!

5. ROUND ROUND ROUND! Don't forget to round! Especially in the places in the NOA sight reduction form that tell you to use the "nearest whole degree".

6. The Equation of Time correction is **only** needed for checking meridian passages, more commonly the Noon Sight for Longitude.

7. In the sight reduction process, you altered the minutes of your LHA to give you a whole-degree number. Did you do the same to your AP Longitude?

# How to Use Other Objects in the Sky

## Shooting the Stars:

Stars are reliable and easy, but it's really tough to see the horizon in the pure inky black of night, unless it's really clear and the Moon is very bright. Most star sights are done at dusk or dawn, when the sun is beyond the horizon, the sky is bright enough to see the horizon, and the stars are just bright enough to show themselves.

Stars ought to be a little less tricky than the Moon or Planets, if you can understand the concept of SHA (aka Sidereal Hour Angle, which is related to LHA, which is a product of GHA). The stars never change position in the sky relative to each other. They simply spin in a circular motion on the same wonky sometimes-24-hour clock that the Earth rotates on.

Their declinations rarely change, either, so they can be listed in the Almanac in a solid constant number. Since the Earth's orbit isn't perfect, there are different SHA and Dec numbers according to seasons. If you look in your almanac, you'll notice that the stars span 2 pages for each set, one page with January-June, and one page July-December. The differences don't make up for much more than 10 minutes in SHA and 1 minute in Dec, but it can affect your readings. The star index, however, is for obscure stars—the main stars are listed in the daily almanac pages in alphabetical order.

This makes them easy to track, but we need one place to relate them all to in order to find where they are when we look at them. If we didn't, the Almanac would take up all the space on your bookshelf, because there are LOTS of stars. So what better candidate for a reference point than our stoned geek friend, Aries!

You will see that stars are listed not in GHA, but SHA. SHA is the direct difference, in degrees of travel West, between LHA Aries and the star's position in the sky.

To get the GHA of your star, you simply look up its SHA in the star tables (its SHA never changes) and add that value to GHA Aries. As with all cyclic 360 degree numbers, if the result is greater than 360, the subtract 360 to find its real value.

So now we use our familiar formula: LHA = GHA (+East, -West) AP Longitude

Since stars do not have v or d corrections to look up, they become slightly faster to use than planets—less onerous tables to trudge through.

That's it—write it into the Sight Reduction tables and off you go. Pretty simple!

Example:
On June 10, 2005, at 04:00:00 we shoot Sirius. GHA Aries of that time is 318 degrees, 36.7 minutes. SHA Sirius is 258 degrees 39.6 minutes, Dec is S16 degrees 43.3 minutes.

318 deg 36.7 min (GHA Aries)
+258 deg 39.6 min (SHA Sirius)
---
576 deg 76.3 min, round to 577 deg, 16.3 min (GHA Sirius)

This is greater than 360, so subtract 360, and arrive at 217 degrees, 16.3 minutes.

*LHA = GHA (+East, -West) AP Longitude*

Let's pull a number out and suppose our AP Longitude is 55 degrees East.

217 deg, 16.3 min (GHA Sirius)
+55 deg, 00 min (AP Longitude, add east)
---
272 deg, 16.3 min (LHA Sirius)

We now have the LHA, Dec, and an angle is on the sextant, so those 3 values can be plugged into your Sight Reduction Tables to yield plotting information.

## More Geek Trivia on Stars:

Stars have an attribute called Magnitude. This is the brightness of the star. The lower the value, the brighter the star (negative values are "highest"). Sirius is the brightest star in the sky, with a magnitude of –1.6. It's easy to find, always following Orion, in line with the 3 stars of his belt.

The "main" stars listed in the daily pages are the brightest by magnitude. They are even labeled as such on the star map so they are easier to find. Yes, the almanac even has star maps! It's such a cool book! Man, I'm such a geek.

Lots of the stars have Arabic names, which have been carried over from the centuries. The Arabs were among the first to name the stars; they used them to navigate across the desert, traveling at night when the temperatures were more forgiving, and resting during the day. Pretty cool.

# Shooting Planets:

Shooting Planets is a little different from shooting the Sun, and here's why: Planets run on their own paths across the sky, at different speeds. They zip across the sky at different rates, climb and descend their declination at different rates, and most of them are too dim to pick out from the rest of the stars.

There are only 4 planets listed in the Almanac, because Mercury is always too close to the sun to be useful, and the others are too far away and/or too dim to see without a powerful telescope. That leaves Venus, Mars, Jupiter, and Saturn.

Venus is a saving grace because it's usually the first thing you see during the evening due to its brightness, so you can get several shots before it's too dark to make out the horizon. It's so bright it simply cannot be confused with any other star. Venus is great —use it as often as you can.

The other planets are dim and hard to find unless you're an astronomy geek. You're probably better off skipping them unless there's some rare conjunction and they are lined up together.

Take a moment to examine a daily almanac page. The planets are on the left page, next to Aries. You'll see the name of the planet, with a + or – number beside them. The number beside the name is the Magnitude of the planet (the lower the brighter).

You'll note on our sample page that Venus has a Magnitude of –4. It's bright! In fact, other than the Sun and Moon, it's the brightest object in the sky.

The planets also have their own GHA and Dec information, and their own "v" and "d" value to at the bottom of the columns to determine corrections in the gray-edged "Increments and Corrections" tables. If you don't remember what the "v or d" corrections are from our Noon Sight explanation, here's a short refresher:

"v" represents the correction in GHA travel an object makes as time passes. "d" represents a change in the Dec as time passes. One looks up v and d the same way (the tables use the same math). If a v or d value in the bottom of the daily column is negative, then you use its absolute value in the Increments and Corrections tables, and stick the negative status on its result. In other words, if its beginning is negative, its result is negative.

Now if you shoot Venus or Mars, there is a tiny little almost negligible correction on the first page of the Almanac, the same page where you get Dip and Sun Semidiameter. Depending on time of year, it can vary up to a whole 0.5 minutes, whoop-de-doo. Remember that your seconds are eliminated from sight reduction for math and sanity's sake, so unless it's a large amount, you should probably forget it. But hey, it's worth checking into nonetheless. We're on the open ocean, we've swabbed the deck so many times you could eat off it and either eaten or re-floated hundreds of suicidal flying fish, and we got nothing better to do than look up onerous corrections to our sights!

Example:
It's still June 10, 2005 (gotta get as much mileage out of that one almanac page as I can!). We shoot Venus at 06:30:00. Suppose our corrected sight gives us an Apparent Altitude of 65 degrees. At the first page of the Almanac, under Venus, Jan1-Sep23, anything over 60 degrees apparent altitude is subject to a +0.1 minute correction. Woo! Aren't you glad you wasted all that time?

According to the Almanac, GHA Venus is 249 degrees 49.2 minutes, Dec is N24 degrees 19.6 minutes. The v = –0.9 and d = 0.1

Looking in the Increments and Corrections pages, we have a whole correction (under Sun/Planets column) of 7 degrees, 30.0 minutes. Now for v of 0.9 (you can't look it up with a negative number so use its absolute value) at 30 minutes 0 seconds, is 0.5 minutes correction. Since v is negative, that becomes a –0.5 minutes correction. Write this down on your sight sheet. It will be summed with GHA.

Now we look up d. At 30 minutes 0 seconds, a d of 0.1 yields a correction of 0.1 minutes. Write this down too. It will be summed with Dec.

249 degrees, 49.2 minutes (GHA Venus)
+ 7 degrees, 30 minutes (Sun/Planets @30 minutes increment)
- 0 deg 0.5 minutes (v corr)
---
256 degrees, 78.7 minutes, rounds to 257 degrees, 18.7 minutes (corrected GHA Venus)

N24 degrees, 19.6 minutes
+ 0 deg 0.1 minutes (d corr)
---
N24 degrees, 19.7 minutes (corrected Dec Venus)

Now since we eliminate seconds or points of minutes from our sight reductions, normally you'd think "Why bother with the v or d corrections?" Well, sometimes, in the case of our GHA, it could sway the minutes to the nearest whole number if you rounded up. And, sometimes, with particularly fast things like the Moon, it can alter your reading by quite a few miles!

Anyhow, now you have a clean GHA and Dec you can use to find your LHA, and plug those values into your sight reduction.

# Shooting the Moon:

Shooting the Moon is like a mix of shooting the Sun and shooting a Planet. It has GHA, Dec, Semi-diameter, like the Sun, and it has "v" and "d" movement like planets.

The Moon has two things that the others do not: One is Parallax, and the other is Phase.

Parallax: Since it's close, the angles you view it at are skewed. Fortunately the Great Geeks of History pulled out all the stops and gave the Moon its own special page in the very back of the almanac.

Phase: The moon isn't always a big bright circle. You can't always shoot the easy Lower Limb like the Sun. If the crescent only shows up in the top half, we have to eat some crow and shoot that Upper Limb.

Take a moment to look at a daily almanac page and find the Moon's columns. It's on the right, next to the Sun's column.

You'll see columns for GHA and Dec just like everything else, but there are columns for v and d, and a new HP column.

The v and d columns are the same v and d correction references you use with the planets. But-- the Moon flies so fast and in such a goofy orbit that the v and d numbers change *hourly*! Some day when it comes crashing down on us, you'll think that the werewolves, crazy human behavior, tides, earthquakes, and other natural disasters it causes were a piece of cake!

Anyhow, pay attention to its v and d values, because they'll throw you WAY off if you let them slide.

Now let's talk about the HP column. HP is used in the Moon's correction tables (last page of the almanac) to find the Parallax correction for either Lower or Upper Limb sights.

Flip to the last page of your almanac. If it's the commercial version, it will be the last page of *data* (the remainder is ads from companies selling you boat stuff, which make the book's price more reasonable).

You'll see the Moon's own table of Altitude Corrections, another Dip table (same table as on the Sun's Altitude Corrections page), and an HP/L U table.

To run the Moon's Altitude Corrections table, move across the top row to find your Apparent Altitude Degrees (sextant reading, + index error, -dip), then scan down until you find your Apparent Altitude Minutes. The corresponding number is your Moon Altitude Correction.

Now you need the HP (Parallax) correction. This is located in the same column as your Apparent Altitude Degrees fell. You'll see a U and an L. This refers to Upper or Lower Limb, whichever you shot. Scan down the side of the table until you find the HP number from the daily almanac page, and then across to U or L. The resulting number is your HP (Parallax) correction.

Now, on the sight sheet, you have values to write down in Altitude and HP. Refraction values are universal, according to the angle you shot at. Now you can find your Height Observed.

Example:
On June 10, 2005, at 20:30:00 we shoot the Moon's upper limb at, say, 33 degrees Apparent Altitude. GHA = 72 degrees 03.5 minutes, Dec = N24 degrees 08.5 minutes. v = 12.2, d = 7.7, and HP = 54.1

Increments and Corrections @30 minutes gives us a whole correction (under Moon) of 7 degrees, 09.5 mins; a v corr of 6.2 minutes; a d corr of 3.9 minutes.

72 deg 03.5 min (GHA Moon)
+ 7 deg 09.5 min (Moon @30 minutes increment)
+ 0 deg 09.5 min (v corr)
_____
79 deg 22.5 min (Corrected GHA Moon)

Now we look in the Moon's table in back, and find the following:
Apparent Altitude of 33 degrees 0 minutes gives us 57.5 minutes Altitude correction. HP of 54.1 gives us a U of 1.5 minutes.

Here's a new onerous rule for you: If you shoot the Moon's Upper Limb, you subtract 30 minutes from your U correction.

33 degrees 0 minutes (App Alt)
+ 0 degrees 57.5 minutes (Alt corr)
+ 0 degrees 1.5 minutes (U corr)
-0 degrees 30 minutes (because we shot Upper Limb)
_____
33 degrees 29 minutes (Height Observed/Ho Moon)

N24 degrees 08.5 minutes (Dec Moon)
+ 0 degrees 3.9 minutes (d corr)
_____
N24 degrees 12.4 minutes (corrected Dec Moon)

Now you have all 3 values needed for your sight reduction!

# Sun-Run-Sun and Running Fixes

A way to figure out where you are during the day, if you're shooting before or after noon, is Sun-Run-Sun. This is basically a series of sun sights, maybe one per hour. Shoot the Sun, run for an hour or so, then shoot the Sun again.

If you plot your DR course on the plotting sheet along with the LOPs of your sights, you can keep a fairly accurate watch of where you are going, tick off marks along that DR course, and use it to calculate your boat's progress. This technique is great if you are approaching landfall and need to keep constant tabs on distance from shore.

No, you won't know exactly minute for minute where you are at any given point in time like a proper 3-target fix will give you, but your positional fix will be based off of the intersection of your DR course and the LOP of your sight at any given time. This is also defined as a Running Fix (the "Run" in Sun-Run-Sun).

If you do a good 3-target fix or noon sight once every 24 hours, with Sun-Run-Sun at morning and evening, you'll never get lost.

Always always ALWAYS keep your DR up to date. Do it at every watch change, do it halfway through your watch, do it as often as you can. It will pay off if you're stuck with overcast skies or inclement weather when the time comes to shoot something in the sky.

# How does the Noon Sight work without Trigonometry? (more optional trivia for hardcore geeks)

The Noon Sight is no different, but since it relies on the perfect alignment between you, the poles, and the Sun, we can skip all that sight reduction stuff and do simple addition. This is why everyone loves the Noon Sight.

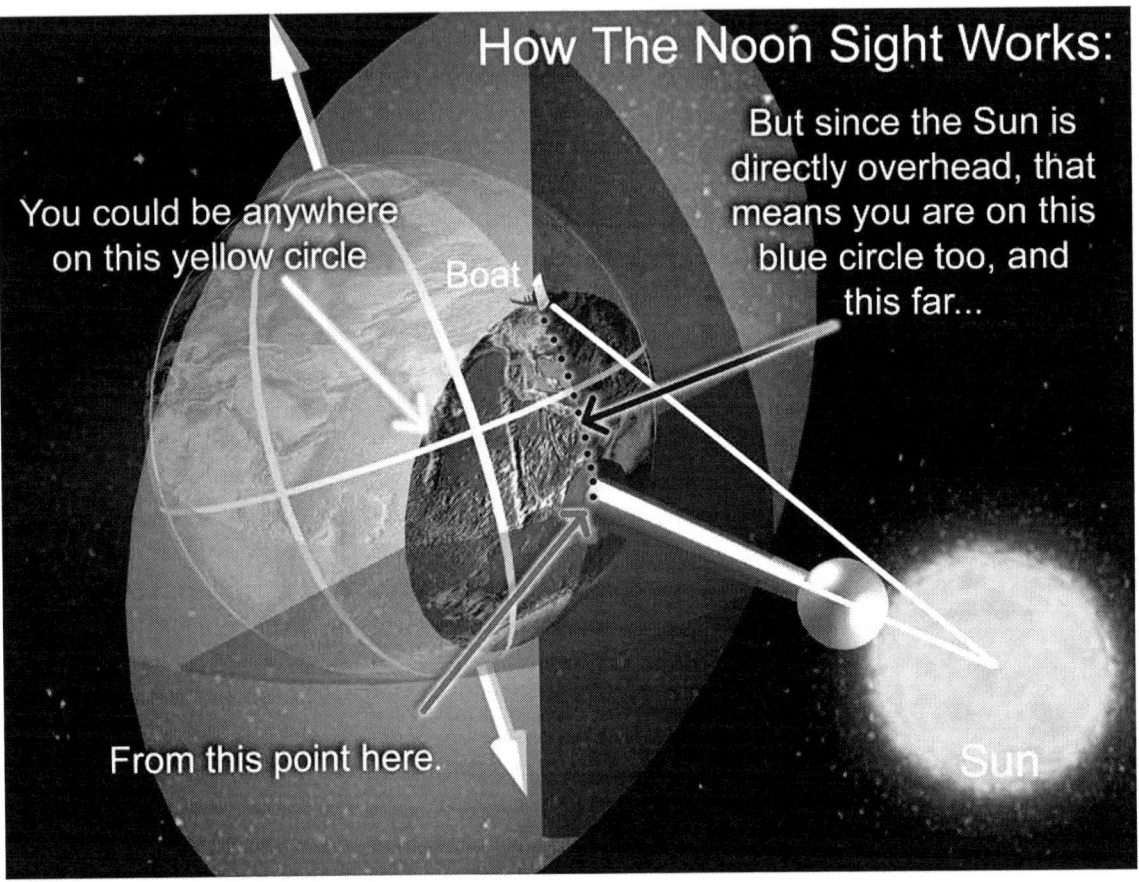

The blue plane represents the Sun's meridian (Longitude). The red plane represents the Sun's GP as it scrolls across the Earth. The yellow plane represents where our sextant sight draws a circle around the GP of the sun, because by geometric laws, we *have* to be that distance from its GP.

Our boat (still beached on the mountain in Russia) knows that it has to be a certain distance from the Sun's GP (base) because that's the core of what our sextant does. The angle tells us so.

We could very well be anywhere on that yellow line, but the Sun is declaring our Local Noon (directly overhead) and therefore on our same Longitude. Since it's Local Noon, that means its GP (flagpole base) is also on our Longitude, and we can measure a straight line down that Longitude, to find how far we are from the Sun's GP in perfect degrees, minutes, and seconds of Latitude.

*Which means you could potentially do a 'noon' sight with any object in the sky!*

If you sight *any* celestial object when its meridian passes yours (ie its 'Local Noon' passage), you can do a 'Noon-Sight-Style' sight with said celestial object, provided you know when it's directly over your meridian. And that's all in the Almanac.

The Sun is easy to do because it's so bloody huge. The moon is easy too. Noting that a particular star is nearly directly overhead is hard but it can save you a lot of headache. Shooting one object a few times to mark its passage directly overhead is a lot easier than running down tables and sight reductions, then plotting the LOPs and intercepts for 2 or more separate objects.

The question then becomes, "Do you have the time and patience to wait for that thing to fly overhead?" Of course you do! You're on a boat in the middle of the ocean—you've got nothing *but* time!

Unfortunately that also means you have time to cram your head full of the rest of the really difficult stuff, *if* you feel like it.

# The World is Your Sextant! (for salty geeks)

If your sextant breaks, or if you're the saltiest of salty dogs, you can even use the horizon as your sextant, at sunset and sunrise (or moonset and moonrise, or the setting and of any listed star), provided your watch is still working. When the sun (or moon) just touches the horizon, that's a lower-limb sight of 0 degrees! Likewise for any other object. Impress your friends. Strike fear into the heart of your crew when you say, "Arr, I don't need no sextant to find where we be, mateys!" Then freak them out and show them your accurate plot!

## Cool Online Resources:

**Free HO229/249 tables!**
The NGA has all of the HO229 and HO249 publications available for free (your tax dollars truly working for a good cause-- get your money's worth!!!) in Adobe PDF file format on their website. While they are clumsy to use on a computer, they can be printed out or used for practice.
http://www.nga.mil/portal/site/maritime/

**Online sight calculators!**
A great way to check your math.
http://www.celnav.de/sightred.htm
http://jacq.istos.com.au/sundry/reduction.html

# Worksheets Galore

Feel free to copy these as much as you like. That's what they are there for. Enjoy!

# All-purpose Sight Worksheet

**Object:**

|  | Date | Time (GMT) |
|---|---|---|
|  |  |  |

### DR / AP

|  | Deg | Min | Sec |
|---|---|---|---|
| N / S |  |  |  |
| E / W |  |  |  |

### Sight

|  | Deg/Hrs | Min | Sec |
|---|---|---|---|
| Sextant reading |  | + | + |
| *add* Index Error | − | − | − |
| *subtract* Dip Correction | = | = | = |
| **Apparent Altitude** |  |  |  |

*use Apparent Altitude to find the following corrections...*

### Corrections

|  |  |  |  |
|---|---|---|---|
| *add* Alt/SD: L / U Limb | + | + | + |
| *add* Refraction | + | + | + |
| *add* HP: L / U (Moon only) | = | = | = |
| *Rule: Subtract 30' if shooting U* |  |  |  |
| **Height Observed (Ho)** |  |  |  |

### Almanac Stuff

|  | Deg | Min | Sec |
|---|---|---|---|
| Dec |  |  |  | d=
| *add or subtract? (according to almanac trend)* | ? | ? | ? |
| d Corr |  |  |  |
| **Corrected Dec** | = | = | = |

Rule: if LHA > 360, replace result with LHA − 360
Rule: if GHA > 360, replace result with GHA − 360

|  |  |  |  | v= |
|---|---|---|---|---|
| GHA |  |  |  |  |
| SHA (star only) | + | + | + |  |
| v Corr or increment | + | + | + |  |
| **Corrected GHA** | = | = | = |  |

### LHA Calculations

|  |  |  |  |
|---|---|---|---|
| GHA |  |  |  |
| DR / AP Longitude | = | = | = |
| *plus East / minus West* |  |  |  |
| **LHA** |  |  |  |

# Advanced Polaris Sight Worksheet

## Sight

|  | Date | Deg/Hrs | Min | Sec |
|---|---|---|---|---|
|  | Time (GMT) |  |  |  |
|  | Sextant reading |  |  |  |
| add | Index Error | + | + | + |
| subtract |  | − | − | − |
| = | **Apparent Altitude** | = | = | = |

*use Apparent Altitude to find the following corrections…*

## Corrections

| | | | | |
|---|---|---|---|---|
| add | Alt/SD : Lower Limb | + | + | + |
| add | Refraction | + | + | + |
| = | **Height Observed (Ho)** | = | = | = |

*use Adjusted Sextant Angle in the next stage….*

## Almanac Stuff

|  |  | Deg | Min | Sec |
|---|---|---|---|---|
|  | GHA Aries |  |  |  |
|  | Assumed Longitude | = | = | = |

*add East, subtract West*

*use LHA Aries to find…*

|  |  |  |  |  |
|---|---|---|---|---|
| LHA Aries |  |  |  |  |
| LHA Aries Correction | + | + | + |
| Adj. Sextant Angle | = | = | = |
| *(from below left)* |  |  |  |
| = "**Lat**" |  |  |  |

*use "Lat" to find…*

| | | | |
|---|---|---|---|
| Lat corr (a1) | + | + | + |
| = Corrected Lat | = | = | = |

*use to find…*

| | | | |
|---|---|---|---|
| Month corr (a2) | + | + | + |
| = Almost done! | = | = | = |

*magical mystery degree* −1

| = **Final Latitude** | | | |

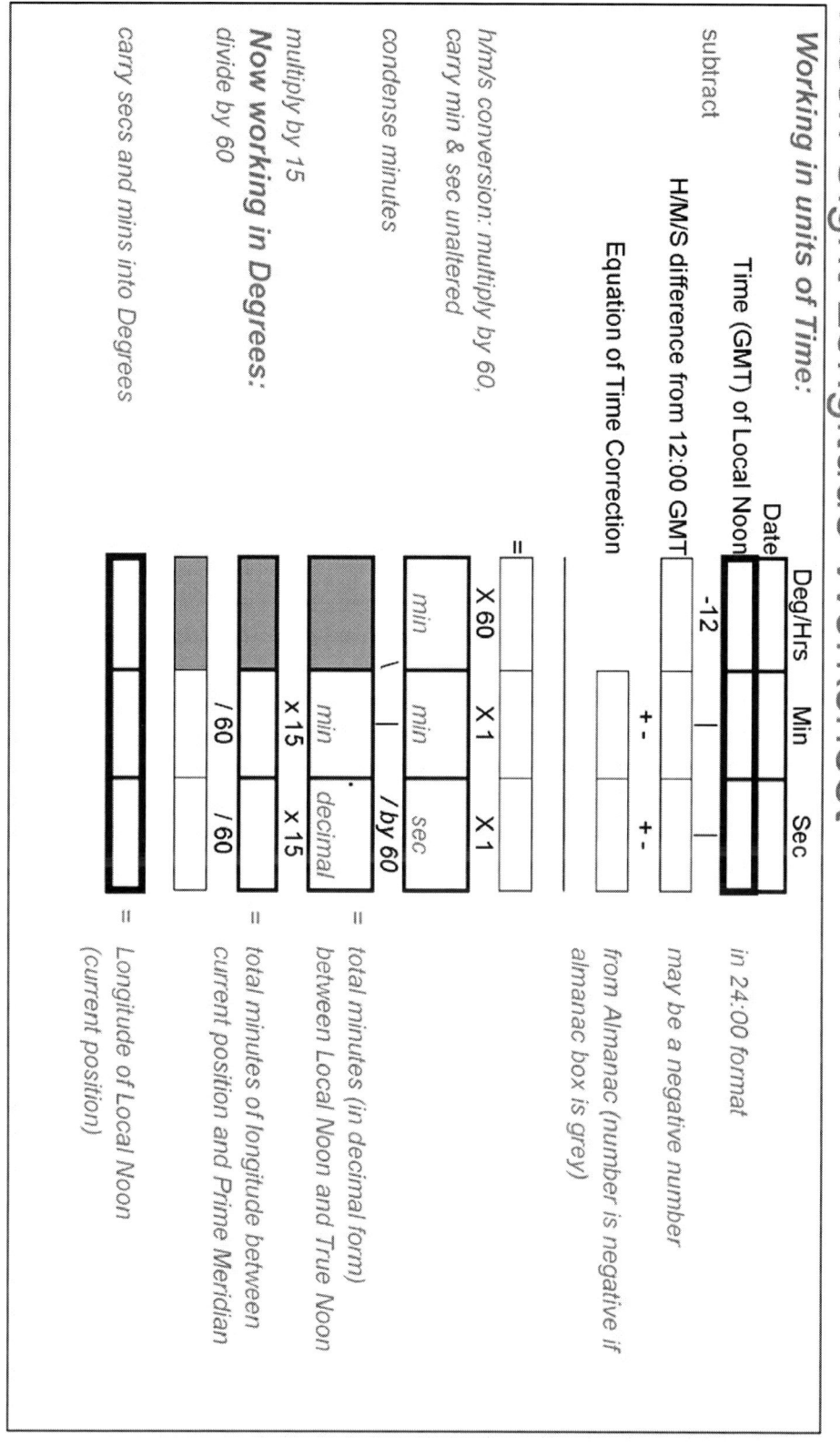

# Noon Sight Latitude Worksheet

## Sight

| | Date | Deg/Hrs | Min | Sec |
|---|---|---|---|---|
| | Time (GMT) | | | |
| | Sextant reading | | | |
| add / subtract | Index Error | - | - | - |
| = | Dip Correction | = | = | = |
| add | Apparent Altitude | | | |

*use Apparent Altitude to find the following corrections...*

## Corrections

| | | Deg | Min | Sec |
|---|---|---|---|---|
| add | Refraction | + | + | + |
| add | Alt/SD : Lower Limb | + | + | + |
| = | Height Observed (Ho) | = | = | = |

*use Adjusted Sextant Angle in the next stage...*

## Calculations

| | | Deg | Min | Sec |
|---|---|---|---|---|
| | Sun's GP Altitude | 90 | 00 | 00 |
| subtract | ...Height Observed (from above) | - | - | - |
| add or subtract? (See math table) | = Distance from Sun's GP Latitude | = ? | = ? | = ? |
| add or subtract? from top right | Corrected Dec Sun | = ? | = ? | = ? |
| | Final Latitude of Observer | = | = | = |

## Almanac Stuff

| | | Deg | Min | Sec |
|---|---|---|---|---|
| | Dec Sun | | | |
| add or subtract? (according to almanac trend) | d Corr | = ? | = ? | = ? |
| | Corrected Dec Sun | = | = | = |

## Declination Math Table

| Hemisphere? You | Sun | Sun's relation to You? | What do you do with the Dec? |
|---|---|---|---|
| N | N | N | Subtract & use abs. value |
| N | N | S | Add |
| N | S | S | Subtract |
| S | S | S | Subtract |
| S | S | N | Add |
| S | N | N | Subtract |
| S | N | S | Subtract & use abs. value |

# Sextant Sights

**Date:**

| Time (GMT) | Object | Reading |
|---|---|---|
|  |  |  |
|  |  |  |
|  |  |  |
|  |  |  |
|  |  |  |
|  |  |  |
|  |  |  |
|  |  |  |
|  |  |  |
|  |  |  |
|  |  |  |
|  |  |  |
|  |  |  |
|  |  |  |
|  |  |  |

**Date:**

| Time (GMT) | Object | Reading |
|---|---|---|
|  |  |  |
|  |  |  |
|  |  |  |
|  |  |  |
|  |  |  |
|  |  |  |
|  |  |  |
|  |  |  |
|  |  |  |
|  |  |  |
|  |  |  |
|  |  |  |
|  |  |  |
|  |  |  |
|  |  |  |

**Date:**

| Time (GMT) | Object | Reading |
|---|---|---|
|  |  |  |
|  |  |  |
|  |  |  |
|  |  |  |
|  |  |  |
|  |  |  |
|  |  |  |
|  |  |  |
|  |  |  |
|  |  |  |
|  |  |  |
|  |  |  |
|  |  |  |
|  |  |  |
|  |  |  |

# NAO CONCISE SIGHT REDUCTION FORM

| Date & UT of observation    h   m   s | Body | Estimated Latitude & Longitude °   '   °   ' |
|---|---|---|

| Step | Calculate Altitude & Azimuth | Summary of Rules & Notes |
|---|---|---|
| Assumed latitude | $Lat =$    ° | Nearest estimated latitude, integral number of degrees. |
| Assumed longitude | $Long =$    °    ' | Choose $Long$ so that $LHA$ has integral number of degrees. |
| **1.** From the almanac: | $Dec =$    °    ' | Record the $Dec$ for use in Step 3. |
| GHA Aries    h | $=$    °    ' | Needed if using $SHA$. Tabular value. |
| Increment    m   s | $=$    °    ' | for minutes and seconds of time. |
| SHA | $SHA =$    °    ' | |
| $GHA = GHA\ Aries + SHA$ | $GHA =$    °    ' | Remove multiples of 360°. |
| Assumed longitude | $Long =$    °    ' | West longitudes are negative. |
| $LHA = GHA + Long$ | $LHA =$    ° | Remove multiples of 360°. |
| **2.** Reduction table, 1$^{st}$ entry $(Lat, LHA) = ($  °,  ° $)$ record $A$, $B$ and $Z_1$. | $A =$   °  '    $A° =$  ° <br>                      $A' =$  ' <br> $B =$   °  ' <br>                      $Z_1 =$  ° | nearest whole degree of $A$. <br> minutes part of $A$. <br> $B$ is minus if $90° < LHA < 270°$. <br> $Z_1$ has the same sign as $B$. |
| **3.** From step 1 <br> $F = B + Dec$ | $Dec =$   °  ' <br> $F =$   °  ' <br>               $F° =$  ° <br>               $F' =$  ' | $Dec$ is minus if contrary to $Lat$. <br> Regard $F$ as positive until step 7. <br> nearest whole degree of $F$. <br> minutes part of $F$. |
| **4.** Reduction table, 2$^{nd}$ entry $(A°, F°) = ($  °,  ° $)$ record $H$, $P$ and $Z_2$. | $H =$   °  '   $P° =$  ° <br>                    $Z_2 =$  ° | nearest whole degree of $P$. |
| **5.** Auxiliary table, 1$^{st}$ entry $(F', P°) = ($  ',  ° $)$ record $corr_1$ | $corr_1 =$   ' | $corr_1$ is minus if $F < 90°$ & $F' > 29'$, or if $F > 90°$ & $F' < 30'$. |
| **6.** Auxiliary table, 2$^{nd}$ entry $(A', Z_2°) = ($  ',  ° $)$ record $corr_2$ | $corr_2 =$   ' | $Z_2°$ nearest whole degree of $Z_2$. <br> $corr_2$ is minus if $A' < 30'$. |
| **7.** Calculated altitude = <br> $H_C = H + corr_1 + corr_2$ | $H_C =$   °  ' | $H_C$ is minus if $F$ is negative, and object is below the horizon. |
| **8.** Azimuth, 1$^{st}$ component <br>                2$^{nd}$ component <br> $Z = Z_1 + Z_2$ <br><br><br><br> True azimuth | $Z_1 =$  ° <br> $Z_2 =$  ° <br> $Z =$  ° <br><br><br><br> $Z_n =$  ° | $Z_1$ has the same sign as $B$. <br> $Z_2$ is minus if $F > 90°$. <br> If $F$ is negative, $Z_2 = 180° - Z_2$. <br> Ignore the sign of $Z$. <br> N $Lat$: If $LHA > 180°$, $Z_n = Z$, or if $LHA < 180°$, $Z_n = 360° - Z$, <br> S $Lat$: If $LHA > 180°$, $Z_n = 180° - Z$, or if $LHA < 180°$, $Z_n = 180° + Z$. <br> ©HMNAO |

For use with *The Nautical Almanac's* Concise Sight Reduction Tables pages 284–318.

*Copyright Council for the Central Laboratory of the Research Councils 2005*

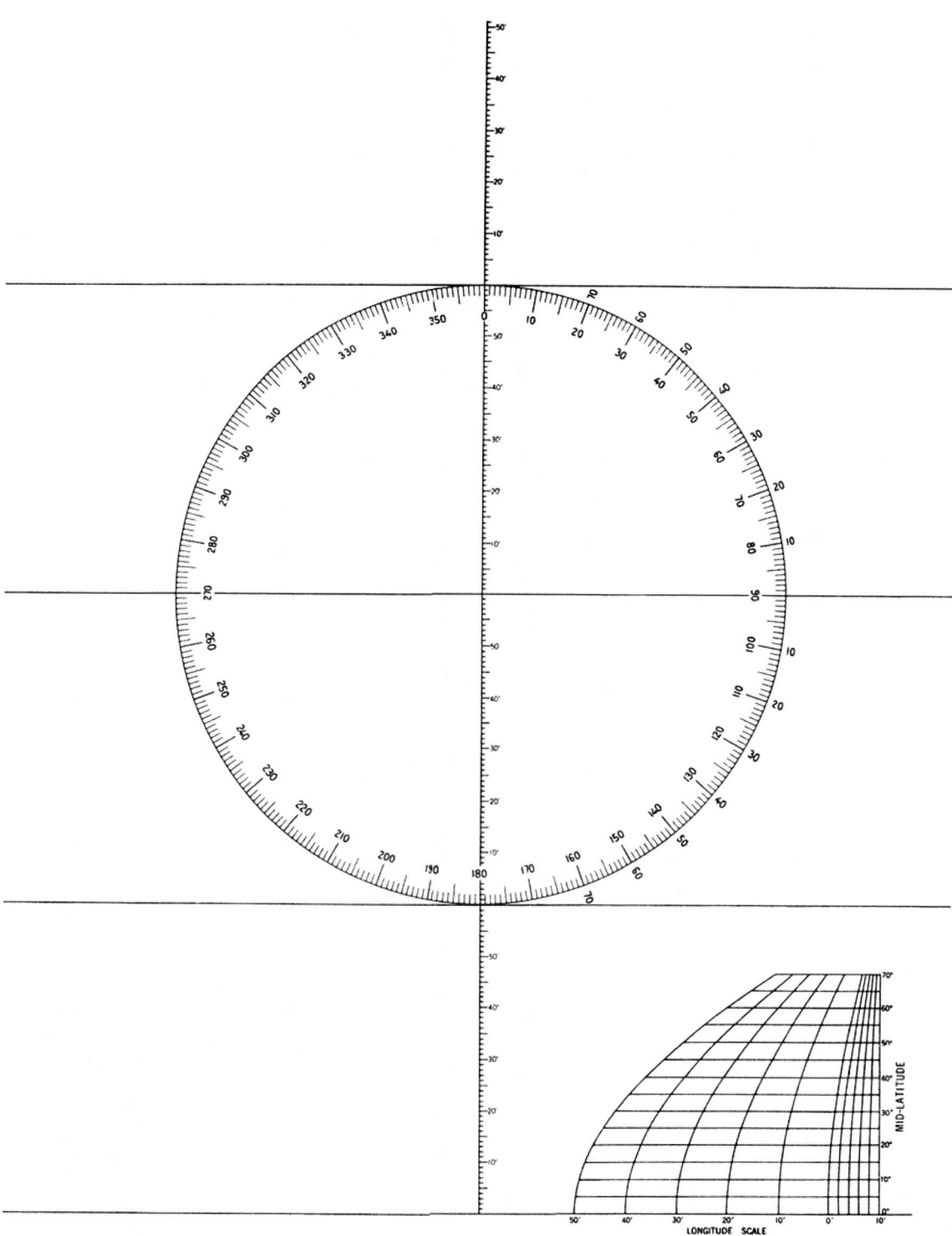

# Almanac Page Samples

These are pages from the 2005 Nautical Almanac. These should cover all the examples and tutorials listed in this book. Obviously, these samples are not to be used for navigation, because June 2005 was 6 months ago when I wrote this. But please do familiarize yourself with how the pages are set up, and to follow along in the tutorials if you don't already have an almanac of your own.

## A2 ALTITUDE CORRECTION TABLES 10°–90°—SUN, STARS, PLANETS

| OCT.—MAR. SUN APR.—SEPT. | | | | | | STARS AND PLANETS | | | | DIP | | | | | |
|---|---|---|---|---|---|---|---|---|---|---|---|---|---|---|---|
| App. Alt. | Lower Limb | Upper Limb | App. Alt. | Lower Limb | Upper Limb | App Alt. | Corr$^n$ | | App. Alt. | Additional Corr$^n$ | Ht. of Eye | Corr$^n$ | Ht. of Eye | Ht. of Eye | Corr$^n$ |
| ° ′ | ′ | ′ | ° ′ | ′ | ′ | ° ′ | ′ | | | **2005** | m | ′ | ft. | m | ′ |
| 9 33 | +10.8 | −21.5 | 9 39 | +10.6 | −21.2 | 9 55 | −5.3 | | | **VENUS** | 2.4 | −2.8 | 8.0 | 1.0 | −1.8 |
| 9 45 | +10.9 | −21.4 | 9 50 | +10.7 | −21.1 | 10 07 | −5.2 | | | Jan. 1–Sept. 23 | 2.6 | −2.9 | 8.6 | 1.5 | −2.2 |
| 9 56 | +11.0 | −21.3 | 10 02 | +10.8 | −21.0 | 10 20 | −5.1 | | | | 2.8 | −3.0 | 9.2 | 2.0 | −2.5 |
| 10 08 | +11.1 | −21.2 | 10 14 | +10.9 | −20.9 | 10 32 | −5.0 | | | ° ′ | 3.0 | −3.1 | 9.8 | 2.5 | −2.8 |
| 10 20 | +11.2 | −21.1 | 10 27 | +11.0 | −20.8 | 10 46 | −4.9 | | | 60 +0.1 | 3.2 | −3.2 | 10.5 | 3.0 | −3.0 |
| 10 33 | +11.3 | −21.0 | 10 40 | +11.1 | −20.7 | 10 59 | −4.8 | | | Sept. 24–Nov. 14 | 3.4 | | 11.2 | See table | |
| 10 46 | +11.4 | −20.9 | 10 53 | +11.2 | −20.6 | 11 14 | −4.7 | | | | 3.6 | −3.3 | 11.9 | ← | |
| 11 00 | +11.5 | −20.8 | 11 07 | +11.3 | −20.5 | 11 29 | −4.6 | | | ° ′ | 3.8 | −3.4 | 12.6 | | |
| 11 15 | +11.6 | −20.7 | 11 22 | +11.4 | −20.4 | 11 44 | −4.5 | | | 41 +0.2 | 4.0 | −3.5 | 13.3 | m | ′ |
| 11 30 | +11.7 | −20.6 | 11 37 | +11.5 | −20.3 | 12 00 | −4.4 | | | 76 +0.1 | 4.3 | −3.6 | 14.1 | 20 | −7.9 |
| 11 45 | +11.8 | −20.5 | 11 53 | +11.6 | −20.2 | 12 17 | −4.3 | | | Nov. 15–Dec. 7 | 4.5 | −3.7 | 14.9 | 22 | −8.3 |
| 12 01 | +11.9 | −20.4 | 12 10 | +11.7 | −20.1 | 12 35 | −4.2 | | | | 4.7 | −3.8 | 15.7 | 24 | −8.6 |
| 12 18 | +12.0 | −20.3 | 12 27 | +11.8 | −20.0 | 12 53 | −4.1 | | | ° ′ | 5.0 | −3.9 | 16.5 | 26 | −9.0 |
| 12 36 | +12.1 | −20.2 | 12 45 | +11.9 | −19.9 | 13 12 | −4.0 | | | 34 +0.3 | 5.2 | −4.0 | 17.4 | 28 | −9.3 |
| 12 54 | +12.2 | −20.1 | 13 04 | +12.0 | −19.8 | 13 32 | −3.9 | | | 60 +0.2 | 5.5 | −4.1 | 18.3 | | |
| 13 14 | +12.3 | −20.0 | 13 24 | +12.1 | −19.7 | 13 53 | −3.8 | | | 80 +0.1 | 5.8 | −4.2 | 19.1 | 30 | −9.6 |
| 13 34 | +12.4 | −19.9 | 13 44 | +12.2 | −19.6 | 14 16 | −3.7 | | | Dec. 8–Dec. 23 | 6.1 | −4.3 | 20.1 | 32 | −10.0 |
| 13 55 | +12.5 | −19.8 | 14 06 | +12.3 | −19.5 | 14 39 | −3.6 | | | ° ′ | 6.3 | −4.4 | 21.0 | 34 | −10.3 |
| 14 17 | +12.6 | −19.7 | 14 29 | +12.4 | −19.4 | 15 03 | −3.5 | | | 29 +0.4 | 6.6 | −4.5 | 22.0 | 36 | −10.6 |
| 14 41 | +12.7 | −19.6 | 14 53 | +12.5 | −19.3 | 15 29 | −3.4 | | | 51 +0.3 | 6.9 | −4.6 | 22.9 | 38 | −10.8 |
| 15 05 | +12.8 | −19.5 | 15 18 | +12.6 | −19.2 | 15 56 | −3.3 | | | 68 +0.2 | 7.2 | −4.7 | 23.9 | | |
| 15 31 | +12.9 | −19.4 | 15 45 | +12.7 | −19.1 | 16 25 | −3.2 | | | 83 +0.1 | 7.5 | −4.8 | 24.9 | 40 | −11.1 |
| 15 59 | +13.0 | −19.3 | 16 13 | +12.8 | −19.0 | 16 55 | −3.1 | | | Dec. 24–Dec. 31 | 7.9 | −4.9 | 26.0 | 42 | −11.4 |
| 16 27 | +13.1 | −19.2 | 16 43 | +12.9 | −18.9 | 17 27 | −3.0 | | | ° ′ | 8.2 | −5.0 | 27.1 | 44 | −11.7 |
| 16 58 | +13.2 | −19.1 | 17 14 | +13.0 | −18.8 | 18 01 | −2.9 | | | 26 +0.5 | 8.5 | −5.1 | 28.1 | 46 | −11.9 |
| 17 30 | +13.3 | −19.0 | 17 47 | +13.1 | −18.7 | 18 37 | −2.8 | | | 46 +0.4 | 8.8 | −5.2 | 29.2 | 48 | −12.2 |
| 18 05 | +13.4 | −18.9 | 18 23 | +13.2 | −18.6 | 19 16 | −2.7 | | | 60 +0.3 | 9.2 | −5.3 | 30.4 | ft. | |
| 18 41 | +13.5 | −18.8 | 19 00 | +13.3 | −18.5 | 19 56 | −2.6 | | | 73 +0.2 | 9.5 | −5.4 | 31.5 | 2 | −1.4 |
| 19 20 | +13.6 | −18.7 | 19 41 | +13.4 | −18.4 | 20 40 | −2.5 | | | 84 +0.1 | 9.9 | −5.5 | 32.7 | 4 | −1.9 |
| 20 02 | +13.7 | −18.6 | 20 24 | +13.5 | −18.3 | 21 27 | −2.4 | | | **MARS** | 10.3 | −5.6 | 33.9 | 6 | −2.4 |
| 20 46 | +13.8 | −18.5 | 21 10 | +13.6 | −18.2 | 22 17 | −2.3 | | | Jan. 1–July 5 | 10.6 | −5.7 | 35.1 | 8 | −2.7 |
| 21 34 | +13.9 | −18.4 | 21 59 | +13.7 | −18.1 | 23 11 | −2.2 | | | ° ′ | 11.0 | −5.8 | 36.3 | 10 | −3.1 |
| 22 25 | +14.0 | −18.3 | 22 52 | +13.8 | −18.0 | 24 09 | −2.1 | | | 60 +0.1 | 11.4 | −5.9 | 37.6 | See table | |
| 23 20 | +14.1 | −18.2 | 23 49 | +13.9 | −17.9 | 25 12 | −2.0 | | | July 6–Sept. 16 | 11.8 | −6.0 | 38.9 | ← | |
| 24 20 | +14.2 | −18.1 | 24 51 | +14.0 | −17.8 | 26 20 | −1.9 | | | Dec. 7–Dec. 31 | 12.2 | −6.1 | 40.1 | ft. | ′ |
| 25 24 | +14.3 | −18.0 | 25 58 | +14.1 | −17.7 | 27 34 | −1.8 | | | ° ′ | 12.6 | −6.2 | 41.5 | 70 | −8.1 |
| 26 34 | +14.4 | −17.9 | 27 11 | +14.2 | −17.6 | 28 54 | −1.7 | | | 41 +0.2 | 13.0 | −6.3 | 42.8 | 75 | −8.4 |
| 27 50 | +14.5 | −17.8 | 28 31 | +14.3 | −17.5 | 30 22 | −1.6 | | | 76 +0.1 | 13.4 | −6.4 | 44.2 | 80 | −8.7 |
| 29 13 | +14.6 | −17.7 | 29 58 | +14.4 | −17.4 | 31 58 | −1.5 | | | Sept. 17–Dec. 6 | 13.8 | −6.5 | 45.5 | 85 | −8.9 |
| 30 44 | +14.7 | −17.6 | 31 33 | +14.5 | −17.3 | 33 43 | −1.4 | | | ° ′ | 14.2 | −6.6 | 46.9 | 90 | −9.2 |
| 32 24 | +14.8 | −17.5 | 33 18 | +14.6 | −17.2 | 35 38 | −1.3 | | | 34 +0.3 | 14.7 | −6.7 | 48.4 | 95 | −9.5 |
| 34 15 | +14.9 | −17.4 | 35 15 | +14.7 | −17.1 | 37 45 | −1.2 | | | 60 +0.2 | 15.1 | −6.8 | 49.8 | | |
| 36 17 | +15.0 | −17.3 | 37 24 | +14.8 | −17.0 | 40 06 | −1.1 | | | 80 +0.1 | 15.5 | −6.9 | 51.3 | 100 | −9.7 |
| 38 34 | +15.1 | −17.2 | 39 48 | +14.9 | −16.9 | 42 42 | −1.0 | | | | 16.0 | −7.0 | 52.8 | 105 | −9.9 |
| 41 06 | +15.2 | −17.1 | 42 28 | +15.0 | −16.8 | 45 34 | −0.9 | | | | 16.5 | −7.1 | 54.3 | 110 | −10.2 |
| 43 56 | +15.3 | −17.0 | 45 29 | +15.1 | −16.7 | 48 45 | −0.8 | | | | 16.9 | −7.2 | 55.8 | 115 | −10.4 |
| 47 07 | +15.4 | −16.9 | 48 52 | +15.2 | −16.6 | 52 16 | −0.7 | | | | 17.4 | −7.3 | 57.4 | 120 | −10.6 |
| 50 43 | +15.5 | −16.8 | 52 41 | +15.3 | −16.5 | 56 09 | −0.6 | | | | 17.9 | −7.4 | 58.9 | 125 | −10.8 |
| 54 46 | +15.6 | −16.7 | 56 59 | +15.4 | −16.4 | 60 26 | −0.5 | | | | 18.4 | −7.5 | 60.5 | | |
| 59 21 | +15.7 | −16.6 | 61 50 | +15.5 | −16.3 | 65 06 | −0.4 | | | | 18.8 | −7.6 | 62.1 | 130 | −11.1 |
| 64 28 | +15.8 | −16.5 | 67 15 | +15.6 | −16.2 | 70 09 | −0.3 | | | | 19.3 | −7.7 | 63.8 | 135 | −11.3 |
| 70 10 | +15.9 | −16.4 | 73 14 | +15.7 | −16.1 | 75 32 | −0.2 | | | | 19.8 | −7.8 | 65.4 | 140 | −11.5 |
| 76 24 | +16.0 | −16.3 | 79 42 | +15.8 | −16.0 | 81 12 | −0.1 | | | | 20.4 | −7.9 | 67.1 | 145 | −11.7 |
| 83 05 | +16.1 | −16.2 | 86 31 | +15.9 | −15.9 | 87 03 | 0.0 | | | | 20.9 | −8.0 | 68.8 | 150 | −11.9 |
| 90 00 | | | 90 00 | | | 90 00 | | | | | 21.4 | −8.1 | 70.5 | 155 | −12.1 |

App. Alt. = Apparent altitude = Sextant altitude corrected for index error and dip.

*Copyright Council for the Central Laboratory of the Research Councils 2004*

## ALTITUDE CORRECTION TABLES 0°–10°—SUN, STARS, PLANETS A3

| App. Alt. | OCT.–MAR. SUN Lower Limb | OCT.–MAR. SUN Upper Limb | APR.–SEPT. SUN Lower Limb | APR.–SEPT. SUN Upper Limb | STARS PLANETS |
|---|---|---|---|---|---|
| ° ′ | ′ | ′ | ′ | ′ | ′ |
| 0 00 | −17·5 | −49·8 | −17·8 | −49·6 | −33·8 |
| 0 03 | 16·9 | 49·2 | 17·2 | 49·0 | 33·2 |
| 0 06 | 16·3 | 48·6 | 16·6 | 48·4 | 32·6 |
| 0 09 | 15·7 | 48·0 | 16·0 | 47·8 | 32·0 |
| 0 12 | 15·2 | 47·5 | 15·4 | 47·2 | 31·5 |
| 0 15 | 14·6 | 46·9 | 14·8 | 46·6 | 30·9 |
| 0 18 | −14·1 | −46·4 | −14·3 | −46·1 | −30·4 |
| 0 21 | 13·5 | 45·8 | 13·8 | 45·6 | 29·8 |
| 0 24 | 13·0 | 45·3 | 13·3 | 45·1 | 29·3 |
| 0 27 | 12·5 | 44·8 | 12·8 | 44·6 | 28·8 |
| 0 30 | 12·0 | 44·3 | 12·3 | 44·1 | 28·3 |
| 0 33 | 11·6 | 43·9 | 11·8 | 43·6 | 27·9 |
| 0 36 | −11·1 | −43·4 | −11·3 | −43·1 | −27·4 |
| 0 39 | 10·6 | 42·9 | 10·9 | 42·7 | 26·9 |
| 0 42 | 10·2 | 42·5 | 10·5 | 42·3 | 26·5 |
| 0 45 | 9·8 | 42·1 | 10·0 | 41·8 | 26·1 |
| 0 48 | 9·4 | 41·7 | 9·6 | 41·4 | 25·7 |
| 0 51 | 9·0 | 41·3 | 9·2 | 41·0 | 25·3 |
| 0 54 | −8·6 | −40·9 | −8·8 | −40·6 | −24·9 |
| 0 57 | 8·2 | 40·5 | 8·4 | 40·2 | 24·5 |
| 1 00 | 7·8 | 40·1 | 8·0 | 39·8 | 24·1 |
| 1 03 | 7·4 | 39·7 | 7·7 | 39·5 | 23·7 |
| 1 06 | 7·1 | 39·4 | 7·3 | 39·1 | 23·4 |
| 1 09 | 6·7 | 39·0 | 7·0 | 38·8 | 23·0 |
| 1 12 | −6·4 | −38·7 | −6·6 | −38·4 | −22·7 |
| 1 15 | 6·0 | 38·3 | 6·3 | 38·1 | 22·3 |
| 1 18 | 5·7 | 38·0 | 6·0 | 37·8 | 22·0 |
| 1 21 | 5·4 | 37·7 | 5·7 | 37·5 | 21·7 |
| 1 24 | 5·1 | 37·4 | 5·3 | 37·1 | 21·4 |
| 1 27 | 4·8 | 37·1 | 5·0 | 36·8 | 21·1 |
| 1 30 | −4·5 | −36·8 | −4·7 | −36·5 | −20·8 |
| 1 35 | 4·0 | 36·3 | 4·3 | 36·1 | 20·3 |
| 1 40 | 3·6 | 35·9 | 3·8 | 35·6 | 19·9 |
| 1 45 | 3·1 | 35·4 | 3·4 | 35·2 | 19·4 |
| 1 50 | 2·7 | 35·0 | 2·9 | 34·7 | 19·0 |
| 1 55 | 2·3 | 34·6 | 2·5 | 34·3 | 18·6 |
| 2 00 | −1·9 | −34·2 | −2·1 | −33·9 | −18·2 |
| 2 05 | 1·5 | 33·8 | 1·7 | 33·5 | 17·8 |
| 2 10 | 1·1 | 33·4 | 1·4 | 33·2 | 17·4 |
| 2 15 | 0·8 | 33·1 | 1·0 | 32·8 | 17·1 |
| 2 20 | 0·4 | 32·7 | 0·7 | 32·5 | 16·7 |
| 2 25 | −0·1 | 32·4 | −0·3 | 32·1 | 16·4 |
| 2 30 | +0·2 | −32·1 | 0·0 | −31·8 | −16·1 |
| 2 35 | 0·5 | 31·8 | +0·3 | 31·5 | 15·8 |
| 2 40 | 0·8 | 31·5 | 0·6 | 31·2 | 15·4 |
| 2 45 | 1·1 | 31·2 | 0·9 | 30·9 | 15·2 |
| 2 50 | 1·4 | 30·9 | 1·2 | 30·6 | 14·9 |
| 2 55 | 1·7 | 30·6 | 1·4 | 30·4 | 14·6 |
| 3 00 | +2·0 | −30·3 | +1·7 | −30·1 | −14·3 |
| 3 05 | 2·2 | 30·1 | 2·0 | 29·8 | 14·1 |
| 3 10 | 2·5 | 29·8 | 2·2 | 29·6 | 13·8 |
| 3 15 | 2·7 | 29·6 | 2·5 | 29·3 | 13·6 |
| 3 20 | 2·9 | 29·4 | 2·7 | 29·1 | 13·4 |
| 3 25 | 3·2 | 29·1 | 2·9 | 28·9 | 13·1 |
| 3 30 | +3·4 | −28·9 | +3·1 | −28·7 | −12·9 |

| App. Alt. | OCT.–MAR. SUN Lower Limb | OCT.–MAR. SUN Upper Limb | APR.–SEPT. SUN Lower Limb | APR.–SEPT. SUN Upper Limb | STARS PLANETS |
|---|---|---|---|---|---|
| ° ′ | ′ | ′ | ′ | ′ | ′ |
| 3 30 | +3·4 | −28·9 | +3·1 | −28·7 | −12·9 |
| 3 35 | 3·6 | 28·7 | 3·3 | 28·5 | 12·7 |
| 3 40 | 3·8 | 28·5 | 3·6 | 28·2 | 12·5 |
| 3 45 | 4·0 | 28·3 | 3·8 | 28·0 | 12·3 |
| 3 50 | 4·2 | 28·1 | 4·0 | 27·8 | 12·1 |
| 3 55 | 4·4 | 27·9 | 4·1 | 27·7 | 11·9 |
| 4 00 | +4·6 | −27·7 | +4·3 | −27·5 | −11·7 |
| 4 05 | 4·8 | 27·5 | 4·5 | 27·3 | 11·5 |
| 4 10 | 4·9 | 27·3 | 4·7 | 27·1 | 11·4 |
| 4 15 | 5·1 | 27·2 | 4·9 | 26·9 | 11·2 |
| 4 20 | 5·3 | 27·0 | 5·0 | 26·8 | 11·0 |
| 4 25 | 5·4 | 26·9 | 5·2 | 26·6 | 10·9 |
| 4 30 | +5·6 | −26·7 | +5·3 | −26·5 | −10·7 |
| 4 35 | 5·7 | 26·6 | 5·5 | 26·3 | 10·6 |
| 4 40 | 5·9 | 26·4 | 5·6 | 26·2 | 10·4 |
| 4 45 | 6·0 | 26·3 | 5·8 | 26·0 | 10·3 |
| 4 50 | 6·2 | 26·1 | 5·9 | 25·9 | 10·1 |
| 4 55 | 6·3 | 26·0 | 6·1 | 25·7 | 10·0 |
| 5 00 | +6·4 | −25·9 | +6·2 | −25·6 | −9·8 |
| 5 05 | 6·6 | 25·7 | 6·3 | 25·5 | 9·7 |
| 5 10 | 6·7 | 25·6 | 6·5 | 25·3 | 9·6 |
| 5 15 | 6·8 | 25·5 | 6·6 | 25·2 | 9·5 |
| 5 20 | 7·0 | 25·3 | 6·7 | 25·1 | 9·3 |
| 5 25 | 7·1 | 25·2 | 6·8 | 25·0 | 9·2 |
| 5 30 | +7·2 | −25·1 | +6·9 | −24·9 | −9·1 |
| 5 35 | 7·3 | 25·0 | 7·1 | 24·7 | 9·0 |
| 5 40 | 7·4 | 24·9 | 7·2 | 24·6 | 8·9 |
| 5 45 | 7·5 | 24·8 | 7·3 | 24·5 | 8·8 |
| 5 50 | 7·6 | 24·7 | 7·4 | 24·4 | 8·7 |
| 5 55 | 7·7 | 24·6 | 7·5 | 24·3 | 8·6 |
| 6 00 | +7·8 | −24·5 | +7·6 | −24·2 | −8·5 |
| 6 10 | 8·0 | 24·3 | 7·8 | 24·0 | 8·3 |
| 6 20 | 8·2 | 24·1 | 8·0 | 23·8 | 8·1 |
| 6 30 | 8·4 | 23·9 | 8·2 | 23·6 | 7·9 |
| 6 40 | 8·6 | 23·7 | 8·3 | 23·5 | 7·7 |
| 6 50 | 8·7 | 23·6 | 8·5 | 23·3 | 7·6 |
| 7 00 | +8·9 | −23·4 | +8·7 | −23·1 | −7·4 |
| 7 10 | 9·1 | 23·2 | 8·8 | 23·0 | 7·2 |
| 7 20 | 9·2 | 23·1 | 9·0 | 22·8 | 7·1 |
| 7 30 | 9·3 | 23·0 | 9·1 | 22·7 | 6·9 |
| 7 40 | 9·5 | 22·8 | 9·2 | 22·6 | 6·8 |
| 7 50 | 9·6 | 22·7 | 9·4 | 22·4 | 6·7 |
| 8 00 | +9·7 | −22·6 | +9·5 | −22·3 | −6·6 |
| 8 10 | 9·9 | 22·4 | 9·6 | 22·2 | 6·4 |
| 8 20 | 10·0 | 22·3 | 9·7 | 22·1 | 6·3 |
| 8 30 | 10·1 | 22·2 | 9·9 | 21·9 | 6·2 |
| 8 40 | 10·2 | 22·1 | 10·0 | 21·8 | 6·1 |
| 8 50 | 10·3 | 22·0 | 10·1 | 21·7 | 6·0 |
| 9 00 | +10·4 | −21·9 | +10·2 | −21·6 | −5·9 |
| 9 10 | 10·5 | 21·8 | 10·3 | 21·5 | 5·8 |
| 9 20 | 10·6 | 21·7 | 10·4 | 21·4 | 5·7 |
| 9 30 | 10·7 | 21·6 | 10·5 | 21·3 | 5·6 |
| 9 40 | 10·8 | 21·5 | 10·6 | 21·2 | 5·5 |
| 9 50 | 10·9 | 21·4 | 10·6 | 21·2 | 5·4 |
| 10 00 | +11·0 | −21·3 | +10·7 | −21·1 | −5·3 |

Additional corrections for temperature and pressure are given on the following page.
For bubble sextant observations ignore dip and use the star corrections for Sun, planets and stars.

*Copyright Council for the Central Laboratory of the Research Councils 2004*

# A4 ALTITUDE CORRECTION TABLES—ADDITIONAL CORRECTIONS
## ADDITIONAL REFRACTION CORRECTIONS FOR NON-STANDARD CONDITIONS

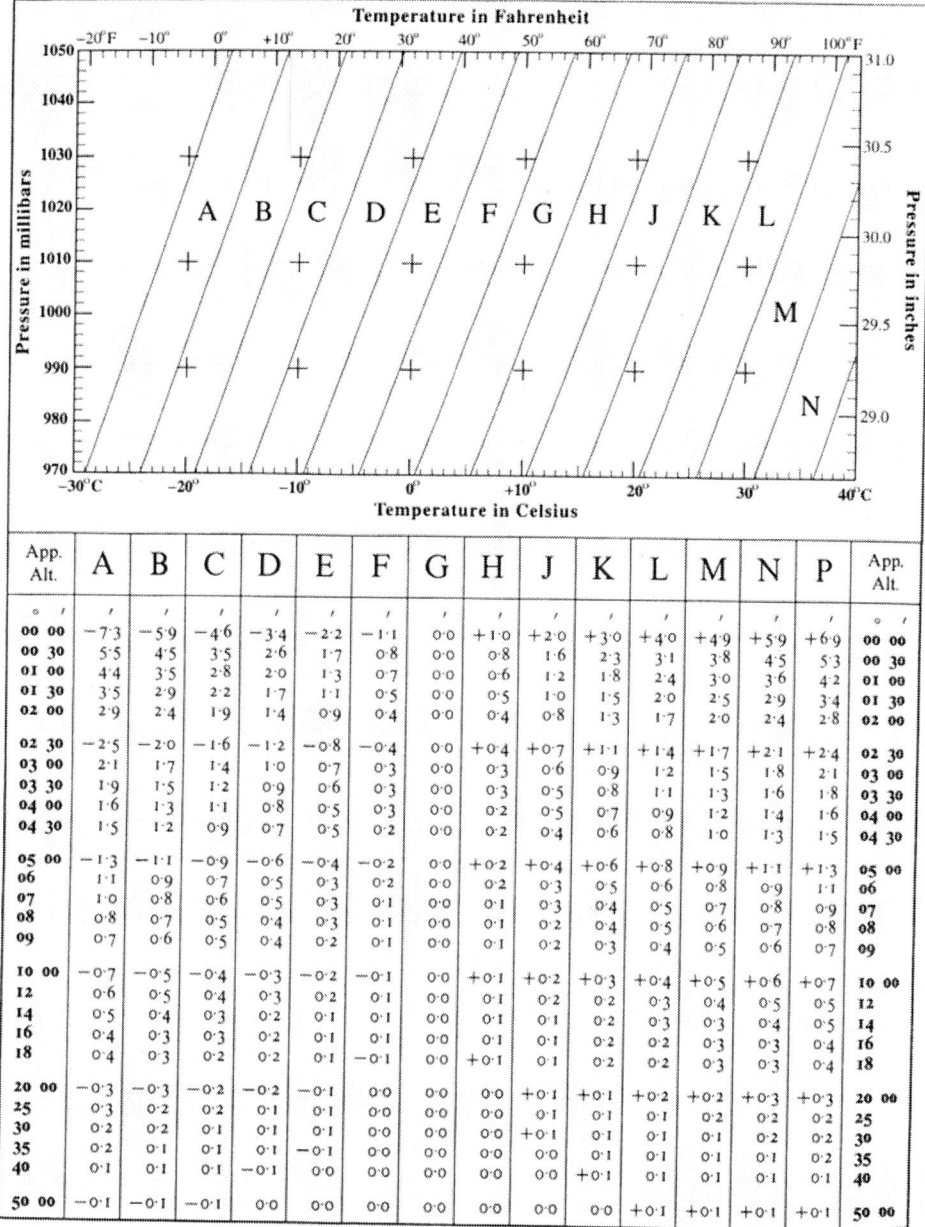

| App. Alt. | A | B | C | D | E | F | G | H | J | K | L | M | N | P | App. Alt. |
|---|---|---|---|---|---|---|---|---|---|---|---|---|---|---|---|
| ° ′ | ′ | ′ | ′ | ′ | ′ | ′ | ′ | ′ | ′ | ′ | ′ | ′ | ′ | ′ | ° ′ |
| 00 00 | −7·3 | −5·9 | −4·6 | −3·4 | −2·2 | −1·1 | 0·0 | +1·0 | +2·0 | +3·0 | +4·0 | +4·9 | +5·9 | +6·9 | 00 00 |
| 00 30 | 5·5 | 4·5 | 3·5 | 2·6 | 1·7 | 0·8 | 0·0 | 0·8 | 1·6 | 2·3 | 3·1 | 3·8 | 4·5 | 5·3 | 00 30 |
| 01 00 | 4·4 | 3·5 | 2·8 | 2·0 | 1·3 | 0·7 | 0·0 | 0·6 | 1·2 | 1·8 | 2·4 | 3·0 | 3·6 | 4·2 | 01 00 |
| 01 30 | 3·5 | 2·9 | 2·2 | 1·7 | 1·1 | 0·5 | 0·0 | 0·5 | 1·0 | 1·5 | 2·0 | 2·5 | 2·9 | 3·4 | 01 30 |
| 02 00 | 2·9 | 2·4 | 1·9 | 1·4 | 0·9 | 0·4 | 0·0 | 0·4 | 0·8 | 1·3 | 1·7 | 2·0 | 2·4 | 2·8 | 02 00 |
| 02 30 | −2·5 | −2·0 | −1·6 | −1·2 | −0·8 | −0·4 | 0·0 | +0·4 | +0·7 | +1·1 | +1·4 | +1·7 | +2·1 | +2·4 | 02 30 |
| 03 00 | 2·1 | 1·7 | 1·4 | 1·0 | 0·7 | 0·3 | 0·0 | 0·3 | 0·6 | 0·9 | 1·2 | 1·5 | 1·8 | 2·1 | 03 00 |
| 03 30 | 1·9 | 1·5 | 1·2 | 0·9 | 0·6 | 0·3 | 0·0 | 0·3 | 0·5 | 0·8 | 1·1 | 1·3 | 1·6 | 1·8 | 03 30 |
| 04 00 | 1·6 | 1·3 | 1·1 | 0·8 | 0·5 | 0·3 | 0·0 | 0·2 | 0·5 | 0·7 | 0·9 | 1·2 | 1·4 | 1·6 | 04 00 |
| 04 30 | 1·5 | 1·2 | 0·9 | 0·7 | 0·5 | 0·2 | 0·0 | 0·2 | 0·4 | 0·6 | 0·8 | 1·0 | 1·3 | 1·5 | 04 30 |
| 05 00 | −1·3 | −1·1 | −0·9 | −0·6 | −0·4 | −0·2 | 0·0 | +0·2 | +0·4 | +0·6 | +0·8 | +0·9 | +1·1 | +1·3 | 05 00 |
| 06 | 1·1 | 0·9 | 0·7 | 0·5 | 0·3 | 0·2 | 0·0 | 0·2 | 0·3 | 0·5 | 0·6 | 0·8 | 0·9 | 1·1 | 06 |
| 07 | 1·0 | 0·8 | 0·6 | 0·5 | 0·3 | 0·1 | 0·0 | 0·1 | 0·3 | 0·4 | 0·5 | 0·7 | 0·8 | 0·9 | 07 |
| 08 | 0·8 | 0·7 | 0·5 | 0·4 | 0·3 | 0·1 | 0·0 | 0·1 | 0·2 | 0·4 | 0·5 | 0·6 | 0·7 | 0·8 | 08 |
| 09 | 0·7 | 0·6 | 0·5 | 0·4 | 0·2 | 0·1 | 0·0 | 0·1 | 0·2 | 0·3 | 0·4 | 0·5 | 0·6 | 0·7 | 09 |
| 10 00 | −0·7 | −0·5 | −0·4 | −0·3 | −0·2 | −0·1 | 0·0 | +0·1 | +0·2 | +0·3 | +0·4 | +0·5 | +0·6 | +0·7 | 10 00 |
| 12 | 0·6 | 0·5 | 0·4 | 0·3 | 0·2 | 0·1 | 0·0 | 0·1 | 0·2 | 0·2 | 0·3 | 0·4 | 0·5 | 0·5 | 12 |
| 14 | 0·5 | 0·4 | 0·3 | 0·2 | 0·1 | 0·1 | 0·0 | 0·1 | 0·1 | 0·2 | 0·3 | 0·3 | 0·4 | 0·5 | 14 |
| 16 | 0·4 | 0·3 | 0·3 | 0·2 | 0·1 | 0·1 | 0·0 | 0·1 | 0·1 | 0·2 | 0·2 | 0·3 | 0·3 | 0·4 | 16 |
| 18 | 0·4 | 0·3 | 0·2 | 0·2 | 0·1 | −0·1 | 0·0 | +0·1 | 0·1 | 0·2 | 0·2 | 0·3 | 0·3 | 0·4 | 18 |
| 20 00 | −0·3 | −0·3 | −0·2 | −0·2 | −0·1 | 0·0 | 0·0 | +0·1 | +0·1 | +0·2 | +0·2 | +0·3 | +0·3 | +0·3 | 20 00 |
| 25 | 0·3 | 0·2 | 0·2 | 0·1 | 0·1 | 0·0 | 0·0 | 0·1 | 0·1 | 0·1 | 0·2 | 0·2 | 0·2 | 0·2 | 25 |
| 30 | 0·2 | 0·2 | 0·1 | 0·1 | 0·1 | 0·0 | 0·0 | 0·0 | +0·1 | 0·1 | 0·1 | 0·1 | 0·2 | 0·2 | 30 |
| 35 | 0·2 | 0·1 | 0·1 | 0·1 | −0·1 | 0·0 | 0·0 | 0·0 | 0·1 | 0·1 | 0·1 | 0·1 | 0·1 | 0·2 | 35 |
| 40 | 0·1 | 0·1 | 0·1 | −0·1 | 0·0 | 0·0 | 0·0 | 0·0 | +0·1 | 0·1 | 0·1 | 0·1 | 0·1 | 0·1 | 40 |
| 50 00 | −0·1 | −0·1 | −0·1 | 0·0 | 0·0 | 0·0 | 0·0 | 0·0 | 0·0 | 0·0 | +0·1 | +0·1 | +0·1 | +0·1 | 50 00 |

The graph is entered with arguments temperature and pressure to find a zone letter; using as arguments this zone letter and apparent altitude (sextant altitude corrected for index error and dip), a correction is taken from the table. This correction is to be applied to the sextant altitude in addition to the corrections for standard conditions (for the Sun, stars and planets from page A2–A3 and for the Moon from pages xxxiv and xxxv).

*Copyright Council for the Central Laboratory of the Research Councils 2004*

## ALTITUDE CORRECTION TABLES 0°–35° — MOON

| App. Alt. | 0°–4° Corrⁿ | 5°–9° Corrⁿ | 10°–14° Corrⁿ | 15°–19° Corrⁿ | 20°–24° Corrⁿ | 25°–29° Corrⁿ | 30°–34° Corrⁿ | App. Alt. |
|---|---|---|---|---|---|---|---|---|
| ′ | ° ′ | ° ′ | ° ′ | ° ′ | ° ′ | ° ′ | ° ′ | ′ |
| 00 | 0  34.5 | 5  58.2 | 10  62.1 | 15  62.8 | 20  62.2 | 25  60.8 | 30  58.9 | 00 |
| 10 | 36.5 | 58.5 | 62.2 | 62.8 | 62.2 | 60.8 | 58.8 | 10 |
| 20 | 38.3 | 58.7 | 62.2 | 62.8 | 62.1 | 60.7 | 58.8 | 20 |
| 30 | 40.0 | 58.9 | 62.3 | 62.8 | 62.1 | 60.7 | 58.7 | 30 |
| 40 | 41.5 | 59.1 | 62.3 | 62.8 | 62.0 | 60.6 | 58.6 | 40 |
| 50 | 42.9 | 59.3 | 62.4 | 62.7 | 62.0 | 60.6 | 58.5 | 50 |
| 00 | 1  44.2 | 6  59.5 | 11  62.4 | 16  62.7 | 21  62.0 | 26  60.5 | 31  58.5 | 00 |
| 10 | 45.4 | 59.7 | 62.4 | 62.7 | 61.9 | 60.4 | 58.4 | 10 |
| 20 | 46.5 | 59.9 | 62.5 | 62.7 | 61.9 | 60.4 | 58.3 | 20 |
| 30 | 47.5 | 60.0 | 62.5 | 62.7 | 61.9 | 60.3 | 58.2 | 30 |
| 40 | 48.4 | 60.2 | 62.5 | 62.7 | 61.8 | 60.3 | 58.2 | 40 |
| 50 | 49.3 | 60.3 | 62.6 | 62.7 | 61.8 | 60.2 | 58.1 | 50 |
| 00 | 2  50.1 | 7  60.5 | 12  62.6 | 17  62.7 | 22  61.7 | 27  60.1 | 32  58.0 | 00 |
| 10 | 50.8 | 60.6 | 62.6 | 62.6 | 61.7 | 60.1 | 57.9 | 10 |
| 20 | 51.5 | 60.7 | 62.6 | 62.6 | 61.6 | 60.0 | 57.8 | 20 |
| 30 | 52.2 | 60.9 | 62.7 | 62.6 | 61.6 | 59.9 | 57.8 | 30 |
| 40 | 52.8 | 61.0 | 62.7 | 62.6 | 61.6 | 59.9 | 57.7 | 40 |
| 50 | 53.4 | 61.1 | 62.7 | 62.6 | 61.5 | 59.8 | 57.6 | 50 |
| 00 | 3  53.9 | 8  61.2 | 13  62.7 | 18  62.5 | 23  61.5 | 28  59.7 | 33  57.5 | 00 |
| 10 | 54.4 | 61.3 | 62.7 | 62.5 | 61.4 | 59.7 | 57.4 | 10 |
| 20 | 54.9 | 61.4 | 62.7 | 62.5 | 61.4 | 59.6 | 57.4 | 20 |
| 30 | 55.3 | 61.5 | 62.8 | 62.5 | 61.3 | 59.5 | 57.3 | 30 |
| 40 | 55.7 | 61.6 | 62.8 | 62.4 | 61.3 | 59.5 | 57.2 | 40 |
| 50 | 56.1 | 61.6 | 62.8 | 62.4 | 61.2 | 59.4 | 57.1 | 50 |
| 00 | 4  56.4 | 9  61.7 | 14  62.8 | 19  62.4 | 24  61.2 | 29  59.3 | 34  57.0 | 00 |
| 10 | 56.8 | 61.8 | 62.8 | 62.4 | 61.1 | 59.3 | 56.9 | 10 |
| 20 | 57.1 | 61.9 | 62.8 | 62.3 | 61.1 | 59.2 | 56.9 | 20 |
| 30 | 57.4 | 61.9 | 62.8 | 62.3 | 61.0 | 59.1 | 56.8 | 30 |
| 40 | 57.7 | 62.0 | 62.8 | 62.3 | 61.0 | 59.1 | 56.7 | 40 |
| 50 | 58.0 | 62.1 | 62.8 | 62.2 | 60.9 | 59.0 | 56.6 | 50 |

| HP | L | U | L | U | L | U | L | U | L | U | L | U | L | U | HP |
|---|---|---|---|---|---|---|---|---|---|---|---|---|---|---|---|
| ′ | ′ | ′ | ′ | ′ | ′ | ′ | ′ | ′ | ′ | ′ | ′ | ′ | ′ | ′ | ′ |
| 54.0 | 0.3 | 0.9 | 0.3 | 0.9 | 0.4 | 1.0 | 0.5 | 1.1 | 0.6 | 1.2 | 0.7 | 1.3 | 0.9 | 1.5 | 54.0 |
| 54.3 | 0.7 | 1.1 | 0.7 | 1.2 | 0.8 | 1.2 | 0.8 | 1.3 | 0.9 | 1.4 | 1.1 | 1.5 | 1.2 | 1.7 | 54.3 |
| 54.6 | 1.1 | 1.4 | 1.1 | 1.4 | 1.1 | 1.4 | 1.2 | 1.5 | 1.3 | 1.6 | 1.4 | 1.7 | 1.5 | 1.8 | 54.6 |
| 54.9 | 1.4 | 1.6 | 1.5 | 1.6 | 1.5 | 1.6 | 1.6 | 1.7 | 1.6 | 1.8 | 1.8 | 1.9 | 1.9 | 2.0 | 54.9 |
| 55.2 | 1.8 | 1.8 | 1.8 | 1.8 | 1.9 | 1.8 | 1.9 | 1.9 | 2.0 | 2.0 | 2.1 | 2.1 | 2.2 | 2.2 | 55.2 |
| 55.5 | 2.2 | 2.0 | 2.2 | 2.0 | 2.3 | 2.1 | 2.3 | 2.1 | 2.4 | 2.2 | 2.4 | 2.3 | 2.5 | 2.4 | 55.5 |
| 55.8 | 2.6 | 2.2 | 2.6 | 2.2 | 2.6 | 2.3 | 2.7 | 2.4 | 2.7 | 2.4 | 2.8 | 2.4 | 2.9 | 2.5 | 55.8 |
| 56.1 | 3.0 | 2.4 | 3.0 | 2.5 | 3.0 | 2.5 | 3.0 | 2.5 | 3.1 | 2.6 | 3.1 | 2.6 | 3.2 | 2.7 | 56.1 |
| 56.4 | 3.3 | 2.7 | 3.4 | 2.7 | 3.4 | 2.7 | 3.4 | 2.7 | 3.4 | 2.8 | 3.5 | 2.8 | 3.5 | 2.9 | 56.4 |
| 56.7 | 3.7 | 2.9 | 3.7 | 2.9 | 3.8 | 2.9 | 3.8 | 2.9 | 3.8 | 3.0 | 3.8 | 3.0 | 3.9 | 3.0 | 56.7 |
| 57.0 | 4.1 | 3.1 | 4.1 | 3.1 | 4.1 | 3.1 | 4.1 | 3.1 | 4.2 | 3.2 | 4.2 | 3.2 | 4.2 | 3.2 | 57.0 |
| 57.3 | 4.5 | 3.3 | 4.5 | 3.3 | 4.5 | 3.3 | 4.5 | 3.3 | 4.5 | 3.3 | 4.5 | 3.4 | 4.6 | 3.4 | 57.3 |
| 57.6 | 4.9 | 3.5 | 4.9 | 3.5 | 4.9 | 3.5 | 4.9 | 3.5 | 4.9 | 3.5 | 4.9 | 3.5 | 4.9 | 3.6 | 57.6 |
| 57.9 | 5.3 | 3.8 | 5.3 | 3.8 | 5.2 | 3.8 | 5.2 | 3.7 | 5.2 | 3.7 | 5.2 | 3.7 | 5.2 | 3.7 | 57.9 |
| 58.2 | 5.6 | 4.0 | 5.6 | 4.0 | 5.6 | 4.0 | 5.6 | 4.0 | 5.6 | 3.9 | 5.6 | 3.9 | 5.6 | 3.9 | 58.2 |
| 58.5 | 6.0 | 4.2 | 6.0 | 4.2 | 6.0 | 4.2 | 6.0 | 4.2 | 6.0 | 4.1 | 5.9 | 4.1 | 5.9 | 4.1 | 58.5 |
| 58.8 | 6.4 | 4.4 | 6.4 | 4.4 | 6.4 | 4.4 | 6.3 | 4.4 | 6.3 | 4.3 | 6.3 | 4.3 | 6.2 | 4.2 | 58.8 |
| 59.1 | 6.8 | 4.6 | 6.8 | 4.6 | 6.7 | 4.6 | 6.7 | 4.6 | 6.7 | 4.5 | 6.6 | 4.5 | 6.6 | 4.4 | 59.1 |
| 59.4 | 7.2 | 4.8 | 7.1 | 4.8 | 7.1 | 4.8 | 7.1 | 4.8 | 7.0 | 4.7 | 7.0 | 4.7 | 6.9 | 4.6 | 59.4 |
| 59.7 | 7.5 | 5.1 | 7.5 | 5.0 | 7.5 | 5.0 | 7.5 | 5.0 | 7.4 | 4.9 | 7.3 | 4.8 | 7.2 | 4.8 | 59.7 |
| 60.0 | 7.9 | 5.3 | 7.9 | 5.3 | 7.9 | 5.2 | 7.8 | 5.2 | 7.8 | 5.1 | 7.7 | 5.0 | 7.6 | 4.9 | 60.0 |
| 60.3 | 8.3 | 5.5 | 8.3 | 5.5 | 8.2 | 5.4 | 8.2 | 5.4 | 8.1 | 5.3 | 8.0 | 5.2 | 7.9 | 5.1 | 60.3 |
| 60.6 | 8.7 | 5.7 | 8.7 | 5.7 | 8.6 | 5.7 | 8.6 | 5.6 | 8.5 | 5.5 | 8.4 | 5.4 | 8.2 | 5.3 | 60.6 |
| 60.9 | 9.1 | 5.9 | 9.0 | 5.9 | 9.0 | 5.9 | 8.9 | 5.8 | 8.8 | 5.7 | 8.7 | 5.6 | 8.6 | 5.4 | 60.9 |
| 61.2 | 9.5 | 6.2 | 9.4 | 6.1 | 9.4 | 6.1 | 9.3 | 6.0 | 9.2 | 5.9 | 9.1 | 5.8 | 8.9 | 5.6 | 61.2 |
| 61.5 | 9.8 | 6.4 | 9.8 | 6.3 | 9.7 | 6.3 | 9.7 | 6.2 | 9.5 | 6.1 | 9.4 | 5.9 | 9.2 | 5.8 | 61.5 |

### DIP

| Ht. of Eye | Corrⁿ | Ht. of Eye | Corrⁿ | Ht. of Eye |
|---|---|---|---|---|
| m | | ft. | | m |
| 2.4 | −2.8 | 8.0 | | 9.5 |
| 2.6 | −2.9 | 8.6 | −5.5 | 9.9 |
| 2.8 | −3.0 | 9.2 | −5.6 | 10.3 |
| 3.0 | −3.1 | 9.8 | −5.7 | 10.6 |
| 3.2 | −3.2 | 10.5 | −5.8 | 11.0 |
| 3.4 | −3.3 | 11.2 | −5.9 | 11.4 |
| 3.6 | −3.4 | 11.9 | −6.0 | 11.8 |
| 3.8 | −3.5 | 12.6 | −6.1 | 12.2 |
| 4.0 | −3.6 | 13.3 | −6.2 | 12.6 |
| 4.3 | −3.7 | 14.1 | −6.3 | 13.0 |
| 4.5 | −3.8 | 14.9 | −6.4 | 13.4 |
| 4.7 | −3.9 | 15.7 | −6.5 | 13.8 |
| 5.0 | −4.0 | 16.5 | −6.6 | 14.2 |
| 5.2 | −4.1 | 17.4 | −6.7 | 14.7 |
| 5.5 | −4.2 | 18.3 | −6.8 | 15.1 |
| 5.8 | −4.3 | 19.1 | −6.9 | 15.5 |
| 6.1 | −4.4 | 20.1 | −7.0 | 16.0 |
| 6.3 | −4.5 | 21.0 | −7.1 | 16.5 |
| 6.6 | −4.6 | 22.0 | −7.2 | 16.9 |
| 6.9 | −4.7 | 22.9 | −7.3 | 17.4 |
| 7.2 | −4.8 | 23.9 | −7.4 | 17.9 |
| 7.5 | −4.9 | 24.9 | −7.5 | 18.4 |
| 7.9 | −5.0 | 26.0 | −7.6 | 18.8 |
| 8.2 | −5.1 | 27.1 | −7.7 | 19.3 |
| 8.5 | −5.2 | 28.1 | −7.8 | 19.8 |
| 8.8 | | 29.2 | −7.9 | 20.4 |
| 9.2 | −5.3 | 30.4 | −8.0 | 20.9 |
| 9.5 | −5.4 | 31.5 | −8.1 | 21.4 |

| Ht. of Eye ft. |
|---|
| 31.5 |
| 32.7 |
| 33.9 |
| 35.1 |
| 36.3 |
| 37.6 |
| 38.9 |
| 40.1 |
| 41.5 |
| 42.8 |
| 44.2 |
| 45.5 |
| 46.9 |
| 48.4 |
| 49.8 |
| 51.3 |
| 52.8 |
| 54.3 |
| 55.8 |
| 57.4 |
| 58.9 |
| 60.5 |
| 62.1 |
| 63.8 |
| 65.4 |
| 67.1 |
| 68.8 |
| 70.5 |

### MOON CORRECTION TABLE

The correction is in two parts; the first correction is taken from the upper part of the table with argument apparent altitude, and the second from the lower part, with argument HP, in the same column as that from which the first correction was taken. Separate corrections are given in the lower part for lower (L) and upper (U) limbs. All corrections are to be **added** to apparent altitude, but 30′ is to be s…
the altitude of the …

For correction…
and temperature s…

For bubble sex…
tions ignore dip, ta…
upper and lower li…
and subtract 15′ fro…

App. Alt. = App…
= Sextant altitude …
index error and di…

# INCREMENTS AND CORRECTIONS

## 30ᵐ

| s | SUN PLANETS | ARIES | MOON | v or d / Corrⁿ | v or d / Corrⁿ | v or d / Corrⁿ |
|---|---|---|---|---|---|---|
| | ° ′ | ° ′ | ° ′ | ′ ′ | ′ ′ | ′ ′ |
| 00 | 7 30·0 | 7 31·2 | 7 09·5 | 0·0 0·0 | 6·0 3·1 | 12·0 6·1 |
| 01 | 7 30·3 | 7 31·5 | 7 09·7 | 0·1 0·1 | 6·1 3·1 | 12·1 6·2 |
| 02 | 7 30·5 | 7 31·7 | 7 10·0 | 0·2 0·1 | 6·2 3·2 | 12·2 6·2 |
| 03 | 7 30·8 | 7 32·0 | 7 10·2 | 0·3 0·2 | 6·3 3·2 | 12·3 6·3 |
| 04 | 7 31·0 | 7 32·2 | 7 10·5 | 0·4 0·2 | 6·4 3·3 | 12·4 6·3 |
| 05 | 7 31·3 | 7 32·5 | 7 10·7 | 0·5 0·3 | 6·5 3·3 | 12·5 6·4 |
| 06 | 7 31·5 | 7 32·7 | 7 10·9 | 0·6 0·3 | 6·6 3·4 | 12·6 6·4 |
| 07 | 7 31·8 | 7 33·0 | 7 11·2 | 0·7 0·4 | 6·7 3·4 | 12·7 6·5 |
| 08 | 7 32·0 | 7 33·2 | 7 11·4 | 0·8 0·4 | 6·8 3·5 | 12·8 6·5 |
| 09 | 7 32·3 | 7 33·5 | 7 11·6 | 0·9 0·5 | 6·9 3·5 | 12·9 6·6 |
| 10 | 7 32·5 | 7 33·7 | 7 11·9 | 1·0 0·5 | 7·0 3·6 | 13·0 6·6 |
| 11 | 7 32·8 | 7 34·0 | 7 12·1 | 1·1 0·6 | 7·1 3·6 | 13·1 6·7 |
| 12 | 7 33·0 | 7 34·2 | 7 12·4 | 1·2 0·6 | 7·2 3·7 | 13·2 6·7 |
| 13 | 7 33·3 | 7 34·5 | 7 12·6 | 1·3 0·7 | 7·3 3·7 | 13·3 6·8 |
| 14 | 7 33·5 | 7 34·7 | 7 12·8 | 1·4 0·7 | 7·4 3·8 | 13·4 6·8 |
| 15 | 7 33·8 | 7 35·0 | 7 13·1 | 1·5 0·8 | 7·5 3·8 | 13·5 6·9 |
| 16 | 7 34·0 | 7 35·2 | 7 13·3 | 1·6 0·8 | 7·6 3·9 | 13·6 6·9 |
| 17 | 7 34·3 | 7 35·5 | 7 13·6 | 1·7 0·9 | 7·7 3·9 | 13·7 7·0 |
| 18 | 7 34·5 | 7 35·7 | 7 13·8 | 1·8 0·9 | 7·8 4·0 | 13·8 7·0 |
| 19 | 7 34·8 | 7 36·0 | 7 14·0 | 1·9 1·0 | 7·9 4·0 | 13·9 7·1 |
| 20 | 7 35·0 | 7 36·2 | 7 14·3 | 2·0 1·0 | 8·0 4·1 | 14·0 7·1 |
| 21 | 7 35·3 | 7 36·5 | 7 14·5 | 2·1 1·1 | 8·1 4·1 | 14·1 7·2 |
| 22 | 7 35·5 | 7 36·7 | 7 14·7 | 2·2 1·1 | 8·2 4·2 | 14·2 7·2 |
| 23 | 7 35·8 | 7 37·0 | 7 15·0 | 2·3 1·2 | 8·3 4·2 | 14·3 7·3 |
| 24 | 7 36·0 | 7 37·2 | 7 15·2 | 2·4 1·2 | 8·4 4·3 | 14·4 7·3 |
| 25 | 7 36·3 | 7 37·5 | 7 15·5 | 2·5 1·3 | 8·5 4·3 | 14·5 7·4 |
| 26 | 7 36·5 | 7 37·7 | 7 15·7 | 2·6 1·3 | 8·6 4·4 | 14·6 7·4 |
| 27 | 7 36·8 | 7 38·0 | 7 15·9 | 2·7 1·4 | 8·7 4·4 | 14·7 7·5 |
| 28 | 7 37·0 | 7 38·3 | 7 16·2 | 2·8 1·4 | 8·8 4·5 | 14·8 7·5 |
| 29 | 7 37·3 | 7 38·5 | 7 16·4 | 2·9 1·5 | 8·9 4·5 | 14·9 7·6 |
| 30 | 7 37·5 | 7 38·8 | 7 16·7 | 3·0 1·5 | 9·0 4·6 | 15·0 7·6 |
| 31 | 7 37·8 | 7 39·0 | 7 16·9 | 3·1 1·6 | 9·1 4·6 | 15·1 7·7 |
| 32 | 7 38·0 | 7 39·3 | 7 17·1 | 3·2 1·6 | 9·2 4·7 | 15·2 7·7 |
| 33 | 7 38·3 | 7 39·5 | 7 17·4 | 3·3 1·7 | 9·3 4·7 | 15·3 7·8 |
| 34 | 7 38·5 | 7 39·8 | 7 17·6 | 3·4 1·7 | 9·4 4·8 | 15·4 7·8 |
| 35 | 7 38·8 | 7 40·0 | 7 17·9 | 3·5 1·8 | 9·5 4·8 | 15·5 7·9 |
| 36 | 7 39·0 | 7 40·3 | 7 18·1 | 3·6 1·8 | 9·6 4·9 | 15·6 7·9 |
| 37 | 7 39·3 | 7 40·5 | 7 18·3 | 3·7 1·9 | 9·7 4·9 | 15·7 8·0 |
| 38 | 7 39·5 | 7 40·8 | 7 18·6 | 3·8 1·9 | 9·8 5·0 | 15·8 8·0 |
| 39 | 7 39·8 | 7 41·0 | 7 18·8 | 3·9 2·0 | 9·9 5·0 | 15·9 8·1 |
| 40 | 7 40·0 | 7 41·3 | 7 19·0 | 4·0 2·0 | 10·0 5·1 | 16·0 8·1 |
| 41 | 7 40·3 | 7 41·5 | 7 19·3 | 4·1 2·1 | 10·1 5·1 | 16·1 8·2 |
| 42 | 7 40·5 | 7 41·8 | 7 19·5 | 4·2 2·1 | 10·2 5·2 | 16·2 8·2 |
| 43 | 7 40·8 | 7 42·0 | 7 19·8 | 4·3 2·2 | 10·3 5·2 | 16·3 8·3 |
| 44 | 7 41·0 | 7 42·3 | 7 20·0 | 4·4 2·2 | 10·4 5·3 | 16·4 8·3 |
| 45 | 7 41·3 | 7 42·5 | 7 20·2 | 4·5 2·3 | 10·5 5·3 | 16·5 8·4 |
| 46 | 7 41·5 | 7 42·8 | 7 20·5 | 4·6 2·3 | 10·6 5·4 | 16·6 8·4 |
| 47 | 7 41·8 | 7 43·0 | 7 20·7 | 4·7 2·4 | 10·7 5·4 | 16·7 8·5 |
| 48 | 7 42·0 | 7 43·3 | 7 21·0 | 4·8 2·4 | 10·8 5·5 | 16·8 8·5 |
| 49 | 7 42·3 | 7 43·5 | 7 21·2 | 4·9 2·5 | 10·9 5·5 | 16·9 8·6 |
| 50 | 7 42·5 | 7 43·8 | 7 21·4 | 5·0 2·5 | 11·0 5·6 | 17·0 8·6 |
| 51 | 7 42·8 | 7 44·0 | 7 21·7 | 5·1 2·6 | 11·1 5·6 | 17·1 8·7 |
| 52 | 7 43·0 | 7 44·3 | 7 21·9 | 5·2 2·6 | 11·2 5·7 | 17·2 8·7 |
| 53 | 7 43·3 | 7 44·5 | 7 22·1 | 5·3 2·7 | 11·3 5·7 | 17·3 8·8 |
| 54 | 7 43·5 | 7 44·8 | 7 22·4 | 5·4 2·7 | 11·4 5·8 | 17·4 8·8 |
| 55 | 7 43·8 | 7 45·0 | 7 22·6 | 5·5 2·8 | 11·5 5·8 | 17·5 8·9 |
| 56 | 7 44·0 | 7 45·3 | 7 22·9 | 5·6 2·8 | 11·6 5·9 | 17·6 8·9 |
| 57 | 7 44·3 | 7 45·5 | 7 23·1 | 5·7 2·9 | 11·7 5·9 | 17·7 9·0 |
| 58 | 7 44·5 | 7 45·8 | 7 23·3 | 5·8 2·9 | 11·8 6·0 | 17·8 9·0 |
| 59 | 7 44·8 | 7 46·0 | 7 23·6 | 5·9 3·0 | 11·9 6·0 | 17·9 9·1 |
| 60 | 7 45·0 | 7 46·3 | 7 23·8 | 6·0 3·1 | 12·0 6·1 | 18·0 9·2 |

## 31ᵐ

| s | SUN PLANETS | ARIES | MOON | v or d / Corrⁿ | v or d / Corrⁿ | v or d / Corrⁿ |
|---|---|---|---|---|---|---|
| | ° ′ | ° ′ | ° ′ | ′ ′ | ′ ′ | ′ ′ |
| 00 | 7 45·0 | 7 46·3 | 7 23·8 | 0·0 0·0 | 6·0 3·2 | 12·0 6·3 |
| 01 | 7 45·3 | 7 46·5 | 7 24·1 | 0·1 0·1 | 6·1 3·2 | 12·1 6·4 |
| 02 | 7 45·5 | 7 46·8 | 7 24·3 | 0·2 0·1 | 6·2 3·3 | 12·2 6·4 |
| 03 | 7 45·8 | 7 47·0 | 7 24·5 | 0·3 0·2 | 6·3 3·3 | 12·3 6·5 |
| 04 | 7 46·0 | 7 47·3 | 7 24·8 | 0·4 0·2 | 6·4 3·4 | 12·4 6·5 |
| 05 | 7 46·3 | 7 47·5 | 7 25·0 | 0·5 0·3 | 6·5 3·4 | 12·5 6·6 |
| 06 | 7 46·5 | 7 47·8 | 7 25·2 | 0·6 0·3 | 6·6 3·5 | 12·6 6·6 |
| 07 | 7 46·8 | 7 48·0 | 7 25·5 | 0·7 0·4 | 6·7 3·5 | 12·7 6·7 |
| 08 | 7 47·0 | 7 48·3 | 7 25·7 | 0·8 0·4 | 6·8 3·6 | 12·8 6·7 |
| 09 | 7 47·3 | 7 48·5 | 7 26·0 | 0·9 0·5 | 6·9 3·6 | 12·9 6·8 |
| 10 | 7 47·5 | 7 48·8 | 7 26·2 | 1·0 0·5 | 7·0 3·7 | 13·0 6·8 |
| 11 | 7 47·8 | 7 49·0 | 7 26·4 | 1·1 0·6 | 7·1 3·7 | 13·1 6·9 |
| 12 | 7 48·0 | 7 49·3 | 7 26·7 | 1·2 0·6 | 7·2 3·8 | 13·2 6·9 |
| 13 | 7 48·3 | 7 49·5 | 7 26·9 | 1·3 0·7 | 7·3 3·8 | 13·3 7·0 |
| 14 | 7 48·5 | 7 49·8 | 7 27·2 | 1·4 0·7 | 7·4 3·9 | 13·4 7·0 |
| 15 | 7 48·8 | 7 50·0 | 7 27·4 | 1·5 0·8 | 7·5 3·9 | 13·5 7·1 |
| 16 | 7 49·0 | 7 50·3 | 7 27·6 | 1·6 0·8 | 7·6 4·0 | 13·6 7·1 |
| 17 | 7 49·3 | 7 50·5 | 7 27·9 | 1·7 0·9 | 7·7 4·0 | 13·7 7·2 |
| 18 | 7 49·5 | 7 50·8 | 7 28·1 | 1·8 0·9 | 7·8 4·1 | 13·8 7·2 |
| 19 | 7 49·8 | 7 51·0 | 7 28·4 | 1·9 1·0 | 7·9 4·1 | 13·9 7·3 |
| 20 | 7 50·0 | 7 51·3 | 7 28·6 | 2·0 1·1 | 8·0 4·2 | 14·0 7·4 |
| 21 | 7 50·3 | 7 51·5 | 7 28·8 | 2·1 1·1 | 8·1 4·3 | 14·1 7·4 |
| 22 | 7 50·5 | 7 51·8 | 7 29·1 | 2·2 1·2 | 8·2 4·3 | 14·2 7·5 |
| 23 | 7 50·8 | 7 52·0 | 7 29·3 | 2·3 1·2 | 8·3 4·4 | 14·3 7·5 |
| 24 | 7 51·0 | 7 52·3 | 7 29·5 | 2·4 1·3 | 8·4 4·4 | 14·4 7·6 |
| 25 | 7 51·3 | 7 52·5 | 7 29·8 | 2·5 1·3 | 8·5 4·5 | 14·5 7·6 |
| 26 | 7 51·5 | 7 52·8 | 7 30·0 | 2·6 1·4 | 8·6 4·5 | 14·6 7·7 |
| 27 | 7 51·8 | 7 53·0 | 7 30·3 | 2·7 1·4 | 8·7 4·6 | 14·7 7·7 |
| 28 | 7 52·0 | 7 53·3 | 7 30·5 | 2·8 1·5 | 8·8 4·6 | 14·8 7·8 |
| 29 | 7 52·3 | 7 53·5 | 7 30·7 | 2·9 1·5 | 8·9 4·7 | 14·9 7·8 |
| 30 | 7 52·5 | 7 53·8 | 7 31·0 | 3·0 1·6 | 9·0 4·7 | 15·0 7·9 |
| 31 | 7 52·8 | 7 54·0 | 7 31·2 | 3·1 1·6 | 9·1 4·8 | 15·1 7·9 |
| 32 | 7 53·0 | 7 54·3 | 7 31·5 | 3·2 1·7 | 9·2 4·8 | 15·2 8·0 |
| 33 | 7 53·3 | 7 54·5 | 7 31·7 | 3·3 1·7 | 9·3 4·9 | 15·3 8·0 |
| 34 | 7 53·5 | 7 54·8 | 7 31·9 | 3·4 1·8 | 9·4 4·9 | 15·4 8·1 |
| 35 | 7 53·8 | 7 55·0 | 7 32·2 | 3·5 1·8 | 9·5 5·0 | 15·5 8·1 |
| 36 | 7 54·0 | 7 55·3 | 7 32·4 | 3·6 1·9 | 9·6 5·0 | 15·6 8·2 |
| 37 | 7 54·3 | 7 55·5 | 7 32·6 | 3·7 1·9 | 9·7 5·1 | 15·7 8·2 |
| 38 | 7 54·5 | 7 55·8 | 7 32·9 | 3·8 2·0 | 9·8 5·1 | 15·8 8·3 |
| 39 | 7 54·8 | 7 56·0 | 7 33·1 | 3·9 2·0 | 9·9 5·2 | 15·9 8·3 |
| 40 | 7 55·0 | 7 56·3 | 7 33·4 | 4·0 2·1 | 10·0 5·3 | 16·0 8·4 |
| 41 | 7 55·3 | 7 56·5 | 7 33·6 | 4·1 2·2 | 10·1 5·3 | 16·1 8·5 |
| 42 | 7 55·5 | 7 56·8 | 7 33·8 | 4·2 2·2 | 10·2 5·4 | 16·2 8·5 |
| 43 | 7 55·8 | 7 57·1 | 7 34·1 | 4·3 2·3 | 10·3 5·4 | 16·3 8·6 |
| 44 | 7 56·0 | 7 57·3 | 7 34·3 | 4·4 2·3 | 10·4 5·5 | 16·4 8·6 |
| 45 | 7 56·3 | 7 57·6 | 7 34·6 | 4·5 2·4 | 10·5 5·5 | 16·5 8·7 |
| 46 | 7 56·5 | 7 57·8 | 7 34·8 | 4·6 2·4 | 10·6 5·6 | 16·6 8·7 |
| 47 | 7 56·8 | 7 58·1 | 7 35·0 | 4·7 2·5 | 10·7 5·6 | 16·7 8·8 |
| 48 | 7 57·0 | 7 58·3 | 7 35·3 | 4·8 2·5 | 10·8 5·7 | 16·8 8·8 |
| 49 | 7 57·3 | 7 58·6 | 7 35·5 | 4·9 2·6 | 10·9 5·7 | 16·9 8·9 |
| 50 | 7 57·5 | 7 58·8 | 7 35·7 | 5·0 2·6 | 11·0 5·8 | 17·0 8·9 |
| 51 | 7 57·8 | 7 59·1 | 7 36·0 | 5·1 2·7 | 11·1 5·8 | 17·1 9·0 |
| 52 | 7 58·0 | 7 59·3 | 7 36·2 | 5·2 2·7 | 11·2 5·9 | 17·2 9·0 |
| 53 | 7 58·3 | 7 59·6 | 7 36·5 | 5·3 2·8 | 11·3 5·9 | 17·3 9·1 |
| 54 | 7 58·5 | 7 59·8 | 7 36·7 | 5·4 2·8 | 11·4 6·0 | 17·4 9·1 |
| 55 | 7 58·8 | 8 00·1 | 7 36·9 | 5·5 2·9 | 11·5 6·0 | 17·5 9·2 |
| 56 | 7 59·0 | 8 00·3 | 7 37·2 | 5·6 2·9 | 11·6 6·1 | 17·6 9·2 |
| 57 | 7 59·3 | 8 00·6 | 7 37·4 | 5·7 3·0 | 11·7 6·1 | 17·7 9·3 |
| 58 | 7 59·5 | 8 00·8 | 7 37·7 | 5·8 3·0 | 11·8 6·2 | 17·8 9·3 |
| 59 | 7 59·8 | 8 01·1 | 7 37·9 | 5·9 3·1 | 11·9 6·2 | 17·9 9·4 |
| 60 | 8 00·0 | 8 01·3 | 7 38·1 | 6·0 3·2 | 12·0 6·3 | 18·0 9·5 |

xvii

*Copyright Council for the Central Laboratory of the Research Councils 2004*

## INCREMENTS AND CORRECTIONS

### 54ᵐ

| s | SUN PLANETS | ARIES | MOON | v or d | Corrⁿ | v or d | Corrⁿ | v or d | Corrⁿ |
|---|---|---|---|---|---|---|---|---|---|
| | ° ′ | ° ′ | ° ′ | ′ | ′ | ′ | ′ | ′ | ′ |
| 00 | 13 30.0 | 13 32.2 | 12 53.1 | 0.0 | 0.0 | 6.0 | 5.5 | 12.0 | 10.9 |
| 01 | 13 30.3 | 13 32.5 | 12 53.3 | 0.1 | 0.1 | 6.1 | 5.5 | 12.1 | 11.0 |
| 02 | 13 30.5 | 13 32.7 | 12 53.6 | 0.2 | 0.2 | 6.2 | 5.6 | 12.2 | 11.1 |
| 03 | 13 30.8 | 13 33.0 | 12 53.8 | 0.3 | 0.3 | 6.3 | 5.7 | 12.3 | 11.2 |
| 04 | 13 31.0 | 13 33.2 | 12 54.1 | 0.4 | 0.4 | 6.4 | 5.8 | 12.4 | 11.3 |
| 05 | 13 31.3 | 13 33.5 | 12 54.3 | 0.5 | 0.5 | 6.5 | 5.9 | 12.5 | 11.4 |
| 06 | 13 31.5 | 13 33.7 | 12 54.5 | 0.6 | 0.5 | 6.6 | 6.0 | 12.6 | 11.4 |
| 07 | 13 31.8 | 13 34.0 | 12 54.8 | 0.7 | 0.6 | 6.7 | 6.1 | 12.7 | 11.5 |
| 08 | 13 32.0 | 13 34.2 | 12 55.0 | 0.8 | 0.7 | 6.8 | 6.2 | 12.8 | 11.6 |
| 09 | 13 32.3 | 13 34.5 | 12 55.2 | 0.9 | 0.8 | 6.9 | 6.3 | 12.9 | 11.7 |
| 10 | 13 32.5 | 13 34.7 | 12 55.5 | 1.0 | 0.9 | 7.0 | 6.4 | 13.0 | 11.8 |
| 11 | 13 32.8 | 13 35.0 | 12 55.7 | 1.1 | 1.0 | 7.1 | 6.4 | 13.1 | 11.9 |
| 12 | 13 33.0 | 13 35.2 | 12 56.0 | 1.2 | 1.1 | 7.2 | 6.5 | 13.2 | 12.0 |
| 13 | 13 33.3 | 13 35.5 | 12 56.2 | 1.3 | 1.2 | 7.3 | 6.6 | 13.3 | 12.1 |
| 14 | 13 33.5 | 13 35.7 | 12 56.4 | 1.4 | 1.3 | 7.4 | 6.7 | 13.4 | 12.2 |
| 15 | 13 33.8 | 13 36.0 | 12 56.7 | 1.5 | 1.4 | 7.5 | 6.8 | 13.5 | 12.3 |
| 16 | 13 34.0 | 13 36.2 | 12 56.9 | 1.6 | 1.5 | 7.6 | 6.9 | 13.6 | 12.4 |
| 17 | 13 34.3 | 13 36.5 | 12 57.2 | 1.7 | 1.5 | 7.7 | 7.0 | 13.7 | 12.4 |
| 18 | 13 34.5 | 13 36.7 | 12 57.4 | 1.8 | 1.6 | 7.8 | 7.1 | 13.8 | 12.5 |
| 19 | 13 34.8 | 13 37.0 | 12 57.6 | 1.9 | 1.7 | 7.9 | 7.2 | 13.9 | 12.6 |
| 20 | 13 35.0 | 13 37.2 | 12 57.9 | 2.0 | 1.8 | 8.0 | 7.3 | 14.0 | 12.7 |
| 21 | 13 35.3 | 13 37.5 | 12 58.1 | 2.1 | 1.9 | 8.1 | 7.4 | 14.1 | 12.8 |
| 22 | 13 35.5 | 13 37.7 | 12 58.3 | 2.2 | 2.0 | 8.2 | 7.4 | 14.2 | 12.9 |
| 23 | 13 35.8 | 13 38.0 | 12 58.6 | 2.3 | 2.1 | 8.3 | 7.5 | 14.3 | 13.0 |
| 24 | 13 36.0 | 13 38.2 | 12 58.8 | 2.4 | 2.2 | 8.4 | 7.6 | 14.4 | 13.1 |
| 25 | 13 36.3 | 13 38.5 | 12 59.1 | 2.5 | 2.3 | 8.5 | 7.7 | 14.5 | 13.2 |
| 26 | 13 36.5 | 13 38.7 | 12 59.3 | 2.6 | 2.4 | 8.6 | 7.8 | 14.6 | 13.3 |
| 27 | 13 36.8 | 13 39.0 | 12 59.5 | 2.7 | 2.5 | 8.7 | 7.9 | 14.7 | 13.4 |
| 28 | 13 37.0 | 13 39.2 | 12 59.8 | 2.8 | 2.5 | 8.8 | 8.0 | 14.8 | 13.4 |
| 29 | 13 37.3 | 13 39.5 | 13 00.0 | 2.9 | 2.6 | 8.9 | 8.1 | 14.9 | 13.5 |
| 30 | 13 37.5 | 13 39.7 | 13 00.3 | 3.0 | 2.7 | 9.0 | 8.2 | 15.0 | 13.6 |
| 31 | 13 37.8 | 13 40.0 | 13 00.5 | 3.1 | 2.8 | 9.1 | 8.3 | 15.1 | 13.7 |
| 32 | 13 38.0 | 13 40.2 | 13 00.7 | 3.2 | 2.9 | 9.2 | 8.4 | 15.2 | 13.8 |
| 33 | 13 38.3 | 13 40.5 | 13 01.0 | 3.3 | 3.0 | 9.3 | 8.4 | 15.3 | 13.9 |
| 34 | 13 38.5 | 13 40.7 | 13 01.2 | 3.4 | 3.1 | 9.4 | 8.5 | 15.4 | 14.0 |
| 35 | 13 38.8 | 13 41.0 | 13 01.5 | 3.5 | 3.2 | 9.5 | 8.6 | 15.5 | 14.1 |
| 36 | 13 39.0 | 13 41.2 | 13 01.7 | 3.6 | 3.3 | 9.6 | 8.7 | 15.6 | 14.2 |
| 37 | 13 39.3 | 13 41.5 | 13 01.9 | 3.7 | 3.4 | 9.7 | 8.8 | 15.7 | 14.3 |
| 38 | 13 39.5 | 13 41.7 | 13 02.2 | 3.8 | 3.5 | 9.8 | 8.9 | 15.8 | 14.4 |
| 39 | 13 39.8 | 13 42.0 | 13 02.4 | 3.9 | 3.5 | 9.9 | 9.0 | 15.9 | 14.4 |
| 40 | 13 40.0 | 13 42.2 | 13 02.6 | 4.0 | 3.6 | 10.0 | 9.1 | 16.0 | 14.5 |
| 41 | 13 40.3 | 13 42.5 | 13 02.9 | 4.1 | 3.7 | 10.1 | 9.2 | 16.1 | 14.6 |
| 42 | 13 40.5 | 13 42.7 | 13 03.1 | 4.2 | 3.8 | 10.2 | 9.3 | 16.2 | 14.7 |
| 43 | 13 40.8 | 13 43.0 | 13 03.4 | 4.3 | 3.9 | 10.3 | 9.4 | 16.3 | 14.8 |
| 44 | 13 41.0 | 13 43.2 | 13 03.6 | 4.4 | 4.0 | 10.4 | 9.4 | 16.4 | 14.9 |
| 45 | 13 41.3 | 13 43.5 | 13 03.8 | 4.5 | 4.1 | 10.5 | 9.5 | 16.5 | 15.0 |
| 46 | 13 41.5 | 13 43.7 | 13 04.1 | 4.6 | 4.2 | 10.6 | 9.6 | 16.6 | 15.1 |
| 47 | 13 41.8 | 13 44.0 | 13 04.3 | 4.7 | 4.3 | 10.7 | 9.7 | 16.7 | 15.2 |
| 48 | 13 42.0 | 13 44.3 | 13 04.6 | 4.8 | 4.4 | 10.8 | 9.8 | 16.8 | 15.3 |
| 49 | 13 42.3 | 13 44.5 | 13 04.8 | 4.9 | 4.5 | 10.9 | 9.9 | 16.9 | 15.4 |
| 50 | 13 42.5 | 13 44.8 | 13 05.0 | 5.0 | 4.5 | 11.0 | 10.0 | 17.0 | 15.4 |
| 51 | 13 42.8 | 13 45.0 | 13 05.3 | 5.1 | 4.6 | 11.1 | 10.1 | 17.1 | 15.5 |
| 52 | 13 43.0 | 13 45.3 | 13 05.5 | 5.2 | 4.7 | 11.2 | 10.2 | 17.2 | 15.6 |
| 53 | 13 43.3 | 13 45.5 | 13 05.7 | 5.3 | 4.8 | 11.3 | 10.3 | 17.3 | 15.7 |
| 54 | 13 43.5 | 13 45.8 | 13 06.0 | 5.4 | 4.9 | 11.4 | 10.4 | 17.4 | 15.8 |
| 55 | 13 43.8 | 13 46.0 | 13 06.2 | 5.5 | 5.0 | 11.5 | 10.4 | 17.5 | 15.9 |
| 56 | 13 44.0 | 13 46.3 | 13 06.5 | 5.6 | 5.1 | 11.6 | 10.5 | 17.6 | 16.0 |
| 57 | 13 44.3 | 13 46.5 | 13 06.7 | 5.7 | 5.2 | 11.7 | 10.6 | 17.7 | 16.1 |
| 58 | 13 44.5 | 13 46.8 | 13 06.9 | 5.8 | 5.3 | 11.8 | 10.7 | 17.8 | 16.2 |
| 59 | 13 44.8 | 13 47.0 | 13 07.2 | 5.9 | 5.4 | 11.9 | 10.8 | 17.9 | 16.3 |
| 60 | 13 45.0 | 13 47.3 | 13 07.4 | 6.0 | 5.5 | 12.0 | 10.9 | 18.0 | 16.4 |

### 55ᵐ

| s | SUN PLANETS | ARIES | MOON | v or d | Corrⁿ | v or d | Corrⁿ | v or d | Corrⁿ |
|---|---|---|---|---|---|---|---|---|---|
| | ° ′ | ° ′ | ° ′ | ′ | ′ | ′ | ′ | ′ | ′ |
| 00 | 13 45.0 | 13 47.3 | 13 07.4 | 0.0 | 0.0 | 6.0 | 5.6 | 12.0 | 11.1 |
| 01 | 13 45.3 | 13 47.5 | 13 07.7 | 0.1 | 0.1 | 6.1 | 5.6 | 12.1 | 11.2 |
| 02 | 13 45.5 | 13 47.8 | 13 07.9 | 0.2 | 0.2 | 6.2 | 5.7 | 12.2 | 11.3 |
| 03 | 13 45.8 | 13 48.0 | 13 08.1 | 0.3 | 0.3 | 6.3 | 5.8 | 12.3 | 11.4 |
| 04 | 13 46.0 | 13 48.3 | 13 08.4 | 0.4 | 0.4 | 6.4 | 5.9 | 12.4 | 11.5 |
| 05 | 13 46.3 | 13 48.5 | 13 08.6 | 0.5 | 0.5 | 6.5 | 6.0 | 12.5 | 11.6 |
| 06 | 13 46.5 | 13 48.8 | 13 08.8 | 0.6 | 0.6 | 6.6 | 6.1 | 12.6 | 11.7 |
| 07 | 13 46.8 | 13 49.0 | 13 09.1 | 0.7 | 0.6 | 6.7 | 6.2 | 12.7 | 11.7 |
| 08 | 13 47.0 | 13 49.3 | 13 09.3 | 0.8 | 0.7 | 6.8 | 6.3 | 12.8 | 11.8 |
| 09 | 13 47.3 | 13 49.5 | 13 09.6 | 0.9 | 0.8 | 6.9 | 6.4 | 12.9 | 11.9 |
| 10 | 13 47.5 | 13 49.8 | 13 09.8 | 1.0 | 0.9 | 7.0 | 6.5 | 13.0 | 12.0 |
| 11 | 13 47.8 | 13 50.0 | 13 10.0 | 1.1 | 1.0 | 7.1 | 6.6 | 13.1 | 12.1 |
| 12 | 13 48.0 | 13 50.3 | 13 10.3 | 1.2 | 1.1 | 7.2 | 6.7 | 13.2 | 12.2 |
| 13 | 13 48.3 | 13 50.5 | 13 10.5 | 1.3 | 1.2 | 7.3 | 6.8 | 13.3 | 12.3 |
| 14 | 13 48.5 | 13 50.8 | 13 10.8 | 1.4 | 1.3 | 7.4 | 6.8 | 13.4 | 12.4 |
| 15 | 13 48.8 | 13 51.0 | 13 11.0 | 1.5 | 1.4 | 7.5 | 6.9 | 13.5 | 12.5 |
| 16 | 13 49.0 | 13 51.3 | 13 11.2 | 1.6 | 1.5 | 7.6 | 7.0 | 13.6 | 12.6 |
| 17 | 13 49.3 | 13 51.5 | 13 11.5 | 1.7 | 1.6 | 7.7 | 7.1 | 13.7 | 12.7 |
| 18 | 13 49.5 | 13 51.8 | 13 11.7 | 1.8 | 1.7 | 7.8 | 7.2 | 13.8 | 12.8 |
| 19 | 13 49.8 | 13 52.0 | 13 12.0 | 1.9 | 1.8 | 7.9 | 7.3 | 13.9 | 12.9 |
| 20 | 13 50.0 | 13 52.3 | 13 12.2 | 2.0 | 1.9 | 8.0 | 7.4 | 14.0 | 13.0 |
| 21 | 13 50.3 | 13 52.5 | 13 12.4 | 2.1 | 1.9 | 8.1 | 7.5 | 14.1 | 13.0 |
| 22 | 13 50.5 | 13 52.8 | 13 12.7 | 2.2 | 2.0 | 8.2 | 7.6 | 14.2 | 13.1 |
| 23 | 13 50.8 | 13 53.0 | 13 12.9 | 2.3 | 2.1 | 8.3 | 7.7 | 14.3 | 13.2 |
| 24 | 13 51.0 | 13 53.3 | 13 13.1 | 2.4 | 2.2 | 8.4 | 7.8 | 14.4 | 13.3 |
| 25 | 13 51.3 | 13 53.5 | 13 13.4 | 2.5 | 2.3 | 8.5 | 7.9 | 14.5 | 13.4 |
| 26 | 13 51.5 | 13 53.8 | 13 13.6 | 2.6 | 2.4 | 8.6 | 8.0 | 14.6 | 13.5 |
| 27 | 13 51.8 | 13 54.0 | 13 13.9 | 2.7 | 2.5 | 8.7 | 8.0 | 14.7 | 13.6 |
| 28 | 13 52.0 | 13 54.3 | 13 14.1 | 2.8 | 2.6 | 8.8 | 8.1 | 14.8 | 13.7 |
| 29 | 13 52.3 | 13 54.5 | 13 14.3 | 2.9 | 2.7 | 8.9 | 8.2 | 14.9 | 13.8 |
| 30 | 13 52.5 | 13 54.8 | 13 14.6 | 3.0 | 2.8 | 9.0 | 8.3 | 15.0 | 13.9 |
| 31 | 13 52.8 | 13 55.0 | 13 14.8 | 3.1 | 2.9 | 9.1 | 8.4 | 15.1 | 14.0 |
| 32 | 13 53.0 | 13 55.3 | 13 15.1 | 3.2 | 3.0 | 9.2 | 8.5 | 15.2 | 14.1 |
| 33 | 13 53.3 | 13 55.5 | 13 15.3 | 3.3 | 3.1 | 9.3 | 8.6 | 15.3 | 14.2 |
| 34 | 13 53.5 | 13 55.8 | 13 15.5 | 3.4 | 3.1 | 9.4 | 8.7 | 15.4 | 14.2 |
| 35 | 13 53.8 | 13 56.0 | 13 15.8 | 3.5 | 3.2 | 9.5 | 8.8 | 15.5 | 14.3 |
| 36 | 13 54.0 | 13 56.3 | 13 16.0 | 3.6 | 3.3 | 9.6 | 8.9 | 15.6 | 14.4 |
| 37 | 13 54.3 | 13 56.5 | 13 16.2 | 3.7 | 3.4 | 9.7 | 9.0 | 15.7 | 14.5 |
| 38 | 13 54.5 | 13 56.8 | 13 16.5 | 3.8 | 3.5 | 9.8 | 9.1 | 15.8 | 14.6 |
| 39 | 13 54.8 | 13 57.0 | 13 16.7 | 3.9 | 3.6 | 9.9 | 9.2 | 15.9 | 14.7 |
| 40 | 13 55.0 | 13 57.3 | 13 17.0 | 4.0 | 3.7 | 10.0 | 9.3 | 16.0 | 14.8 |
| 41 | 13 55.3 | 13 57.5 | 13 17.2 | 4.1 | 3.8 | 10.1 | 9.3 | 16.1 | 14.9 |
| 42 | 13 55.5 | 13 57.8 | 13 17.4 | 4.2 | 3.9 | 10.2 | 9.4 | 16.2 | 15.0 |
| 43 | 13 55.8 | 13 58.0 | 13 17.7 | 4.3 | 4.0 | 10.3 | 9.5 | 16.3 | 15.1 |
| 44 | 13 56.0 | 13 58.3 | 13 17.9 | 4.4 | 4.1 | 10.4 | 9.6 | 16.4 | 15.2 |
| 45 | 13 56.3 | 13 58.5 | 13 18.2 | 4.5 | 4.2 | 10.5 | 9.7 | 16.5 | 15.3 |
| 46 | 13 56.5 | 13 58.8 | 13 18.4 | 4.6 | 4.3 | 10.6 | 9.8 | 16.6 | 15.4 |
| 47 | 13 56.8 | 13 59.0 | 13 18.6 | 4.7 | 4.3 | 10.7 | 9.9 | 16.7 | 15.4 |
| 48 | 13 57.0 | 13 59.3 | 13 18.9 | 4.8 | 4.4 | 10.8 | 10.0 | 16.8 | 15.5 |
| 49 | 13 57.3 | 13 59.5 | 13 19.1 | 4.9 | 4.5 | 10.9 | 10.1 | 16.9 | 15.6 |
| 50 | 13 57.5 | 13 59.8 | 13 19.3 | 5.0 | 4.6 | 11.0 | 10.2 | 17.0 | 15.7 |
| 51 | 13 57.8 | 14 00.0 | 13 19.6 | 5.1 | 4.7 | 11.1 | 10.3 | 17.1 | 15.8 |
| 52 | 13 58.0 | 14 00.3 | 13 19.8 | 5.2 | 4.8 | 11.2 | 10.4 | 17.2 | 15.9 |
| 53 | 13 58.3 | 14 00.5 | 13 20.1 | 5.3 | 4.9 | 11.3 | 10.5 | 17.3 | 16.0 |
| 54 | 13 58.5 | 14 00.8 | 13 20.3 | 5.4 | 5.0 | 11.4 | 10.5 | 17.4 | 16.1 |
| 55 | 13 58.8 | 14 01.0 | 13 20.5 | 5.5 | 5.1 | 11.5 | 10.6 | 17.5 | 16.2 |
| 56 | 13 59.0 | 14 01.3 | 13 20.8 | 5.6 | 5.2 | 11.6 | 10.7 | 17.6 | 16.3 |
| 57 | 13 59.3 | 14 01.5 | 13 21.0 | 5.7 | 5.3 | 11.7 | 10.8 | 17.7 | 16.4 |
| 58 | 13 59.5 | 14 01.8 | 13 21.3 | 5.8 | 5.4 | 11.8 | 10.9 | 17.8 | 16.5 |
| 59 | 13 59.8 | 14 02.0 | 13 21.5 | 5.9 | 5.5 | 11.9 | 11.0 | 17.9 | 16.6 |
| 60 | 14 00.0 | 14 02.3 | 13 21.7 | 6.0 | 5.6 | 12.0 | 11.1 | 18.0 | 16.7 |

## INCREMENTS AND CORRECTIONS

### 56ᵐ

| s | SUN PLANETS | ARIES | MOON | v or d | Corrⁿ | v or d | Corrⁿ | v or d | Corrⁿ |
|---|---|---|---|---|---|---|---|---|---|
| | ° ′ | ° ′ | ° ′ | ′ | ′ | ′ | ′ | ′ | ′ |
| 00 | 14 00·0 | 14 02·3 | 13 21·7 | 0·0 | 0·0 | 6·0 | 5·7 | 12·0 | 11·3 |
| 01 | 14 00·3 | 14 02·6 | 13 22·0 | 0·1 | 0·1 | 6·1 | 5·7 | 12·1 | 11·4 |
| 02 | 14 00·5 | 14 02·8 | 13 22·2 | 0·2 | 0·2 | 6·2 | 5·8 | 12·2 | 11·5 |
| 03 | 14 00·8 | 14 03·1 | 13 22·4 | 0·3 | 0·3 | 6·3 | 5·9 | 12·3 | 11·6 |
| 04 | 14 01·0 | 14 03·3 | 13 22·7 | 0·4 | 0·4 | 6·4 | 6·0 | 12·4 | 11·7 |
| 05 | 14 01·3 | 14 03·6 | 13 22·9 | 0·5 | 0·5 | 6·5 | 6·1 | 12·5 | 11·8 |
| 06 | 14 01·5 | 14 03·8 | 13 23·2 | 0·6 | 0·6 | 6·6 | 6·2 | 12·6 | 11·9 |
| 07 | 14 01·8 | 14 04·1 | 13 23·4 | 0·7 | 0·7 | 6·7 | 6·3 | 12·7 | 12·0 |
| 08 | 14 02·0 | 14 04·3 | 13 23·6 | 0·8 | 0·8 | 6·8 | 6·4 | 12·8 | 12·1 |
| 09 | 14 02·3 | 14 04·6 | 13 23·9 | 0·9 | 0·8 | 6·9 | 6·5 | 12·9 | 12·1 |
| 10 | 14 02·5 | 14 04·8 | 13 24·1 | 1·0 | 0·9 | 7·0 | 6·6 | 13·0 | 12·2 |
| 11 | 14 02·8 | 14 05·1 | 13 24·4 | 1·1 | 1·0 | 7·1 | 6·7 | 13·1 | 12·3 |
| 12 | 14 03·0 | 14 05·3 | 13 24·6 | 1·2 | 1·1 | 7·2 | 6·8 | 13·2 | 12·4 |
| 13 | 14 03·3 | 14 05·6 | 13 24·8 | 1·3 | 1·2 | 7·3 | 6·9 | 13·3 | 12·5 |
| 14 | 14 03·5 | 14 05·8 | 13 25·1 | 1·4 | 1·3 | 7·4 | 7·0 | 13·4 | 12·6 |
| 15 | 14 03·8 | 14 06·1 | 13 25·3 | 1·5 | 1·4 | 7·5 | 7·1 | 13·5 | 12·7 |
| 16 | 14 04·0 | 14 06·3 | 13 25·6 | 1·6 | 1·5 | 7·6 | 7·2 | 13·6 | 12·8 |
| 17 | 14 04·3 | 14 06·6 | 13 25·8 | 1·7 | 1·6 | 7·7 | 7·3 | 13·7 | 12·9 |
| 18 | 14 04·5 | 14 06·8 | 13 26·0 | 1·8 | 1·7 | 7·8 | 7·3 | 13·8 | 13·0 |
| 19 | 14 04·8 | 14 07·1 | 13 26·3 | 1·9 | 1·8 | 7·9 | 7·4 | 13·9 | 13·1 |
| 20 | 14 05·0 | 14 07·3 | 13 26·5 | 2·0 | 1·9 | 8·0 | 7·5 | 14·0 | 13·2 |
| 21 | 14 05·3 | 14 07·6 | 13 26·7 | 2·1 | 2·0 | 8·1 | 7·6 | 14·1 | 13·3 |
| 22 | 14 05·5 | 14 07·8 | 13 27·0 | 2·2 | 2·1 | 8·2 | 7·7 | 14·2 | 13·4 |
| 23 | 14 05·8 | 14 08·1 | 13 27·2 | 2·3 | 2·2 | 8·3 | 7·8 | 14·3 | 13·5 |
| 24 | 14 06·0 | 14 08·3 | 13 27·5 | 2·4 | 2·3 | 8·4 | 7·9 | 14·4 | 13·6 |
| 25 | 14 06·3 | 14 08·6 | 13 27·7 | 2·5 | 2·4 | 8·5 | 8·0 | 14·5 | 13·7 |
| 26 | 14 06·5 | 14 08·8 | 13 27·9 | 2·6 | 2·4 | 8·6 | 8·1 | 14·6 | 13·7 |
| 27 | 14 06·8 | 14 09·1 | 13 28·2 | 2·7 | 2·5 | 8·7 | 8·2 | 14·7 | 13·8 |
| 28 | 14 07·0 | 14 09·3 | 13 28·4 | 2·8 | 2·6 | 8·8 | 8·3 | 14·8 | 13·9 |
| 29 | 14 07·3 | 14 09·6 | 13 28·7 | 2·9 | 2·7 | 8·9 | 8·4 | 14·9 | 14·0 |
| 30 | 14 07·5 | 14 09·8 | 13 28·9 | 3·0 | 2·8 | 9·0 | 8·5 | 15·0 | 14·1 |
| 31 | 14 07·8 | 14 10·1 | 13 29·1 | 3·1 | 2·9 | 9·1 | 8·6 | 15·1 | 14·2 |
| 32 | 14 08·0 | 14 10·3 | 13 29·4 | 3·2 | 3·0 | 9·2 | 8·7 | 15·2 | 14·3 |
| 33 | 14 08·3 | 14 10·6 | 13 29·6 | 3·3 | 3·1 | 9·3 | 8·8 | 15·3 | 14·4 |
| 34 | 14 08·5 | 14 10·8 | 13 29·8 | 3·4 | 3·2 | 9·4 | 8·9 | 15·4 | 14·5 |
| 35 | 14 08·8 | 14 11·1 | 13 30·1 | 3·5 | 3·3 | 9·5 | 8·9 | 15·5 | 14·6 |
| 36 | 14 09·0 | 14 11·3 | 13 30·3 | 3·6 | 3·4 | 9·6 | 9·0 | 15·6 | 14·7 |
| 37 | 14 09·3 | 14 11·6 | 13 30·6 | 3·7 | 3·5 | 9·7 | 9·1 | 15·7 | 14·8 |
| 38 | 14 09·5 | 14 11·8 | 13 30·8 | 3·8 | 3·6 | 9·8 | 9·2 | 15·8 | 14·9 |
| 39 | 14 09·8 | 14 12·1 | 13 31·0 | 3·9 | 3·7 | 9·9 | 9·3 | 15·9 | 15·0 |
| 40 | 14 10·0 | 14 12·3 | 13 31·3 | 4·0 | 3·8 | 10·0 | 9·4 | 16·0 | 15·1 |
| 41 | 14 10·3 | 14 12·6 | 13 31·5 | 4·1 | 3·9 | 10·1 | 9·5 | 16·1 | 15·2 |
| 42 | 14 10·5 | 14 12·8 | 13 31·8 | 4·2 | 4·0 | 10·2 | 9·6 | 16·2 | 15·3 |
| 43 | 14 10·8 | 14 13·1 | 13 32·0 | 4·3 | 4·0 | 10·3 | 9·7 | 16·3 | 15·4 |
| 44 | 14 11·0 | 14 13·3 | 13 32·2 | 4·4 | 4·1 | 10·4 | 9·8 | 16·4 | 15·4 |
| 45 | 14 11·3 | 14 13·6 | 13 32·5 | 4·5 | 4·2 | 10·5 | 9·9 | 16·5 | 15·5 |
| 46 | 14 11·5 | 14 13·8 | 13 32·7 | 4·6 | 4·3 | 10·6 | 10·0 | 16·6 | 15·6 |
| 47 | 14 11·8 | 14 14·1 | 13 32·9 | 4·7 | 4·4 | 10·7 | 10·1 | 16·7 | 15·7 |
| 48 | 14 12·0 | 14 14·3 | 13 33·2 | 4·8 | 4·5 | 10·8 | 10·2 | 16·8 | 15·8 |
| 49 | 14 12·3 | 14 14·6 | 13 33·4 | 4·9 | 4·6 | 10·9 | 10·3 | 16·9 | 15·9 |
| 50 | 14 12·5 | 14 14·8 | 13 33·7 | 5·0 | 4·7 | 11·0 | 10·4 | 17·0 | 16·0 |
| 51 | 14 12·8 | 14 15·1 | 13 33·9 | 5·1 | 4·8 | 11·1 | 10·5 | 17·1 | 16·1 |
| 52 | 14 13·0 | 14 15·3 | 13 34·1 | 5·2 | 4·9 | 11·2 | 10·5 | 17·2 | 16·2 |
| 53 | 14 13·3 | 14 15·6 | 13 34·4 | 5·3 | 5·0 | 11·3 | 10·6 | 17·3 | 16·3 |
| 54 | 14 13·5 | 14 15·8 | 13 34·6 | 5·4 | 5·1 | 11·4 | 10·7 | 17·4 | 16·4 |
| 55 | 14 13·8 | 14 16·1 | 13 34·9 | 5·5 | 5·2 | 11·5 | 10·8 | 17·5 | 16·5 |
| 56 | 14 14·0 | 14 16·3 | 13 35·1 | 5·6 | 5·3 | 11·6 | 10·9 | 17·6 | 16·6 |
| 57 | 14 14·3 | 14 16·6 | 13 35·3 | 5·7 | 5·4 | 11·7 | 11·0 | 17·7 | 16·7 |
| 58 | 14 14·5 | 14 16·8 | 13 35·6 | 5·8 | 5·5 | 11·8 | 11·1 | 17·8 | 16·8 |
| 59 | 14 14·8 | 14 17·1 | 13 35·8 | 5·9 | 5·6 | 11·9 | 11·2 | 17·9 | 16·9 |
| 60 | 14 15·0 | 14 17·3 | 13 36·1 | 6·0 | 5·7 | 12·0 | 11·3 | 18·0 | 17·0 |

### 57ᵐ

| s | SUN PLANETS | ARIES | MOON | v or d | Corrⁿ | v or d | Corrⁿ | v or d | Corrⁿ |
|---|---|---|---|---|---|---|---|---|---|
| | ° ′ | ° ′ | ° ′ | ′ | ′ | ′ | ′ | ′ | ′ |
| 00 | 14 15·0 | 14 17·3 | 13 36·1 | 0·0 | 0·0 | 6·0 | 5·8 | 12·0 | 11·5 |
| 01 | 14 15·3 | 14 17·6 | 13 36·3 | 0·1 | 0·1 | 6·1 | 5·8 | 12·1 | 11·6 |
| 02 | 14 15·5 | 14 17·8 | 13 36·5 | 0·2 | 0·2 | 6·2 | 5·9 | 12·2 | 11·7 |
| 03 | 14 15·8 | 14 18·1 | 13 36·8 | 0·3 | 0·3 | 6·3 | 6·0 | 12·3 | 11·8 |
| 04 | 14 16·0 | 14 18·3 | 13 37·0 | 0·4 | 0·4 | 6·4 | 6·1 | 12·4 | 11·9 |
| 05 | 14 16·3 | 14 18·6 | 13 37·2 | 0·5 | 0·5 | 6·5 | 6·2 | 12·5 | 12·0 |
| 06 | 14 16·5 | 14 18·8 | 13 37·5 | 0·6 | 0·6 | 6·6 | 6·3 | 12·6 | 12·1 |
| 07 | 14 16·8 | 14 19·1 | 13 37·7 | 0·7 | 0·7 | 6·7 | 6·4 | 12·7 | 12·2 |
| 08 | 14 17·0 | 14 19·3 | 13 38·0 | 0·8 | 0·8 | 6·8 | 6·5 | 12·8 | 12·3 |
| 09 | 14 17·3 | 14 19·6 | 13 38·2 | 0·9 | 0·9 | 6·9 | 6·6 | 12·9 | 12·4 |
| 10 | 14 17·5 | 14 19·8 | 13 38·4 | 1·0 | 1·0 | 7·0 | 6·7 | 13·0 | 12·5 |
| 11 | 14 17·8 | 14 20·1 | 13 38·7 | 1·1 | 1·1 | 7·1 | 6·8 | 13·1 | 12·6 |
| 12 | 14 18·0 | 14 20·3 | 13 38·9 | 1·2 | 1·2 | 7·2 | 6·9 | 13·2 | 12·7 |
| 13 | 14 18·3 | 14 20·6 | 13 39·2 | 1·3 | 1·2 | 7·3 | 7·0 | 13·3 | 12·7 |
| 14 | 14 18·5 | 14 20·9 | 13 39·4 | 1·4 | 1·3 | 7·4 | 7·1 | 13·4 | 12·8 |
| 15 | 14 18·8 | 14 21·1 | 13 39·6 | 1·5 | 1·4 | 7·5 | 7·2 | 13·5 | 12·9 |
| 16 | 14 19·0 | 14 21·4 | 13 39·9 | 1·6 | 1·5 | 7·6 | 7·3 | 13·6 | 13·0 |
| 17 | 14 19·3 | 14 21·6 | 13 40·1 | 1·7 | 1·6 | 7·7 | 7·4 | 13·7 | 13·1 |
| 18 | 14 19·5 | 14 21·9 | 13 40·3 | 1·8 | 1·7 | 7·8 | 7·5 | 13·8 | 13·2 |
| 19 | 14 19·8 | 14 22·1 | 13 40·6 | 1·9 | 1·8 | 7·9 | 7·6 | 13·9 | 13·3 |
| 20 | 14 20·0 | 14 22·4 | 13 40·8 | 2·0 | 1·9 | 8·0 | 7·7 | 14·0 | 13·4 |
| 21 | 14 20·3 | 14 22·6 | 13 41·1 | 2·1 | 2·0 | 8·1 | 7·8 | 14·1 | 13·5 |
| 22 | 14 20·5 | 14 22·9 | 13 41·3 | 2·2 | 2·1 | 8·2 | 7·9 | 14·2 | 13·6 |
| 23 | 14 20·8 | 14 23·1 | 13 41·5 | 2·3 | 2·2 | 8·3 | 8·0 | 14·3 | 13·7 |
| 24 | 14 21·0 | 14 23·4 | 13 41·8 | 2·4 | 2·3 | 8·4 | 8·1 | 14·4 | 13·8 |
| 25 | 14 21·3 | 14 23·6 | 13 42·0 | 2·5 | 2·4 | 8·5 | 8·1 | 14·5 | 13·9 |
| 26 | 14 21·5 | 14 23·9 | 13 42·3 | 2·6 | 2·5 | 8·6 | 8·2 | 14·6 | 14·0 |
| 27 | 14 21·8 | 14 24·1 | 13 42·5 | 2·7 | 2·6 | 8·7 | 8·3 | 14·7 | 14·1 |
| 28 | 14 22·0 | 14 24·4 | 13 42·7 | 2·8 | 2·7 | 8·8 | 8·4 | 14·8 | 14·2 |
| 29 | 14 22·3 | 14 24·6 | 13 43·0 | 2·9 | 2·8 | 8·9 | 8·5 | 14·9 | 14·3 |
| 30 | 14 22·5 | 14 24·9 | 13 43·2 | 3·0 | 2·9 | 9·0 | 8·6 | 15·0 | 14·4 |
| 31 | 14 22·8 | 14 25·1 | 13 43·4 | 3·1 | 3·0 | 9·1 | 8·7 | 15·1 | 14·5 |
| 32 | 14 23·0 | 14 25·4 | 13 43·7 | 3·2 | 3·1 | 9·2 | 8·8 | 15·2 | 14·6 |
| 33 | 14 23·3 | 14 25·6 | 13 43·9 | 3·3 | 3·2 | 9·3 | 8·9 | 15·3 | 14·7 |
| 34 | 14 23·5 | 14 25·9 | 13 44·2 | 3·4 | 3·3 | 9·4 | 9·0 | 15·4 | 14·8 |
| 35 | 14 23·8 | 14 26·1 | 13 44·4 | 3·5 | 3·4 | 9·5 | 9·1 | 15·5 | 14·9 |
| 36 | 14 24·0 | 14 26·4 | 13 44·6 | 3·6 | 3·5 | 9·6 | 9·2 | 15·6 | 15·0 |
| 37 | 14 24·3 | 14 26·6 | 13 44·9 | 3·7 | 3·5 | 9·7 | 9·3 | 15·7 | 15·0 |
| 38 | 14 24·5 | 14 26·9 | 13 45·1 | 3·8 | 3·6 | 9·8 | 9·4 | 15·8 | 15·1 |
| 39 | 14 24·8 | 14 27·1 | 13 45·4 | 3·9 | 3·7 | 9·9 | 9·5 | 15·9 | 15·2 |
| 40 | 14 25·0 | 14 27·4 | 13 45·6 | 4·0 | 3·8 | 10·0 | 9·6 | 16·0 | 15·3 |
| 41 | 14 25·3 | 14 27·6 | 13 45·8 | 4·1 | 3·9 | 10·1 | 9·7 | 16·1 | 15·4 |
| 42 | 14 25·5 | 14 27·9 | 13 46·1 | 4·2 | 4·0 | 10·2 | 9·8 | 16·2 | 15·5 |
| 43 | 14 25·8 | 14 28·1 | 13 46·3 | 4·3 | 4·1 | 10·3 | 9·9 | 16·3 | 15·6 |
| 44 | 14 26·0 | 14 28·4 | 13 46·5 | 4·4 | 4·2 | 10·4 | 10·0 | 16·4 | 15·7 |
| 45 | 14 26·3 | 14 28·6 | 13 46·8 | 4·5 | 4·3 | 10·5 | 10·1 | 16·5 | 15·8 |
| 46 | 14 26·5 | 14 28·9 | 13 47·0 | 4·6 | 4·4 | 10·6 | 10·2 | 16·6 | 15·9 |
| 47 | 14 26·8 | 14 29·1 | 13 47·3 | 4·7 | 4·5 | 10·7 | 10·3 | 16·7 | 16·0 |
| 48 | 14 27·0 | 14 29·4 | 13 47·5 | 4·8 | 4·6 | 10·8 | 10·4 | 16·8 | 16·1 |
| 49 | 14 27·3 | 14 29·6 | 13 47·7 | 4·9 | 4·7 | 10·9 | 10·4 | 16·9 | 16·2 |
| 50 | 14 27·5 | 14 29·9 | 13 48·0 | 5·0 | 4·8 | 11·0 | 10·5 | 17·0 | 16·3 |
| 51 | 14 27·8 | 14 30·1 | 13 48·2 | 5·1 | 4·9 | 11·1 | 10·6 | 17·1 | 16·4 |
| 52 | 14 28·0 | 14 30·4 | 13 48·5 | 5·2 | 5·0 | 11·2 | 10·7 | 17·2 | 16·5 |
| 53 | 14 28·3 | 14 30·6 | 13 48·7 | 5·3 | 5·1 | 11·3 | 10·8 | 17·3 | 16·6 |
| 54 | 14 28·5 | 14 30·9 | 13 48·9 | 5·4 | 5·2 | 11·4 | 10·9 | 17·4 | 16·7 |
| 55 | 14 28·8 | 14 31·1 | 13 49·2 | 5·5 | 5·3 | 11·5 | 11·0 | 17·5 | 16·8 |
| 56 | 14 29·0 | 14 31·4 | 13 49·4 | 5·6 | 5·4 | 11·6 | 11·1 | 17·6 | 16·9 |
| 57 | 14 29·3 | 14 31·6 | 13 49·7 | 5·7 | 5·5 | 11·7 | 11·2 | 17·7 | 17·0 |
| 58 | 14 29·5 | 14 31·9 | 13 49·9 | 5·8 | 5·6 | 11·8 | 11·3 | 17·8 | 17·1 |
| 59 | 14 29·8 | 14 32·1 | 13 50·1 | 5·9 | 5·7 | 11·9 | 11·4 | 17·9 | 17·2 |
| 60 | 14 30·0 | 14 32·4 | 13 50·4 | 6·0 | 5·8 | 12·0 | 11·5 | 18·0 | 17·3 |

## POLARIS (POLE STAR) TABLES, 2005
### FOR DETERMINING LATITUDE FROM SEXTANT ALTITUDE AND FOR AZIMUTH

| LHA ARIES | 120°–129° | 130°–139° | 140°–149° | 150°–159° | 160°–169° | 170°–179° | 180°–189° | 190°–199° | 200°–209° | 210°–219° | 220°–229° | 230°–239° |
|---|---|---|---|---|---|---|---|---|---|---|---|---|
| ° | $a_0$ ° ′ | $a_0$ ° ′ | $a_0$ ° ′ | $a_0$ ° ′ | $a_0$ ° ′ | $a_0$ ° ′ | $a_0$ ° ′ | $a_0$ ° ′ | $a_0$ ° ′ | $a_0$ ° ′ | $a_0$ ° ′ | $a_0$ ° ′ |
| 0 | 0 52·2 | 0 59·6 | 1 07·0 | 1 14·1 | 1 20·7 | 1 26·7 | 1 31·9 | 1 36·0 | 1 39·0 | 1 40·8 | 1 41·4 | 1 40·7 |
| 1 | 52·9 | 1 00·3 | 07·7 | 14·8 | 21·4 | 27·3 | 32·3 | 36·4 | 39·3 | 41·0 | 41·4 | 40·5 |
| 2 | 53·6 | 01·1 | 08·4 | 15·5 | 22·0 | 27·8 | 32·8 | 36·7 | 39·5 | 41·1 | 41·4 | 40·4 |
| 3 | 54·4 | 01·8 | 09·1 | 16·1 | 22·6 | 28·4 | 33·2 | 37·0 | 39·7 | 41·1 | 41·3 | 40·2 |
| 4 | 55·1 | 02·5 | 09·8 | 16·8 | 23·2 | 28·9 | 33·6 | 37·3 | 39·9 | 41·2 | 41·3 | 40·0 |
| 5 | 0 55·9 | 1 03·3 | 1 10·6 | 1 17·5 | 1 23·8 | 1 29·4 | 1 34·1 | 1 37·7 | 1 40·1 | 1 41·3 | 1 41·2 | 1 39·9 |
| 6 | 56·6 | 04·0 | 11·3 | 18·1 | 24·4 | 29·9 | 34·5 | 38·0 | 40·3 | 41·3 | 41·1 | 39·6 |
| 7 | 57·3 | 04·8 | 12·0 | 18·8 | 25·0 | 30·4 | 34·9 | 38·2 | 40·4 | 41·4 | 41·0 | 39·4 |
| 8 | 58·1 | 05·5 | 12·7 | 19·4 | 25·6 | 30·9 | 35·3 | 38·5 | 40·6 | 41·4 | 40·9 | 39·2 |
| 9 | 58·8 | 06·2 | 13·4 | 20·1 | 26·2 | 31·4 | 35·6 | 38·8 | 40·7 | 41·4 | 40·8 | 39·0 |
| 10 | 0 59·6 | 1 07·0 | 1 14·1 | 1 20·7 | 1 26·7 | 1 31·9 | 1 36·0 | 1 39·0 | 1 40·8 | 1 41·4 | 1 40·7 | 1 38·7 |

| Lat. | $a_1$ | $a_1$ | $a_1$ | $a_1$ | $a_1$ | $a_1$ | $a_1$ | $a_1$ | $a_1$ | $a_1$ | $a_1$ | $a_1$ |
|---|---|---|---|---|---|---|---|---|---|---|---|---|
| ° | ′ | ′ | ′ | ′ | ′ | ′ | ′ | ′ | ′ | ′ | ′ | ′ |
| 0 | 0·3 | 0·3 | 0·3 | 0·3 | 0·4 | 0·4 | 0·5 | 0·5 | 0·6 | 0·6 | 0·6 | 0·6 |
| 10 | ·3 | ·3 | ·4 | ·4 | ·4 | ·5 | ·5 | ·6 | ·6 | ·6 | ·6 | ·6 |
| 20 | ·4 | ·4 | ·4 | ·4 | ·5 | ·5 | ·5 | ·6 | ·6 | ·6 | ·6 | ·6 |
| 30 | ·4 | ·4 | ·4 | ·5 | ·5 | ·5 | ·5 | ·6 | ·6 | ·6 | ·6 | ·6 |
| 40 | 0·5 | 0·5 | 0·5 | 0·5 | 0·5 | 0·6 | 0·6 | 0·6 | 0·6 | 0·6 | 0·6 | 0·6 |
| 45 | ·5 | ·5 | ·6 | ·6 | ·6 | ·6 | ·6 | ·6 | ·6 | ·6 | ·6 | ·6 |
| 50 | ·6 | ·6 | ·6 | ·6 | ·6 | ·6 | ·6 | ·6 | ·6 | ·6 | ·6 | ·6 |
| 55 | ·7 | ·7 | ·7 | ·7 | ·6 | ·6 | ·6 | ·6 | ·6 | ·6 | ·6 | ·6 |
| 60 | ·7 | ·7 | ·7 | ·7 | ·7 | ·7 | ·6 | ·6 | ·6 | ·6 | ·6 | ·6 |
| 62 | 0·8 | 0·8 | 0·8 | 0·7 | 0·7 | 0·7 | 0·7 | 0·6 | 0·6 | 0·6 | 0·6 | 0·6 |
| 64 | ·8 | ·8 | ·8 | ·8 | ·7 | ·7 | ·7 | ·6 | ·6 | ·6 | ·6 | ·6 |
| 66 | ·9 | ·9 | ·9 | ·8 | ·8 | ·7 | ·7 | ·6 | ·6 | ·6 | ·6 | ·6 |
| 68 | 0·9 | 0·9 | 0·9 | 0·9 | 0·8 | 0·8 | 0·7 | 0·7 | 0·6 | 0·6 | 0·6 | 0·6 |

| Month | $a_2$ | $a_2$ | $a_2$ | $a_2$ | $a_2$ | $a_2$ | $a_2$ | $a_2$ | $a_2$ | $a_2$ | $a_2$ | $a_2$ |
|---|---|---|---|---|---|---|---|---|---|---|---|---|
| Jan. | 0·6 | 0·6 | 0·6 | 0·6 | 0·6 | 0·5 | 0·5 | 0·5 | 0·5 | 0·5 | 0·5 | 0·5 |
| Feb. | ·8 | ·8 | ·7 | ·7 | ·7 | ·6 | ·6 | ·5 | ·5 | ·5 | ·4 | ·4 |
| Mar. | 0·9 | 0·9 | 0·9 | 0·8 | ·8 | ·8 | ·7 | ·7 | ·6 | ·6 | ·5 | ·5 |
| Apr. | 1·0 | 1·0 | 1·0 | 1·0 | 0·9 | 0·9 | 0·9 | 0·8 | 0·7 | 0·7 | 0·6 | 0·6 |
| May | 0·9 | 1·0 | 1·0 | 1·0 | 1·0 | 1·0 | 1·0 | 0·9 | 0·9 | ·8 | ·8 | ·7 |
| June | ·8 | 0·9 | 0·9 | 1·0 | 1·0 | 1·0 | 1·0 | 1·0 | 1·0 | 0·9 | ·9 | ·8 |
| July | 0·7 | 0·7 | 0·8 | 0·8 | 0·9 | 0·9 | 0·9 | 1·0 | 1·0 | 1·0 | 0·9 | 0·9 |
| Aug. | ·5 | ·5 | ·6 | ·7 | ·7 | ·8 | ·8 | 0·9 | 0·9 | 0·9 | ·9 | ·9 |
| Sept. | ·3 | ·4 | ·4 | ·5 | ·5 | ·6 | ·6 | ·7 | ·7 | ·8 | ·8 | ·9 |
| Oct. | 0·3 | 0·3 | 0·3 | 0·3 | 0·3 | 0·4 | 0·4 | 0·5 | 0·6 | 0·6 | 0·7 | 0·7 |
| Nov. | ·2 | ·2 | ·2 | ·2 | ·2 | ·2 | ·3 | ·3 | ·4 | ·4 | ·5 | ·6 |
| Dec. | 0·3 | 0·2 | 0·2 | 0·2 | 0·1 | 0·1 | 0·2 | 0·2 | 0·2 | 0·3 | 0·3 | 0·4 |

| Lat. | AZIMUTH | | | | | | | | | | | |
|---|---|---|---|---|---|---|---|---|---|---|---|---|
| ° | ° | ° | ° | ° | ° | ° | ° | ° | ° | ° | ° | ° |
| 0 | 359·3 | 359·3 | 359·3 | 359·4 | 359·4 | 359·5 | 359·6 | 359·7 | 359·8 | 359·9 | 0·1 | 0·2 |
| 20 | 359·2 | 359·2 | 359·3 | 359·3 | 359·4 | 359·5 | 359·6 | 359·7 | 359·8 | 359·9 | 0·1 | 0·2 |
| 40 | 359·1 | 359·1 | 359·1 | 359·2 | 359·3 | 359·4 | 359·5 | 359·6 | 359·8 | 359·9 | 0·1 | 0·2 |
| 50 | 358·9 | 358·9 | 358·9 | 359·0 | 359·1 | 359·2 | 359·4 | 359·6 | 359·7 | 359·9 | 0·1 | 0·3 |
| 55 | 358·8 | 358·8 | 358·8 | 358·9 | 359·0 | 359·1 | 359·3 | 359·5 | 359·7 | 359·9 | 0·1 | 0·3 |
| 60 | 358·6 | 358·6 | 358·6 | 358·7 | 358·9 | 359·0 | 359·2 | 359·4 | 359·7 | 359·9 | 0·1 | 0·4 |
| 65 | 358·3 | 358·3 | 358·4 | 358·5 | 358·7 | 358·8 | 359·1 | 359·3 | 359·6 | 359·9 | 0·2 | 0·4 |

ILLUSTRATION

On 2005 April 21 at 23$^h$ 18$^m$ 56$^s$ UT in longitude W 37° 14′ the apparent altitude (corrected for refraction), $H_0$, of Polaris was 49° 31′·6

| From the daily pages: | ° | ′ | | $H_0$ | 49° | 31·6 |
|---|---|---|---|---|---|---|
| GHA Aries (23$^h$) | 195 | 06·6 | | $a_0$ (argument 162° 37′) | 1 | 22·4 |
| Increment (18$^m$ 56$^s$) | 4 | 44·8 | | $a_1$ (Lat 50° approx.) | | 0·6 |
| Longitude (west) | −37 | 14 | | $a_2$ (April) | | 0·9 |
| LHA Aries | 162 | 37 | | Sum − 1° = Lat = | 49 | 55·5 |

*Copyright Council for the Central Laboratory of the Research Councils 2004*

## 2005 JUNE 9, 10, 11 (THURS., FRI., SAT.)

| UT | ARIES GHA | VENUS −3.7 GHA | Dec | MARS +0.2 GHA | Dec | JUPITER −2.2 GHA | Dec | SATURN +0.2 GHA | Dec | STARS Name | SHA | Dec |
|---|---|---|---|---|---|---|---|---|---|---|---|---|
| d h | ° ′ | ° ′ | ° ′ | ° ′ | ° ′ | ° ′ | ° ′ | ° ′ | ° ′ | | ° ′ | ° ′ |
| 9 00 | 257 27.7 | 160 15.8 N24 | 22.3 | 258 33.4 S 2 | 55.4 | 68 41.2 S 2 | 15.5 | 140 02.9 N21 | 16.7 | Acamar | 315 23.3 | S40 16.8 |
| 01 | 272 30.2 | 175 14.9 | 22.3 | 273 34.3 | 54.7 | 83 43.6 | 15.5 | 155 05.1 | 16.7 | Achernar | 335 31.5 | S57 12.3 |
| 02 | 287 32.6 | 190 14.0 | 22.2 | 288 35.1 | 54.1 | 98 46.0 | 15.6 | 170 07.2 | 16.6 | Acrux | 173 16.5 | S63 08.0 |
| 03 | 302 35.1 | 205 13.2 .. | 22.1 | 303 35.9 .. | 53.4 | 113 48.5 .. | 15.6 | 185 09.4 .. | 16.6 | Adhara | 255 17.8 | S28 58.7 |
| 04 | 317 37.6 | 220 12.3 | 22.0 | 318 36.8 | 52.7 | 128 50.9 | 15.6 | 200 11.6 | 16.5 | Aldebaran | 290 57.0 | N16 31.3 |
| 05 | 332 40.0 | 235 11.4 | 22.0 | 333 37.6 | 52.1 | 143 53.4 | 15.6 | 215 13.7 | 16.5 | | | |
| 06 | 347 42.5 | 250 10.5 N24 | 21.9 | 348 38.5 S 2 | 51.4 | 158 55.8 S 2 | 15.6 | 230 15.9 N21 | 16.4 | Alioth | 166 25.6 | N55 56.1 |
| 07 | 2 45.0 | 265 09.6 | 21.8 | 3 39.3 | 50.8 | 173 58.3 | 15.7 | 245 18.1 | 16.4 | Alkaid | 153 03.3 | N49 17.3 |
| T 08 | 17 47.4 | 280 08.7 | 21.7 | 18 40.2 | 50.1 | 189 00.7 | 15.7 | 260 20.2 | 16.3 | Al Na'ir | 27 51.2 | S46 55.9 |
| H 09 | 32 49.9 | 295 07.8 .. | 21.6 | 33 41.0 .. | 49.4 | 204 03.1 .. | 15.7 | 275 22.4 .. | 16.3 | Alnilam | 275 53.1 | S 1 11.8 |
| U 10 | 47 52.4 | 310 06.9 | 21.6 | 48 41.8 | 48.8 | 219 05.6 | 15.7 | 290 24.6 | 16.2 | Alphard | 218 02.4 | S 8 40.9 |
| R 11 | 62 54.8 | 325 06.1 | 21.5 | 63 42.7 | 48.1 | 234 08.0 | 15.8 | 305 26.7 | 16.2 | | | |
| S 12 | 77 57.3 | 340 05.2 N24 | 21.4 | 78 43.5 S 2 | 47.4 | 249 10.5 S 2 | 15.8 | 320 28.9 N21 | 16.1 | Alphecca | 126 15.9 | N26 41.8 |
| D 13 | 92 59.7 | 355 04.3 | 21.3 | 93 44.4 | 46.8 | 264 12.9 | 15.8 | 335 31.1 | 16.1 | Alpheratz | 357 50.2 | N29 07.0 |
| A 14 | 108 02.2 | 10 03.4 | 21.2 | 108 45.2 | 46.1 | 279 15.3 | 15.8 | 350 33.2 | 16.0 | Altair | 62 14.1 | N 8 52.8 |
| Y 15 | 123 04.7 | 25 02.5 .. | 21.1 | 123 46.1 .. | 45.5 | 294 17.8 .. | 15.8 | 5 35.4 .. | 16.0 | Ankaa | 353 21.8 | S42 16.4 |
| 16 | 138 07.1 | 40 01.6 | 21.0 | 138 46.9 | 44.8 | 309 20.2 | 15.9 | 20 37.6 | 15.9 | Antares | 112 33.6 | S26 26.8 |
| 17 | 153 09.6 | 55 00.7 | 20.9 | 153 47.8 | 44.1 | 324 22.6 | 15.9 | 35 39.7 | 15.9 | | | |
| 18 | 168 12.1 | 69 59.8 N24 | 20.8 | 168 48.6 S 2 | 43.5 | 339 25.1 S 2 | 15.9 | 50 41.9 N21 | 15.8 | Arcturus | 146 01.2 | N19 09.3 |
| 19 | 183 14.5 | 84 59.0 | 20.7 | 183 49.4 | 42.8 | 354 27.5 | 15.9 | 65 44.1 | 15.8 | Atria | 107 40.7 | S69 02.4 |
| 20 | 198 17.0 | 99 58.1 | 20.7 | 198 50.3 | 42.1 | 9 30.0 | 16.0 | 80 46.2 | 15.7 | Avior | 234 21.3 | S59 31.7 |
| 21 | 213 19.5 | 114 57.2 .. | 20.6 | 213 51.1 .. | 41.5 | 24 32.4 .. | 16.0 | 95 48.4 .. | 15.7 | Bellatrix | 278 39.1 | N 6 21.4 |
| 22 | 228 21.9 | 129 56.3 | 20.5 | 228 52.0 | 40.8 | 39 34.8 | 16.0 | 110 50.6 | 15.6 | Betelgeuse | 271 08.4 | N 7 24.6 |
| 23 | 243 24.4 | 144 55.4 | 20.4 | 243 52.8 | 40.2 | 54 37.3 | 16.0 | 125 52.7 | 15.6 | | | |
| 10 00 | 258 26.9 | 159 54.5 N24 | 20.3 | 258 53.7 S 2 | 39.5 | 69 39.7 S 2 | 16.1 | 140 54.9 N21 | 15.6 | Canopus | 263 59.5 | S52 41.9 |
| 01 | 273 29.3 | 174 53.6 | 20.2 | 273 54.5 | 38.8 | 84 42.1 | 16.1 | 155 57.1 | 15.5 | Capella | 280 44.3 | N46 00.3 |
| 02 | 288 31.8 | 189 52.8 | 20.0 | 288 55.4 | 38.2 | 99 44.6 | 16.1 | 170 59.2 | 15.5 | Deneb | 49 35.6 | N45 17.7 |
| 03 | 303 34.2 | 204 51.9 .. | 19.9 | 303 56.2 .. | 37.5 | 114 47.0 .. | 16.1 | 186 01.4 .. | 15.4 | Denebola | 182 40.0 | N14 32.6 |
| 04 | 318 36.7 | 219 51.0 | 19.8 | 318 57.1 | 36.9 | 129 49.4 | 16.1 | 201 03.6 | 15.4 | Diphda | 349 02.2 | S17 57.3 |
| 05 | 333 39.2 | 234 50.1 | 19.7 | 333 57.9 | 36.2 | 144 51.9 | 16.2 | 216 05.7 | 15.3 | | | |
| 06 | 348 41.6 | 249 49.2 N24 | 19.6 | 348 58.8 S 2 | 35.5 | 159 54.3 S 2 | 16.2 | 231 07.9 N21 | 15.3 | Dubhe | 193 59.0 | N61 43.6 |
| 07 | 3 44.1 | 264 48.3 | 19.5 | 3 59.6 | 34.9 | 174 56.7 | 16.2 | 246 10.1 | 15.2 | Elnath | 278 21.0 | N28 36.8 |
| 08 | 18 46.6 | 279 47.5 | 19.4 | 19 00.4 | 34.2 | 189 59.2 | 16.2 | 261 12.2 | 15.2 | Eltanin | 90 48.5 | N51 29.1 |
| F 09 | 33 49.0 | 294 46.6 .. | 19.3 | 34 01.3 .. | 33.5 | 205 01.6 .. | 16.3 | 276 14.4 .. | 15.1 | Enif | 33 53.2 | N 9 53.8 |
| R 10 | 48 51.5 | 309 45.7 | 19.2 | 49 02.1 | 32.9 | 220 04.0 | 16.3 | 291 16.6 | 15.1 | Fomalhaut | 15 30.7 | S29 35.5 |
| I 11 | 63 54.0 | 324 44.8 | 19.1 | 64 03.0 | 32.2 | 235 06.5 | 16.3 | 306 18.7 | 15.0 | | | |
| D 12 | 78 56.4 | 339 43.9 N24 | 18.9 | 79 03.8 S 2 | 31.6 | 250 08.9 S 2 | 16.3 | 321 20.9 N21 | 15.0 | Gacrux | 172 08.1 | S57 08.9 |
| A 13 | 93 58.9 | 354 43.0 | 18.8 | 94 04.7 | 30.9 | 265 11.3 | 16.4 | 336 23.1 | 14.9 | Gienah | 175 58.8 | S17 34.4 |
| Y 14 | 109 01.4 | 9 42.1 | 18.7 | 109 05.5 | 30.2 | 280 13.8 | 16.4 | 351 25.2 | 14.9 | Hadar | 148 56.7 | S60 24.2 |
| 15 | 124 03.8 | 24 41.3 .. | 18.6 | 124 06.4 .. | 29.6 | 295 16.2 .. | 16.4 | 6 27.4 .. | 14.8 | Hamal | 328 08.2 | N23 29.2 |
| 16 | 139 06.3 | 39 40.4 | 18.5 | 139 07.2 | 28.9 | 310 18.6 | 16.4 | 21 29.6 | 14.8 | Kaus Aust. | 83 51.7 | S34 23.0 |
| 17 | 154 08.7 | 54 39.5 | 18.3 | 154 08.1 | 28.2 | 325 21.1 | 16.5 | 36 31.7 | 14.7 | | | |
| 18 | 169 11.2 | 69 38.6 N24 | 18.2 | 169 08.9 S 2 | 27.6 | 340 23.5 S 2 | 16.5 | 51 33.9 N21 | 14.7 | Kochab | 137 18.3 | N74 08.1 |
| 19 | 184 13.7 | 84 37.7 | 18.1 | 184 09.8 | 26.9 | 355 25.9 | 16.5 | 66 36.1 | 14.6 | Markab | 13 44.6 | N15 13.9 |
| 20 | 199 16.1 | 99 36.9 | 18.0 | 199 10.6 | 26.3 | 10 28.4 | 16.6 | 81 38.2 | 14.6 | Menkar | 314 21.9 | N 4 06.7 |
| 21 | 214 18.6 | 114 36.0 .. | 17.8 | 214 11.5 .. | 25.6 | 25 30.8 .. | 16.6 | 96 40.4 .. | 14.5 | Menkent | 148 14.8 | S36 24.0 |
| 22 | 229 21.1 | 129 35.1 | 17.7 | 229 12.3 | 24.9 | 40 33.2 | 16.6 | 111 42.5 | 14.5 | Miaplacidus | 221 41.9 | S69 44.5 |
| 23 | 244 23.5 | 144 34.2 | 17.6 | 244 13.2 | 24.3 | 55 35.7 | 16.6 | 126 44.7 | 14.4 | | | |
| 11 00 | 259 26.0 | 159 33.3 N24 | 17.5 | 259 14.0 S 2 | 23.6 | 70 38.1 S 2 | 16.7 | 141 46.9 N21 | 14.4 | Mirfak | 308 50.0 | N49 52.7 |
| 01 | 274 28.5 | 174 32.4 | 17.3 | 274 14.9 | 23.0 | 85 40.5 | 16.7 | 156 49.0 | 14.3 | Nunki | 76 05.7 | S26 17.5 |
| 02 | 289 30.9 | 189 31.6 | 17.2 | 289 15.7 | 22.3 | 100 42.9 | 16.7 | 171 51.2 | 14.3 | Peacock | 53 28.5 | S56 43.0 |
| 03 | 304 33.4 | 204 30.7 .. | 17.1 | 304 16.6 .. | 21.6 | 115 45.4 .. | 16.7 | 186 53.4 .. | 14.2 | Pollux | 243 35.7 | N28 01.0 |
| 04 | 319 35.9 | 219 29.8 | 16.9 | 319 17.4 | 21.0 | 130 47.8 | 16.8 | 201 55.5 | 14.2 | Procyon | 245 06.6 | N 5 12.8 |
| 05 | 334 38.3 | 234 28.9 | 16.8 | 334 18.3 | 20.3 | 145 50.2 | 16.8 | 216 57.7 | 14.1 | | | |
| 06 | 349 40.8 | 249 28.0 N24 | 16.6 | 349 19.1 S 2 | 19.7 | 160 52.7 S 2 | 16.8 | 231 59.9 N21 | 14.1 | Rasalhague | 96 11.9 | N12 33.2 |
| 07 | 4 43.2 | 264 27.2 | 16.5 | 4 20.0 | 19.0 | 175 55.1 | 16.9 | 247 02.0 | 14.0 | Regulus | 207 50.3 | N11 56.6 |
| S 08 | 19 45.7 | 279 26.3 | 16.4 | 19 20.8 | 18.3 | 190 57.5 | 16.9 | 262 04.2 | 14.0 | Rigel | 281 18.4 | S 8 11.6 |
| A 09 | 34 48.2 | 294 25.4 .. | 16.2 | 34 21.7 .. | 17.7 | 205 59.9 .. | 16.9 | 277 06.3 .. | 13.9 | Rigil Kent. | 140 00.2 | S60 51.7 |
| T 10 | 49 50.6 | 309 24.5 | 16.1 | 49 22.5 | 17.0 | 221 02.4 | 16.9 | 292 08.5 | 13.9 | Sabik | 102 19.4 | S15 44.0 |
| U 11 | 64 53.1 | 324 23.6 | 15.9 | 64 23.4 | 16.3 | 236 04.8 | 17.0 | 307 10.7 | 13.8 | | | |
| R 12 | 79 55.6 | 339 22.8 N24 | 15.8 | 79 24.2 S 2 | 15.7 | 251 07.2 S 2 | 17.0 | 322 12.8 N21 | 13.8 | Schedar | 349 48.2 | N56 33.7 |
| D 13 | 94 58.0 | 354 21.9 | 15.6 | 94 25.1 | 15.0 | 266 09.6 | 17.0 | 337 15.0 | 13.7 | Shaula | 96 30.0 | S37 06.6 |
| A 14 | 110 00.5 | 9 21.0 | 15.5 | 109 25.9 | 14.4 | 281 12.1 | 17.0 | 352 17.2 | 13.7 | Sirius | 258 39.6 | S16 43.3 |
| Y 15 | 125 03.0 | 24 20.1 .. | 15.3 | 124 26.8 .. | 13.7 | 296 14.5 .. | 17.1 | 7 19.3 .. | 13.6 | Spica | 158 37.7 | S11 11.5 |
| 16 | 140 05.4 | 39 19.2 | 15.2 | 139 27.6 | 13.0 | 311 16.9 | 17.1 | 22 21.5 | 13.6 | Suhail | 222 57.5 | S43 27.4 |
| 17 | 155 07.9 | 54 18.4 | 15.0 | 154 28.5 | 12.4 | 326 19.3 | 17.1 | 37 23.7 | 13.5 | | | |
| 18 | 170 10.4 | 69 17.5 N24 | 14.9 | 169 29.3 S 2 | 11.7 | 341 21.8 S 2 | 17.2 | 52 25.8 N21 | 13.5 | Vega | 80 42.8 | N38 47.1 |
| 19 | 185 12.8 | 84 16.6 | 14.7 | 184 30.2 | 11.1 | 356 24.2 | 17.2 | 67 28.0 | 13.4 | Zuben'ubi | 137 12.1 | S16 04.0 |
| 20 | 200 15.3 | 99 15.7 | 14.6 | 199 31.0 | 10.4 | 11 26.6 | 17.2 | 82 30.1 | 13.4 | | SHA | Mer.Pass. |
| 21 | 215 17.7 | 114 14.8 .. | 14.4 | 214 31.9 .. | 09.7 | 26 29.0 .. | 17.3 | 97 32.3 .. | 13.3 | | ° ′ | h m |
| 22 | 230 20.2 | 129 14.0 | 14.3 | 229 32.7 | 09.1 | 41 31.5 | 17.3 | 112 34.5 | 13.3 | Venus | 261 27.7 | 13 21 |
| 23 | 245 22.7 | 144 13.1 | 14.1 | 244 33.6 | 08.4 | 56 33.9 | 17.3 | 127 36.6 | 13.2 | Mars | 0 26.8 | 6 44 |
| | h m | | | | | | | | | Jupiter | 171 12.8 | 19 18 |
| Mer. Pass. | 6 45.1 | v −0.9 | d 0.1 | v 0.8 | d 0.7 | v 2.4 | d 0.0 | v 2.2 | d 0.0 | Saturn | 242 28.1 | 14 34 |

*Copyright Council for the Central Laboratory of the Research Councils 2004*

## 2005 JUNE 9, 10, 11 (THURS., FRI., SAT.)

| UT | SUN GHA | SUN Dec | MOON GHA | MOON v | MOON Dec | MOON d | MOON HP | Lat. | Twilight Naut. | Twilight Civil | Sunrise | Moonrise 9 | Moonrise 10 | Moonrise 11 | Moonrise 12 |
|---|---|---|---|---|---|---|---|---|---|---|---|---|---|---|---|
| d h | ° ′ | ° ′ | ° ′ | ′ | ° ′ | ′ | ′ | ° | h m | h m | h m | h m | h m | h m | h m |
|  |  |  |  |  |  |  |  | N 72 | ▭ | ▭ | ▭ | ▭ | ▭ | ▭ | ▭ |
| 9 00 | 180 12.8 | N22 55.4 | 154 13.1 | 9.7 | N27 54.2 | 2.4 | 54.4 | N 70 | ▭ | ▭ | ▭ | ▭ | ▭ | ▭ | 05 35 |
| 01 | 195 12.7 | 55.6 | 168 41.8 | 9.6 | 27 51.8 | 2.5 | 54.4 | 68 | ▭ | ▭ | ▭ | ▭ | ▭ | ▭ | 06 28 |
| 02 | 210 12.6 | 55.8 | 183 10.4 | 9.7 | 27 49.3 | 2.6 | 54.4 | 66 | //// | //// | 00 27 | ▭ | ▭ | 04 43 | 07 00 |
| 03 | 225 12.5 | 56.0 | 197 39.1 | 9.8 | 27 46.7 | 2.8 | 54.4 | 64 | //// | //// | 01 39 | ▭ | ▭ | 05 33 | 07 24 |
| 04 | 240 12.3 | 56.2 | 212 07.9 | 9.8 | 27 43.9 | 3.0 | 54.3 | 62 | //// | //// | 02 14 | 02 24 | 04 19 | 06 04 | 07 42 |
| 05 | 255 12.2 | 56.4 | 226 36.7 | 9.8 | 27 40.9 | 3.0 | 54.3 | 60 | //// | 01 02 | 02 39 | 03 30 | 04 55 | 06 27 | 07 57 |
| 06 | 270 12.1 | N22 56.6 | 241 05.5 | 9.9 | N27 37.9 | 3.2 | 54.3 | N 58 | //// | 01 46 | 02 59 | 04 04 | 05 21 | 06 45 | 08 10 |
| 07 | 285 12.0 | 56.8 | 255 34.4 | 10.0 | 27 34.7 | 3.3 | 54.3 | 56 | //// | 02 14 | 03 15 | 04 29 | 05 42 | 07 01 | 08 21 |
| T 08 | 300 11.9 | 57.0 | 270 03.4 | 9.9 | 27 31.4 | 3.5 | 54.3 | 54 | 00 57 | 02 35 | 03 29 | 04 49 | 05 59 | 07 14 | 08 31 |
| H 09 | 315 11.7 | 57.2 | 284 32.3 | 10.1 | 27 27.9 | 3.6 | 54.3 | 52 | 01 37 | 02 52 | 03 41 | 05 06 | 06 13 | 07 26 | 08 39 |
| U 10 | 330 11.6 | 57.4 | 299 01.4 | 10.1 | 27 24.3 | 3.7 | 54.3 | 50 | 02 03 | 03 07 | 03 51 | 05 20 | 06 26 | 07 36 | 08 47 |
| R 11 | 345 11.5 | 57.7 | 313 30.5 | 10.1 | 27 20.6 | 3.9 | 54.3 | 45 | 02 47 | 03 36 | 04 13 | 05 50 | 06 52 | 07 57 | 09 03 |
| S 12 | 0 11.4 | N22 57.9 | 327 59.6 | 10.2 | N27 16.7 | 4.0 | 54.3 | N 40 | 03 17 | 03 58 | 04 31 | 06 13 | 07 12 | 08 14 | 09 17 |
| D 13 | 15 11.2 | 58.1 | 342 28.8 | 10.2 | 27 12.7 | 4.1 | 54.3 | 35 | 03 39 | 04 16 | 04 46 | 06 31 | 07 29 | 08 29 | 09 28 |
| A 14 | 30 11.1 | 58.3 | 356 58.0 | 10.3 | 27 08.6 | 4.2 | 54.3 | 30 | 03 58 | 04 31 | 04 58 | 06 48 | 07 44 | 08 41 | 09 38 |
| Y 15 | 45 11.0 | 58.5 | 11 27.3 | 10.4 | 27 04.4 | 4.4 | 54.2 | 20 | 04 26 | 04 55 | 05 20 | 07 15 | 08 09 | 09 02 | 09 54 |
| 16 | 60 10.9 | 58.7 | 25 56.7 | 10.4 | 27 00.0 | 4.5 | 54.2 | N 10 | 04 49 | 05 16 | 05 39 | 07 38 | 08 30 | 09 21 | 10 09 |
| 17 | 75 10.7 | 58.9 | 40 26.1 | 10.4 | 26 55.5 | 4.6 | 54.2 | 0 | 05 07 | 05 33 | 05 56 | 08 00 | 08 50 | 09 38 | 10 23 |
| 18 | 90 10.6 | N22 59.1 | 54 55.5 | 10.6 | N26 50.9 | 4.8 | 54.2 | S 10 | 05 24 | 05 50 | 06 13 | 08 22 | 09 10 | 09 55 | 10 36 |
| 19 | 105 10.5 | 59.2 | 69 25.1 | 10.5 | 26 46.1 | 4.9 | 54.2 | 20 | 05 40 | 06 07 | 06 31 | 08 45 | 09 32 | 10 13 | 10 51 |
| 20 | 120 10.4 | 59.4 | 83 54.6 | 10.7 | 26 41.2 | 5.0 | 54.2 | 30 | 05 56 | 06 26 | 06 52 | 09 13 | 09 56 | 10 34 | 11 07 |
| 21 | 135 10.2 | 59.6 | 98 24.3 | 10.7 | 26 36.2 | 5.1 | 54.2 | 35 | 06 04 | 06 36 | 07 04 | 09 29 | 10 11 | 10 46 | 11 17 |
| 22 | 150 10.1 | 22 59.8 | 112 54.0 | 10.7 | 26 31.1 | 5.2 | 54.2 | 40 | 06 14 | 06 47 | 07 18 | 09 47 | 10 27 | 11 00 | 11 27 |
| 23 | 165 10.0 | 23 00.0 | 127 23.7 | 10.8 | 26 25.9 | 5.4 | 54.2 | 45 | 06 24 | 07 01 | 07 34 | 10 10 | 10 47 | 11 16 | 11 40 |
| 10 00 | 180 09.9 | N23 00.2 | 141 53.5 | 10.9 | N26 20.5 | 5.5 | 54.2 | S 50 | 06 35 | 07 16 | 07 55 | 10 38 | 11 12 | 11 37 | 11 55 |
| 01 | 195 09.7 | 00.4 | 156 23.4 | 11.0 | 26 15.0 | 5.6 | 54.2 | 52 | 06 40 | 07 24 | 08 04 | 10 52 | 11 24 | 11 46 | 12 03 |
| 02 | 210 09.6 | 00.6 | 170 53.4 | 11.0 | 26 09.4 | 5.8 | 54.2 | 54 | 06 46 | 07 32 | 08 15 | 11 09 | 11 37 | 11 57 | 12 11 |
| 03 | 225 09.5 | 00.8 | 185 23.4 | 11.0 | 26 03.6 | 5.8 | 54.2 | 56 | 06 52 | 07 41 | 08 27 | 11 28 | 11 53 | 12 09 | 12 19 |
| 04 | 240 09.4 | 01.0 | 199 53.4 | 11.2 | 25 57.8 | 6.0 | 54.2 | 58 | 06 58 | 07 50 | 08 42 | 11 52 | 12 12 | 12 23 | 12 29 |
| 05 | 255 09.2 | 01.2 | 214 23.6 | 11.2 | 25 51.8 | 6.1 | 54.1 | S 60 | 07 05 | 08 02 | 08 59 | 12 23 | 12 35 | 12 39 | 12 41 |

| UT | SUN GHA | SUN Dec | MOON GHA | MOON v | MOON Dec | MOON d | MOON HP | Lat. | Sunset | Twilight Civil | Twilight Naut. | Moonset 9 | Moonset 10 | Moonset 11 | Moonset 12 |
|---|---|---|---|---|---|---|---|---|---|---|---|---|---|---|---|
| 06 | 270 09.1 | N23 01.4 | 228 53.8 | 11.2 | N25 45.7 | 6.2 | 54.1 |  |  |  |  |  |  |  |  |
| 07 | 285 09.0 | 01.6 | 243 24.0 | 11.4 | 25 39.5 | 6.3 | 54.1 |  |  |  |  |  |  |  |  |
| 08 | 300 08.9 | 01.7 | 257 54.4 | 11.3 | 25 33.2 | 6.5 | 54.1 | ° | h m | h m | h m | h m | h m | h m | h m |
| F 09 | 315 08.7 | 01.9 | 272 24.7 | 11.5 | 25 26.7 | 6.5 | 54.1 | N 72 | ▭ | ▭ | ▭ | ▭ | ▭ | ▭ | ▭ |
| R 10 | 330 08.6 | 02.1 | 286 55.2 | 11.5 | 25 20.2 | 6.7 | 54.1 | N 70 | ▭ | ▭ | ▭ | ▭ | ▭ | ▭ | 03 05 |
| I 11 | 345 08.5 | 02.3 | 301 25.7 | 11.6 | 25 13.5 | 6.8 | 54.1 | 68 | ▭ | ▭ | ▭ | ▭ | ▭ | ▭ | 02 11 |
| D 12 | 0 08.4 | N23 02.5 | 315 56.3 | 11.7 | N25 06.7 | 6.8 | 54.1 | 66 | 23 39 | //// | //// | ▭ | ▭ | 02 21 | 01 38 |
| A 13 | 15 08.2 | 02.7 | 330 27.0 | 11.7 | 24 59.9 | 7.0 | 54.1 | 64 | 22 21 | //// | //// | ▭ | ▭ | 01 31 | 01 14 |
| Y 14 | 30 08.1 | 02.9 | 344 57.7 | 11.8 | 24 52.9 | 7.2 | 54.1 | 62 | 21 46 | //// | //// | 01 13 | 01 04 | 00 59 | 00 54 |
| 15 | 45 08.0 | 03.0 | 359 28.5 | 11.9 | 24 45.7 | 7.2 | 54.1 | 60 | 21 21 | 22 59 | //// | 00 07 | 00 27 | 00 35 | 00 38 |
| 16 | 60 07.9 | 03.2 | 13 59.4 | 11.9 | 24 38.5 | 7.3 | 54.1 | N 58 | 21 01 | 22 14 | //// | 24 01 | 00 01 | 00 16 | 00 25 |
| 17 | 75 07.7 | 03.4 | 28 30.3 | 12.0 | 24 31.2 | 7.5 | 54.1 | 56 | 20 45 | 21 46 | //// | 23 40 | 24 00 | 00 00 | 00 13 |
| 18 | 90 07.6 | N23 03.6 | 43 01.3 | 12.1 | N24 23.7 | 7.5 | 54.1 | 54 | 20 31 | 21 24 | 23 04 | 23 23 | 23 46 | 24 03 | 00 03 |
| 19 | 105 07.5 | 03.8 | 57 32.4 | 12.1 | 24 16.2 | 7.7 | 54.1 | 52 | 20 19 | 21 07 | 22 23 | 23 08 | 23 34 | 23 54 | 24 08 |
| 20 | 120 07.3 | 03.9 | 72 03.5 | 12.2 | 24 08.5 | 7.7 | 54.1 | 50 | 20 08 | 20 52 | 21 56 | 22 55 | 23 24 | 23 45 | 24 02 |
| 21 | 135 07.2 | 04.1 | 86 34.7 | 12.3 | 24 00.8 | 7.9 | 54.1 | 45 | 19 46 | 20 23 | 21 12 | 22 28 | 23 01 | 23 28 | 23 49 |
| 22 | 150 07.1 | 04.3 | 101 06.0 | 12.3 | 23 52.9 | 7.9 | 54.1 | N 40 | 19 28 | 20 01 | 20 42 | 22 07 | 22 43 | 23 13 | 23 39 |
| 23 | 165 07.0 | 04.5 | 115 37.3 | 12.4 | 23 45.0 | 8.1 | 54.1 | 35 | 19 14 | 19 43 | 20 20 | 21 49 | 22 28 | 23 01 | 23 29 |
| 11 00 | 180 06.8 | N23 04.7 | 130 08.7 | 12.5 | N23 36.9 | 8.2 | 54.1 | 30 | 19 01 | 19 28 | 20 01 | 21 34 | 22 15 | 22 50 | 23 21 |
| 01 | 195 06.7 | 04.8 | 144 40.2 | 12.5 | 23 28.7 | 8.2 | 54.1 | 20 | 18 39 | 19 04 | 19 33 | 21 08 | 21 52 | 22 31 | 23 07 |
| 02 | 210 06.6 | 05.0 | 159 11.7 | 12.6 | 23 20.5 | 8.4 | 54.1 | N 10 | 18 20 | 18 43 | 19 10 | 20 46 | 21 32 | 22 15 | 22 55 |
| 03 | 225 06.5 | 05.2 | 173 43.3 | 12.7 | 23 12.1 | 8.5 | 54.1 | 0 | 18 03 | 18 26 | 18 52 | 20 25 | 21 14 | 22 00 | 22 43 |
| 04 | 240 06.3 | 05.4 | 188 15.0 | 12.8 | 23 03.6 | 8.6 | 54.1 | S 10 | 17 46 | 18 09 | 18 35 | 20 04 | 20 55 | 21 44 | 22 32 |
| 05 | 255 06.2 | 05.5 | 202 46.8 | 12.8 | 22 55.0 | 8.6 | 54.1 | 20 | 17 28 | 17 52 | 18 19 | 19 41 | 20 35 | 21 28 | 22 19 |
| 06 | 270 06.1 | N23 05.7 | 217 18.6 | 12.9 | N22 46.4 | 8.8 | 54.1 | 30 | 17 07 | 17 33 | 18 03 | 19 15 | 20 12 | 21 09 | 22 05 |
| 07 | 285 05.9 | 05.9 | 231 50.5 | 12.9 | 22 37.6 | 8.9 | 54.1 | 35 | 16 55 | 17 23 | 17 54 | 18 59 | 19 58 | 20 57 | 21 56 |
| S 08 | 300 05.8 | 06.0 | 246 22.4 | 13.0 | 22 28.7 | 8.9 | 54.1 | 40 | 16 41 | 17 11 | 17 45 | 18 41 | 19 42 | 20 44 | 21 46 |
| A 09 | 315 05.7 | 06.2 | 260 54.4 | 13.1 | 22 19.8 | 9.1 | 54.1 | 45 | 16 24 | 16 58 | 17 35 | 18 19 | 19 23 | 20 29 | 21 35 |
| T 10 | 330 05.6 | 06.4 | 275 26.5 | 13.2 | 22 10.7 | 9.1 | 54.1 | S 50 | 16 04 | 16 42 | 17 24 | 17 51 | 18 59 | 20 10 | 21 21 |
| U 11 | 345 05.4 | 06.6 | 289 58.7 | 13.2 | 22 01.6 | 9.2 | 54.1 | 52 | 15 54 | 16 35 | 17 19 | 17 37 | 18 47 | 20 01 | 21 15 |
| R 12 | 0 05.3 | N23 06.7 | 304 30.9 | 13.3 | N21 52.4 | 9.4 | 54.1 | 54 | 15 44 | 16 27 | 17 13 | 17 21 | 18 34 | 19 51 | 21 07 |
| D 13 | 15 05.2 | 06.9 | 319 03.2 | 13.3 | 21 43.0 | 9.4 | 54.1 | 56 | 15 31 | 16 18 | 17 07 | 17 02 | 18 19 | 19 39 | 20 59 |
| A 14 | 30 05.1 | 07.1 | 333 35.5 | 13.5 | 21 33.6 | 9.5 | 54.1 | 58 | 15 17 | 16 08 | 17 00 | 16 38 | 18 01 | 19 26 | 20 50 |
| Y 15 | 45 04.9 | 07.2 | 348 08.0 | 13.4 | 21 24.1 | 9.6 | 54.1 | S 60 | 15 00 | 15 57 | 16 53 | 16 07 | 17 38 | 19 10 | 20 39 |
| 16 | 60 04.8 | 07.4 | 2 40.4 | 13.6 | 21 14.5 | 9.7 | 54.1 |  |  |  |  |  |  |  |  |
| 17 | 75 04.7 | 07.6 | 17 13.0 | 13.6 | 21 04.8 | 9.7 | 54.1 |  | SUN | | | MOON | | | |
| 18 | 90 04.5 | N23 07.7 | 31 45.6 | 13.7 | N20 55.1 | 9.9 | 54.1 | Day | Eqn. of Time | | Mer. Pass. | Mer. Pass. Upper | Mer. Pass. Lower | Age | Phase |
| 19 | 105 04.4 | 07.9 | 46 18.3 | 13.7 | 20 45.2 | 9.9 | 54.1 |  | 00ʰ | 12ʰ |  |  |  |  |  |
| 20 | 120 04.3 | 08.0 | 60 51.0 | 13.8 | 20 35.3 | 10.1 | 54.1 | d | m s | m s | h m | h m | h m | d | % |
| 21 | 135 04.2 | 08.2 | 75 23.8 | 13.9 | 20 25.2 | 10.1 | 54.1 | 9 | 00 52 | 00 46 | 11 59 | 14 13 | 01 47 | 03 | 6 |
| 22 | 150 04.0 | 08.4 | 89 56.7 | 13.9 | 20 15.1 | 10.2 | 54.1 | 10 | 00 40 | 00 34 | 11 59 | 15 02 | 02 38 | 04 | 12 |
| 23 | 165 03.9 | 08.5 | 104 29.6 | 14.0 | N20 04.9 | 10.3 | 54.1 | 11 | 00 28 | 00 21 | 12 00 | 15 49 | 03 26 | 05 | 19 |
|  | SD 15.8 | d 0.2 | SD 14.8 |  | 14.7 |  | 14.7 |  |  |  |  |  |  |  |  |

*Copyright Council for the Central Laboratory of the Research Councils 2004*

# SIGHT REDUCTION TABLE

LATITUDE / A: 48° – 53°

B: (−) for 90° < LHA < 270°
Dec:(−) for Lat. contrary name

$Z_1$: same sign as B
$Z_2$: (−) for F > 90°

| Lat. / A | 48° | | | 49° | | | 50° | | | 51° | | | 52° | | | 53° | | | Lat. / A |
|---|---|---|---|---|---|---|---|---|---|---|---|---|---|---|---|---|---|---|---|
| LHA/F | A/H | B/P | $Z_1/Z_2$ | A/H | B/P | $Z_1/Z_2$ | A/H | B/P | $Z_1/Z_2$ | A/H | B/P | $Z_1/Z_2$ | A/H | B/P | $Z_1/Z_2$ | A/H | B/P | $Z_1/Z_2$ | LHA |
| 0 / 180 | 0 00 | 42 00 | 90·0 | 0 00 | 41 00 | 90·0 | 0 00 | 40 00 | 90·0 | 0 00 | 39 00 | 90·0 | 0 00 | 38 00 | 90·0 | 0 00 | 37 00 | 90·0 | 180 / 360 |
| 1 / 179 | 0 40 | 42 00 | 89·3 | 0 39 | 41 00 | 89·3 | 0 39 | 40 00 | 89·2 | 0 38 | 39 00 | 89·2 | 0 37 | 38 00 | 89·2 | 0 36 | 37 00 | 89·2 | 181 / 359 |
| 2 / 178 | 1 20 | 41 59 | 88·5 | 1 19 | 40 59 | 88·5 | 1 17 | 39 59 | 88·5 | 1 16 | 38 59 | 88·4 | 1 14 | 37 59 | 88·4 | 1 12 | 36 59 | 88·4 | 182 / 358 |
| 3 / 177 | 2 00 | 41 58 | 87·8 | 1 58 | 40 58 | 87·7 | 1 56 | 39 58 | 87·7 | 1 53 | 38 58 | 87·6 | 1 51 | 37 58 | 87·6 | 1 48 | 36 58 | 87·6 | 183 / 357 |
| 4 / 176 | 2 41 | 41 56 | 87·0 | 2 37 | 40 56 | 87·0 | 2 34 | 39 56 | 86·9 | 2 31 | 38 56 | 86·9 | 2 28 | 37 56 | 86·8 | 2 24 | 36 56 | 86·8 | 184 / 356 |
| 5 / 175 | 3 21 | 41 53 | 86·3 | 3 17 | 40 54 | 86·2 | 3 13 | 39 54 | 86·2 | 3 09 | 38 54 | 86·1 | 3 05 | 37 54 | 86·1 | 3 00 | 36 54 | 86·0 | 185 / 355 |
| 6 / 174 | 4 01 | 41 51 | 85·5 | 3 56 | 40 51 | 85·5 | 3 51 | 39 51 | 85·4 | 3 46 | 38 51 | 85·3 | 3 41 | 37 51 | 85·3 | 3 36 | 36 51 | 85·2 | 186 / 354 |
| 7 / 173 | 4 41 | 41 47 | 84·8 | 4 35 | 40 47 | 84·7 | 4 30 | 39 47 | 84·6 | 4 24 | 38 47 | 84·5 | 4 18 | 37 48 | 84·5 | 4 12 | 36 48 | 84·4 | 187 / 353 |
| 8 / 172 | 5 21 | 41 43 | 84·0 | 5 15 | 40 43 | 83·9 | 5 08 | 39 43 | 83·9 | 5 01 | 38 44 | 83·8 | 4 55 | 37 44 | 83·7 | 4 48 | 36 44 | 83·6 | 188 / 352 |
| 9 / 171 | 6 01 | 41 39 | 83·3 | 5 53 | 40 39 | 83·2 | 5 46 | 39 39 | 83·1 | 5 39 | 38 39 | 83·0 | 5 32 | 37 39 | 82·9 | 5 24 | 36 40 | 82·8 | 189 / 351 |
| 10 / 170 | 6 40 | 41 34 | 82·5 | 6 32 | 40 34 | 82·4 | 6 25 | 39 34 | 82·3 | 6 16 | 38 34 | 82·2 | 6 08 | 37 35 | 82·1 | 6 00 | 36 35 | 82·0 | 190 / 350 |
| 11 / 169 | 7 20 | 41 28 | 81·8 | 7 11 | 40 28 | 81·7 | 7 03 | 39 29 | 81·5 | 6 54 | 38 29 | 81·4 | 6 45 | 37 29 | 81·3 | 6 36 | 36 29 | 81·2 | 191 / 349 |
| 12 / 168 | 8 00 | 41 22 | 81·0 | 7 50 | 40 22 | 80·9 | 7 41 | 39 23 | 80·8 | 7 31 | 38 23 | 80·6 | 7 21 | 37 23 | 80·5 | 7 11 | 36 24 | 80·4 | 192 / 348 |
| 13 / 167 | 8 39 | 41 16 | 80·3 | 8 29 | 40 16 | 80·1 | 8 19 | 39 16 | 80·0 | 8 08 | 38 16 | 79·9 | 7 58 | 37 17 | 79·7 | 7 47 | 36 17 | 79·6 | 193 / 347 |
| 14 / 166 | 9 19 | 41 09 | 79·5 | 9 08 | 40 09 | 79·3 | 8 57 | 39 09 | 79·2 | 8 45 | 38 09 | 79·0 | 8 34 | 37 10 | 78·9 | 8 22 | 36 10 | 78·7 | 194 / 346 |
| 15 / 165 | 9 58 | 41 01 | 78·7 | 9 47 | 40 01 | 78·6 | 9 35 | 39 02 | 78·4 | 9 22 | 38 02 | 78·2 | 9 10 | 37 02 | 78·1 | 8 58 | 36 03 | 77·9 | 195 / 345 |
| 16 / 164 | 10 38 | 40 53 | 78·0 | 10 25 | 39 53 | 77·8 | 10 12 | 38 53 | 77·6 | 9 59 | 37 54 | 77·4 | 9 46 | 36 54 | 77·3 | 9 33 | 35 55 | 77·1 | 196 / 344 |
| 17 / 163 | 11 17 | 40 44 | 77·2 | 11 04 | 39 44 | 77·0 | 10 50 | 38 45 | 76·8 | 10 36 | 37 45 | 76·6 | 10 22 | 36 46 | 76·5 | 10 08 | 35 47 | 76·3 | 197 / 343 |
| 18 / 162 | 11 56 | 40 34 | 76·4 | 11 42 | 39 35 | 76·2 | 11 27 | 38 35 | 76·0 | 11 13 | 37 36 | 75·8 | 10 58 | 36 37 | 75·6 | 10 43 | 35 38 | 75·5 | 198 / 342 |
| 19 / 161 | 12 35 | 40 25 | 75·6 | 12 20 | 39 25 | 75·4 | 12 05 | 38 26 | 75·2 | 11 49 | 37 26 | 75·0 | 11 34 | 36 27 | 74·8 | 11 18 | 35 28 | 74·6 | 199 / 341 |
| 20 / 160 | 13 14 | 40 14 | 74·9 | 12 58 | 39 15 | 74·6 | 12 42 | 38 15 | 74·4 | 12 26 | 37 16 | 74·2 | 12 09 | 36 17 | 74·0 | 11 53 | 35 18 | 73·8 | 200 / 340 |
| 21 / 159 | 13 52 | 40 03 | 74·1 | 13 36 | 39 04 | 73·8 | 13 19 | 38 04 | 73·6 | 13 02 | 37 05 | 73·4 | 12 45 | 36 06 | 73·2 | 12 27 | 35 08 | 73·0 | 201 / 339 |
| 22 / 158 | 14 31 | 39 51 | 73·3 | 14 14 | 38 52 | 73·0 | 13 56 | 37 53 | 72·8 | 13 38 | 36 54 | 72·6 | 13 20 | 35 55 | 72·3 | 13 02 | 34 56 | 72·1 | 202 / 338 |
| 23 / 157 | 15 09 | 39 39 | 72·5 | 14 51 | 38 40 | 72·2 | 14 33 | 37 41 | 72·0 | 14 14 | 36 42 | 71·7 | 13 55 | 35 43 | 71·5 | 13 36 | 34 45 | 71·3 | 203 / 337 |
| 24 / 156 | 15 48 | 39 26 | 71·7 | 15 29 | 38 27 | 71·4 | 15 09 | 37 28 | 71·2 | 14 50 | 36 30 | 70·9 | 14 30 | 35 31 | 70·7 | 14 10 | 34 33 | 70·4 | 204 / 336 |
| 25 / 155 | 16 26 | 39 13 | 70·9 | 16 06 | 38 14 | 70·6 | 15 46 | 38 15 | 70·6 | 15 25 | 36 17 | 70·1 | 15 05 | 35 18 | 69·8 | 14 44 | 34 20 | 69·6 | 205 / 335 |
| 26 / 154 | 17 03 | 38 59 | 70·1 | 16 43 | 38 00 | 69·8 | 16 22 | 37 01 | 69·5 | 16 01 | 36 03 | 69·2 | 15 39 | 35 05 | 69·0 | 15 18 | 34 07 | 68·7 | 206 / 334 |
| 27 / 153 | 17 41 | 38 44 | 69·3 | 17 20 | 37 46 | 69·0 | 16 58 | 36 47 | 68·7 | 16 36 | 35 49 | 68·4 | 16 14 | 34 51 | 68·1 | 15 51 | 33 53 | 67·9 | 207 / 333 |
| 28 / 152 | 18 19 | 38 29 | 68·4 | 17 56 | 37 30 | 68·1 | 17 34 | 36 32 | 67·8 | 17 11 | 35 34 | 67·5 | 16 48 | 34 36 | 67·3 | 16 25 | 33 38 | 67·0 | 208 / 332 |
| 29 / 151 | 18 56 | 38 13 | 67·6 | 18 33 | 37 15 | 67·3 | 18 09 | 36 16 | 67·0 | 17 46 | 35 18 | 66·7 | 17 22 | 34 21 | 66·4 | 16 58 | 33 23 | 66·1 | 209 / 331 |
| 30 / 150 | 19 33 | 37 57 | 66·8 | 19 09 | 36 58 | 66·5 | 18 45 | 36 00 | 66·1 | 18 20 | 35 03 | 65·8 | 17 56 | 34 05 | 65·5 | 17 31 | 33 08 | 65·2 | 210 / 330 |
| 31 / 149 | 20 10 | 37 40 | 65·9 | 19 45 | 36 41 | 65·6 | 19 20 | 35 44 | 65·3 | 18 55 | 34 46 | 64·9 | 18 29 | 33 49 | 64·6 | 18 03 | 32 52 | 64·4 | 211 / 329 |
| 32 / 148 | 20 46 | 37 22 | 65·1 | 20 21 | 36 24 | 64·8 | 19 55 | 35 26 | 64·4 | 19 29 | 34 29 | 64·1 | 19 02 | 33 32 | 63·8 | 18 36 | 32 35 | 63·5 | 212 / 328 |
| 33 / 147 | 21 22 | 37 03 | 64·2 | 20 56 | 36 06 | 63·9 | 20 30 | 35 08 | 63·6 | 20 03 | 34 11 | 63·2 | 19 35 | 33 14 | 62·9 | 19 08 | 32 18 | 62·6 | 213 / 327 |
| 34 / 146 | 21 58 | 36 44 | 63·4 | 21 31 | 35 47 | 63·1 | 21 04 | 34 49 | 62·7 | 20 36 | 33 53 | 62·3 | 20 08 | 32 56 | 62·0 | 19 40 | 32 00 | 61·7 | 214 / 326 |
| 35 / 145 | 22 34 | 36 25 | 62·5 | 22 06 | 35 27 | 62·1 | 21 38 | 34 30 | 61·8 | 21 10 | 33 33 | 61·4 | 20 41 | 32 37 | 61·1 | 20 12 | 31 41 | 60·8 | 215 / 325 |
| 36 / 144 | 23 10 | 36 04 | 61·6 | 22 41 | 35 07 | 61·3 | 22 12 | 34 10 | 60·9 | 21 43 | 33 14 | 60·5 | 21 13 | 32 18 | 60·2 | 20 43 | 31 22 | 59·9 | 216 / 324 |
| 37 / 143 | 23 45 | 35 43 | 60·8 | 23 15 | 34 46 | 60·4 | 22 45 | 33 50 | 60·0 | 22 15 | 32 53 | 59·6 | 21 45 | 31 58 | 59·3 | 21 14 | 31 02 | 58·9 | 217 / 323 |
| 38 / 142 | 24 20 | 35 21 | 59·9 | 23 49 | 34 25 | 59·5 | 23 19 | 33 28 | 59·1 | 22 48 | 32 33 | 58·7 | 22 16 | 31 37 | 58·4 | 21 45 | 30 42 | 58·0 | 218 / 322 |
| 39 / 141 | 24 54 | 34 59 | 59·0 | 24 23 | 34 02 | 58·6 | 23 52 | 33 07 | 58·2 | 23 20 | 32 11 | 57·8 | 22 48 | 31 16 | 57·5 | 22 15 | 30 21 | 57·1 | 219 / 321 |
| 40 / 140 | 25 28 | 34 36 | 58·1 | 24 57 | 33 40 | 57·7 | 24 24 | 32 44 | 57·3 | 23 52 | 31 49 | 56·9 | 23 19 | 30 54 | 56·5 | 22 45 | 30 00 | 56·2 | 220 / 320 |
| 41 / 139 | 26 02 | 34 12 | 57·1 | 25 30 | 33 16 | 56·7 | 24 57 | 32 21 | 56·3 | 24 23 | 31 26 | 55·9 | 23 49 | 30 32 | 55·6 | 23 15 | 29 38 | 55·2 | 221 / 319 |
| 42 / 138 | 26 36 | 33 47 | 56·2 | 26 02 | 32 52 | 55·8 | 25 28 | 31 57 | 55·4 | 24 54 | 31 02 | 55·0 | 24 20 | 30 08 | 54·6 | 23 45 | 29 15 | 54·3 | 222 / 318 |
| 43 / 137 | 27 09 | 33 22 | 55·3 | 26 35 | 32 27 | 54·9 | 26 00 | 31 32 | 54·5 | 25 25 | 30 38 | 54·1 | 24 50 | 29 45 | 53·7 | 24 14 | 28 52 | 53·3 | 223 / 317 |
| 44 / 136 | 27 42 | 32 56 | 54·3 | 27 07 | 32 01 | 53·9 | 26 31 | 31 07 | 53·5 | 25 55 | 30 13 | 53·1 | 25 19 | 29 20 | 52·7 | 24 43 | 28 28 | 52·4 | 224 / 316 |
| 45 / 135 | 28 14 | 32 29 | 53·4 | 27 38 | 31 35 | 53·0 | 27 02 | 30 41 | 52·5 | 26 25 | 29 48 | 52·1 | 25 48 | 28 55 | 51·8 | 25 11 | 28 03 | 51·4 | 225 / 315 |

## SIGHT REDUCTION TABLE

| Lat./A LHA/F | 30° A/H | B/P | Z₁/Z₂ | 31° A/H | B/P | Z₁/Z₂ | 32° A/H | B/P | Z₁/Z₂ | 33° A/H | B/P | Z₁/Z₂ | 34° A/H | B/P | Z₁/Z₂ | 35° A/H | B/P | Z₁/Z₂ | Lat./A LHA |
|---|---|---|---|---|---|---|---|---|---|---|---|---|---|---|---|---|---|---|---|
| 45 135 | 37 46 | 50 46 | 63·4 | 37 19 | 49 39 | 62·7 | 36 51 | 48 32 | 62·1 | 36 22 | 47 26 | 61·4 | 35 53 | 46 21 | 60·8 | 35 24 | 45 17 | 60·2 | 225 315 |
| 46 134 | 38 32 | 50 16 | 62·6 | 38 04 | 49 08 | 61·9 | 37 36 | 48 02 | 61·2 | 37 06 | 46 56 | 60·6 | 36 37 | 45 51 | 59·9 | 36 06 | 44 46 | 59·3 | 226 314 |
| 47 133 | 39 18 | 49 45 | 61·8 | 38 49 | 48 37 | 61·1 | 38 20 | 47 30 | 60·4 | 37 50 | 46 24 | 59·7 | 37 19 | 45 19 | 59·1 | 36 48 | 44 15 | 58·4 | 227 313 |
| 48 132 | 40 04 | 49 13 | 61·0 | 39 34 | 48 05 | 60·2 | 39 04 | 46 58 | 59·5 | 38 33 | 45 51 | 58·8 | 38 02 | 44 46 | 58·2 | 37 30 | 43 42 | 57·5 | 228 312 |
| 49 131 | 40 49 | 48 39 | 60·1 | 40 19 | 47 31 | 59·4 | 39 48 | 46 24 | 58·6 | 39 16 | 45 18 | 57·9 | 38 44 | 44 12 | 57·2 | 38 11 | 43 08 | 56·6 | 229 311 |
| 50 130 | 41 34 | 48 04 | 59·2 | 41 03 | 46 56 | 58·5 | 40 31 | 45 49 | 57·7 | 39 59 | 44 42 | 57·0 | 39 26 | 43 37 | 56·3 | 38 52 | 42 33 | 55·6 | 230 310 |
| 51 129 | 42 18 | 47 28 | 58·3 | 41 46 | 46 20 | 57·5 | 41 14 | 45 12 | 56·8 | 40 41 | 44 06 | 56·1 | 40 07 | 43 01 | 55·4 | 39 32 | 41 57 | 54·7 | 231 309 |
| 52 128 | 43 02 | 46 50 | 57·4 | 42 29 | 45 42 | 56·6 | 41 56 | 44 34 | 55·9 | 41 22 | 43 28 | 55·1 | 40 47 | 42 23 | 54·4 | 40 12 | 41 19 | 53·7 | 232 308 |
| 53 127 | 43 46 | 46 11 | 56·4 | 43 12 | 45 03 | 55·6 | 42 38 | 43 55 | 54·9 | 42 03 | 42 49 | 54·1 | 41 28 | 41 44 | 53·4 | 40 52 | 40 41 | 52·7 | 233 307 |
| 54 126 | 44 29 | 45 31 | 55·5 | 43 54 | 44 22 | 54·7 | 43 19 | 43 15 | 53·9 | 42 44 | 42 09 | 53·1 | 42 07 | 41 04 | 52·4 | 41 30 | 40 01 | 51·7 | 234 306 |
| 55 125 | 45 11 | 44 49 | 54·5 | 44 36 | 43 40 | 53·7 | 44 00 | 42 33 | 52·9 | 43 24 | 41 27 | 52·1 | 42 46 | 40 23 | 51·4 | 42 09 | 39 19 | 50·7 | 235 305 |
| 56 124 | 45 53 | 44 05 | 53·5 | 45 17 | 42 57 | 52·6 | 44 40 | 41 50 | 51·8 | 44 03 | 40 44 | 51·1 | 43 25 | 39 40 | 50·3 | 42 46 | 38 37 | 49·6 | 236 304 |
| 57 123 | 46 35 | 43 20 | 52·4 | 45 58 | 42 11 | 51·6 | 45 20 | 41 05 | 50·8 | 44 42 | 39 59 | 50·0 | 44 03 | 38 55 | 49·3 | 43 24 | 37 53 | 48·5 | 237 303 |
| 58 122 | 47 16 | 42 33 | 51·3 | 46 38 | 41 25 | 50·5 | 45 59 | 40 18 | 49·7 | 45 20 | 39 13 | 48·9 | 44 40 | 38 09 | 48·2 | 44 00 | 37 07 | 47·5 | 238 302 |
| 59 121 | 47 56 | 41 44 | 50·2 | 47 17 | 40 36 | 49·4 | 46 38 | 39 30 | 48·6 | 45 58 | 38 25 | 47·8 | 45 17 | 37 22 | 47·1 | 44 36 | 36 20 | 46·3 | 239 301 |
| 60 120 | 48 35 | 40 54 | 49·1 | 47 56 | 39 46 | 48·3 | 47 16 | 38 40 | 47·5 | 46 35 | 37 36 | 46·7 | 45 53 | 36 33 | 46·0 | 45 11 | 35 32 | 45·2 | 240 300 |
| 61 119 | 49 14 | 40 01 | 47·9 | 48 34 | 38 54 | 47·1 | 47 53 | 37 48 | 46·3 | 47 11 | 36 45 | 45·5 | 46 29 | 35 42 | 44·7 | 45 46 | 34 42 | 44·0 | 241 299 |
| 62 118 | 49 53 | 39 07 | 46·8 | 49 11 | 38 00 | 45·9 | 48 29 | 36 55 | 45·1 | 47 46 | 35 52 | 44·3 | 47 03 | 34 50 | 43·6 | 46 19 | 33 50 | 42·8 | 242 298 |
| 63 117 | 50 30 | 38 11 | 45·5 | 49 48 | 37 04 | 44·7 | 49 05 | 36 00 | 43·9 | 48 21 | 34 57 | 43·1 | 47 37 | 33 57 | 42·3 | 46 53 | 32 57 | 41·6 | 243 297 |
| 64 116 | 51 07 | 37 13 | 44·3 | 50 23 | 36 07 | 43·4 | 49 40 | 35 03 | 42·6 | 48 55 | 34 01 | 41·8 | 48 10 | 33 01 | 41·1 | 47 25 | 32 03 | 40·4 | 244 296 |
| 65 115 | 51 43 | 36 12 | 43·0 | 50 58 | 35 07 | 42·2 | 50 14 | 34 04 | 41·3 | 49 28 | 33 03 | 40·6 | 48 43 | 32 04 | 39·8 | 47 56 | 31 07 | 39·1 | 245 295 |
| 66 114 | 52 18 | 35 10 | 41·7 | 51 33 | 34 06 | 40·8 | 50 47 | 33 04 | 40·0 | 50 01 | 32 04 | 39·3 | 49 14 | 31 05 | 38·5 | 48 27 | 30 09 | 37·8 | 246 294 |
| 67 113 | 52 52 | 34 05 | 40·3 | 52 06 | 33 02 | 39·5 | 51 19 | 32 01 | 38·7 | 50 34 | 31 02 | 37·9 | 49 44 | 30 05 | 37·2 | 48 56 | 29 10 | 36·5 | 247 293 |
| 68 112 | 53 25 | 32 59 | 38·9 | 52 38 | 31 56 | 38·1 | 51 50 | 30 57 | 37·3 | 51 02 | 29 59 | 36·6 | 50 14 | 29 03 | 35·8 | 49 25 | 28 09 | 35·2 | 248 292 |
| 69 111 | 53 57 | 31 50 | 37·5 | 53 09 | 30 49 | 36·7 | 52 21 | 29 50 | 35·9 | 51 32 | 28 53 | 35·2 | 50 43 | 27 59 | 34·5 | 49 53 | 27 06 | 33·8 | 249 291 |
| 70 110 | 54 28 | 30 39 | 36·1 | 53 39 | 29 39 | 35·2 | 52 50 | 28 42 | 34·5 | 52 00 | 27 46 | 33·8 | 51 10 | 26 53 | 33·1 | 50 20 | 26 02 | 32·4 | 250 290 |
| 71 109 | 54 58 | 29 25 | 34·6 | 54 08 | 28 27 | 33·8 | 53 18 | 27 31 | 33·0 | 52 28 | 26 37 | 32·3 | 51 37 | 25 46 | 31·6 | 50 46 | 24 56 | 31·0 | 251 289 |
| 72 108 | 55 27 | 28 09 | 33·0 | 54 37 | 27 13 | 32·2 | 53 46 | 26 19 | 31·5 | 52 55 | 25 27 | 30·8 | 52 03 | 24 37 | 30·2 | 51 10 | 23 49 | 29·5 | 252 288 |
| 73 107 | 55 55 | 26 51 | 31·4 | 55 03 | 25 57 | 30·7 | 54 12 | 25 04 | 30·0 | 53 19 | 24 14 | 29·3 | 52 27 | 23 26 | 28·7 | 51 34 | 22 40 | 28·1 | 253 287 |
| 74 106 | 56 21 | 25 31 | 29·8 | 55 29 | 24 39 | 29·1 | 54 36 | 23 48 | 28·4 | 53 43 | 23 00 | 27·8 | 52 50 | 22 14 | 27·1 | 51 57 | 21 29 | 26·6 | 254 286 |
| 75 105 | 56 46 | 24 09 | 28·2 | 55 53 | 23 18 | 27·5 | 55 00 | 22 30 | 26·8 | 54 06 | 21 44 | 26·2 | 53 12 | 21 00 | 25·6 | 52 18 | 20 17 | 25·0 | 255 285 |
| 76 104 | 57 10 | 22 44 | 26·5 | 56 16 | 21 56 | 25·8 | 55 22 | 21 10 | 25·2 | 54 28 | 20 26 | 24·6 | 53 33 | 19 44 | 24·0 | 52 38 | 19 04 | 23·5 | 256 284 |
| 77 103 | 57 33 | 21 17 | 24·8 | 56 38 | 20 31 | 24·1 | 55 43 | 19 48 | 23·5 | 54 48 | 19 06 | 23·0 | 53 53 | 18 27 | 22·4 | 52 57 | 17 49 | 21·9 | 257 283 |
| 78 102 | 57 54 | 19 48 | 23·0 | 56 59 | 19 05 | 22·4 | 56 03 | 18 24 | 21·9 | 55 07 | 17 45 | 21·3 | 54 11 | 17 08 | 20·8 | 53 15 | 16 32 | 20·3 | 258 282 |
| 79 101 | 58 15 | 18 17 | 21·2 | 57 19 | 17 37 | 20·7 | 56 21 | 16 59 | 20·1 | 55 25 | 16 22 | 19·6 | 54 28 | 15 48 | 19·1 | 53 31 | 15 15 | 18·7 | 259 281 |
| 80 100 | 58 32 | 16 44 | 19·4 | 57 37 | 16 07 | 18·9 | 56 38 | 15 32 | 18·4 | 55 41 | 14 58 | 17·9 | 54 44 | 14 26 | 17·5 | 53 47 | 13 56 | 17·1 | 260 280 |
| 81 99 | 58 48 | 15 10 | 17·6 | 57 51 | 14 36 | 17·1 | 56 53 | 14 03 | 16·6 | 55 56 | 13 33 | 16·2 | 54 58 | 13 03 | 15·8 | 54 00 | 12 36 | 15·4 | 261 279 |
| 82 98 | 59 03 | 13 33 | 15·7 | 58 05 | 13 02 | 15·3 | 57 07 | 12 33 | 14·9 | 56 09 | 12 06 | 14·5 | 55 11 | 11 40 | 14·1 | 54 13 | 11 14 | 13·8 | 262 278 |
| 83 97 | 59 16 | 11 55 | 13·8 | 58 18 | 11 28 | 13·4 | 57 19 | 11 02 | 13·0 | 56 21 | 10 38 | 12·7 | 55 22 | 10 14 | 12·4 | 54 24 | 9 52 | 12·1 | 263 277 |
| 84 96 | 59 28 | 10 16 | 11·9 | 58 29 | 9 52 | 11·5 | 57 30 | 9 30 | 11·2 | 56 31 | 9 09 | 10·9 | 55 32 | 8 49 | 10·6 | 54 33 | 8 29 | 10·4 | 264 276 |
| 85 95 | 59 37 | 8 35 | 9·9 | 58 38 | 8 15 | 9·6 | 57 39 | 7 56 | 9·4 | 56 40 | 7 39 | 9·1 | 55 41 | 7 22 | 8·9 | 54 41 | 7 06 | 8·7 | 265 275 |
| 86 94 | 59 46 | 6 53 | 8·0 | 58 46 | 6 37 | 7·7 | 57 47 | 6 22 | 7·5 | 56 47 | 6 08 | 7·3 | 55 48 | 5 54 | 7·1 | 54 48 | 5 41 | 7·0 | 266 274 |
| 87 93 | 59 52 | 5 11 | 6·0 | 58 52 | 4 59 | 5·8 | 57 52 | 4 47 | 5·6 | 56 53 | 4 36 | 5·5 | 55 53 | 4 26 | 5·4 | 54 53 | 4 16 | 5·2 | 267 273 |
| 88 92 | 59 56 | 3 28 | 4·0 | 58 57 | 3 19 | 3·9 | 57 57 | 3 12 | 3·8 | 56 57 | 3 05 | 3·7 | 55 57 | 2 58 | 3·6 | 54 57 | 2 51 | 3·5 | 268 272 |
| 89 91 | 59 59 | 1 44 | 2·0 | 58 59 | 1 40 | 1·9 | 57 59 | 1 36 | 1·9 | 56 59 | 1 32 | 1·8 | 55 59 | 1 29 | 1·8 | 54 59 | 1 26 | 1·7 | 269 271 |
| 90 90 | 60 00 | 0 00 | 0·0 | 59 00 | 0 00 | 0·0 | 58 00 | 0 00 | 0·0 | 57 00 | 0 00 | 0·0 | 56 00 | 0 00 | 0·0 | 55 00 | 0 00 | 0·0 | 270 270 |

N. Lat.: for LHA > 180° ... $Z_n = Z$
for LHA < 180° ... $Z_n = 360° − Z$

S. Lat.: for LHA > 180° ... $Z_n = 180° − Z$
for LHA < 180° ... $Z_n = 180° + Z$

## SIGHT REDUCTION TABLE

| Lat. / A | 48° | | | 49° | | | 50° | | | 51° | | | 52° | | | 53° | | | Lat. / A |
|---|---|---|---|---|---|---|---|---|---|---|---|---|---|---|---|---|---|---|---|
| LHA/F | A/H | B/P | $Z_1/Z_2$ | A/H | B/P | $Z_1/Z_2$ | A/H | B/P | $Z_1/Z_2$ | A/H | B/P | $Z_1/Z_2$ | A/H | B/P | $Z_1/Z_2$ | A/H | B/P | $Z_1/Z_2$ | LHA |
| ° | ° ′ | ° ′ | ° | ° ′ | ° ′ | ° | ° ′ | ° ′ | ° | ° ′ | ° ′ | ° | ° ′ | ° ′ | ° | ° ′ | ° ′ | ° | ° |
| 45 | 28 14 | 32 29 | 53.4 | 27 38 | 31 35 | 53.0 | 27 02 | 30 41 | 52.5 | 26 25 | 29 48 | 52.1 | 25 48 | 28 55 | 51.8 | 25 11 | 28 03 | 51.4 | 225 | 315 |
| 46 | 28 46 | 32 01 | 52.4 | 28 10 | 31 08 | 52.0 | 27 32 | 30 14 | 51.6 | 26 55 | 29 22 | 51.2 | 26 17 | 28 29 | 50.8 | 25 39 | 27 38 | 50.4 | 226 | 314 |
| 47 | 29 18 | 31 33 | 51.4 | 28 40 | 30 40 | 51.0 | 28 02 | 29 47 | 50.6 | 27 24 | 28 55 | 50.2 | 26 46 | 28 03 | 49.8 | 26 07 | 27 12 | 49.4 | 227 | 313 |
| 48 | 29 49 | 31 04 | 50.5 | 29 11 | 30 11 | 50.0 | 28 32 | 29 19 | 49.6 | 27 53 | 28 27 | 49.2 | 27 14 | 27 36 | 48.8 | 26 34 | 26 46 | 48.4 | 228 | 312 |
| 49 | 30 20 | 30 34 | 49.5 | 29 41 | 29 42 | 49.0 | 29 01 | 28 50 | 48.6 | 28 21 | 27 59 | 48.2 | 27 41 | 27 08 | 47.8 | 27 01 | 26 18 | 47.4 | 229 | 311 |
| 50 | 30 50 | 30 04 | 48.5 | 30 10 | 29 12 | 48.0 | 29 30 | 28 20 | 47.6 | 28 49 | 27 30 | 47.2 | 28 08 | 26 40 | 46.8 | 27 27 | 25 51 | 46.4 | 230 | 310 |
| 51 | 31 20 | 29 32 | 47.5 | 30 39 | 28 41 | 47.0 | 29 58 | 27 50 | 46.6 | 29 17 | 27 00 | 46.2 | 28 35 | 26 11 | 45.8 | 27 53 | 25 22 | 45.4 | 231 | 309 |
| 52 | 31 49 | 29 00 | 46.4 | 31 08 | 28 09 | 46.0 | 30 26 | 27 19 | 45.6 | 29 44 | 26 30 | 45.2 | 29 01 | 25 41 | 44.8 | 28 19 | 24 53 | 44.4 | 232 | 308 |
| 53 | 32 18 | 28 27 | 45.4 | 31 36 | 27 37 | 45.0 | 30 53 | 26 48 | 44.6 | 30 10 | 25 59 | 44.1 | 29 27 | 25 11 | 43.7 | 28 44 | 24 24 | 43.3 | 233 | 307 |
| 54 | 32 46 | 27 53 | 44.4 | 32 03 | 27 04 | 43.9 | 31 20 | 26 15 | 43.5 | 30 36 | 25 27 | 43.1 | 29 52 | 24 40 | 42.7 | 29 10 | 23 56 | 42.3 | 234 | 306 |
| 55 | 33 14 | 27 19 | 43.3 | 32 30 | 26 30 | 42.9 | 31 46 | 25 42 | 42.4 | 31 02 | 24 55 | 42.0 | 30 17 | 24 08 | 41.6 | 29 32 | 23 23 | 41.2 | 235 | 305 |
| 56 | 33 42 | 26 44 | 42.2 | 32 57 | 25 55 | 41.8 | 32 12 | 25 08 | 41.4 | 31 27 | 24 22 | 41.0 | 30 41 | 23 36 | 40.6 | 29 56 | 22 51 | 40.2 | 236 | 304 |
| 57 | 34 08 | 26 07 | 41.1 | 33 23 | 25 20 | 40.7 | 32 37 | 24 34 | 40.3 | 31 51 | 23 48 | 39.9 | 31 05 | 23 03 | 39.5 | 30 19 | 22 19 | 39.1 | 237 | 303 |
| 58 | 34 34 | 25 30 | 40.1 | 33 48 | 24 44 | 39.6 | 33 02 | 23 58 | 39.2 | 32 15 | 23 14 | 38.8 | 31 28 | 22 30 | 38.4 | 30 41 | 21 46 | 38.0 | 238 | 302 |
| 59 | 35 00 | 24 53 | 39.0 | 34 13 | 24 07 | 38.5 | 33 26 | 23 22 | 38.1 | 32 39 | 22 38 | 37.7 | 31 51 | 21 55 | 37.3 | 31 03 | 21 13 | 37.0 | 239 | 301 |
| 60 | 35 25 | 24 14 | 37.8 | 34 37 | 23 30 | 37.4 | 33 50 | 22 46 | 37.0 | 33 02 | 22 03 | 36.6 | 32 13 | 21 20 | 36.2 | 31 25 | 20 39 | 35.9 | 240 | 300 |
| 61 | 35 49 | 23 35 | 36.7 | 35 01 | 22 52 | 36.3 | 34 12 | 22 08 | 35.9 | 33 24 | 21 26 | 35.5 | 32 35 | 20 45 | 35.1 | 31 46 | 20 04 | 34.8 | 241 | 299 |
| 62 | 36 13 | 22 55 | 35.6 | 35 24 | 22 12 | 35.2 | 34 35 | 21 30 | 34.8 | 33 45 | 20 49 | 34.4 | 32 56 | 20 09 | 34.0 | 32 06 | 19 29 | 33.7 | 242 | 298 |
| 63 | 36 36 | 22 14 | 34.4 | 35 46 | 21 32 | 34.0 | 34 56 | 20 51 | 33.6 | 34 06 | 20 11 | 33.3 | 33 16 | 19 32 | 32.9 | 32 26 | 18 53 | 32.5 | 243 | 297 |
| 64 | 36 58 | 21 32 | 33.3 | 36 08 | 20 52 | 32.9 | 35 17 | 20 12 | 32.5 | 34 27 | 19 33 | 32.1 | 33 36 | 18 54 | 31.8 | 32 45 | 18 17 | 31.4 | 244 | 296 |
| 65 | 37 20 | 20 50 | 32.1 | 36 28 | 20 10 | 31.7 | 35 38 | 19 32 | 31.3 | 34 47 | 18 54 | 31.0 | 33 55 | 18 16 | 30.6 | 33 03 | 17 40 | 30.3 | 245 | 295 |
| 66 | 37 41 | 20 07 | 30.9 | 36 49 | 19 28 | 30.5 | 35 58 | 18 51 | 30.2 | 35 06 | 18 14 | 29.8 | 34 13 | 17 38 | 29.5 | 33 21 | 17 02 | 29.1 | 246 | 294 |
| 67 | 38 01 | 19 23 | 29.7 | 37 09 | 18 46 | 29.4 | 36 17 | 18 09 | 29.0 | 35 24 | 17 33 | 28.6 | 34 31 | 16 59 | 28.3 | 33 38 | 16 24 | 27.9 | 247 | 293 |
| 68 | 38 21 | 18 38 | 28.5 | 37 28 | 18 02 | 28.2 | 36 35 | 17 27 | 27.8 | 35 42 | 16 53 | 27.5 | 34 48 | 16 19 | 27.1 | 33 55 | 15 46 | 26.8 | 248 | 292 |
| 69 | 38 40 | 17 53 | 27.3 | 37 46 | 17 18 | 27.0 | 36 53 | 16 44 | 26.6 | 35 59 | 16 11 | 26.3 | 35 05 | 15 38 | 26.0 | 34 11 | 15 07 | 25.7 | 249 | 291 |
| 70 | 38 58 | 17 07 | 26.1 | 38 04 | 16 33 | 25.7 | 37 10 | 16 01 | 25.4 | 36 15 | 15 29 | 25.1 | 35 21 | 14 58 | 24.8 | 34 26 | 14 27 | 24.5 | 250 | 290 |
| 71 | 39 15 | 16 20 | 24.9 | 38 20 | 15 48 | 24.5 | 37 26 | 15 17 | 24.2 | 36 31 | 14 46 | 23.9 | 35 36 | 14 16 | 23.6 | 34 41 | 13 47 | 23.3 | 251 | 289 |
| 72 | 39 31 | 15 33 | 23.6 | 38 36 | 15 02 | 23.3 | 37 41 | 14 32 | 23.0 | 36 46 | 14 03 | 22.7 | 35 50 | 13 34 | 22.4 | 34 55 | 13 07 | 22.1 | 252 | 288 |
| 73 | 39 47 | 14 45 | 22.4 | 38 51 | 14 16 | 22.1 | 37 56 | 13 47 | 21.8 | 37 00 | 13 19 | 21.5 | 36 04 | 12 52 | 21.2 | 35 08 | 12 25 | 20.9 | 253 | 287 |
| 74 | 40 02 | 13 56 | 21.1 | 39 06 | 13 28 | 20.8 | 38 10 | 13 01 | 20.5 | 37 13 | 12 35 | 20.3 | 36 17 | 12 09 | 20.0 | 35 21 | 11 44 | 19.8 | 254 | 286 |
| 75 | 40 16 | 13 07 | 19.8 | 39 19 | 12 41 | 19.5 | 38 23 | 12 15 | 19.3 | 37 26 | 11 50 | 19.0 | 36 29 | 11 26 | 18.8 | 35 33 | 11 02 | 18.5 | 255 | 285 |
| 76 | 40 29 | 12 17 | 18.5 | 39 32 | 11 53 | 18.3 | 38 35 | 11 28 | 18.0 | 37 38 | 11 05 | 17.8 | 36 41 | 10 42 | 17.6 | 35 44 | 10 20 | 17.3 | 256 | 284 |
| 77 | 40 41 | 11 27 | 17.3 | 39 44 | 11 04 | 17.0 | 38 47 | 10 41 | 16.8 | 37 49 | 10 19 | 16.5 | 36 52 | 9 58 | 16.3 | 35 54 | 9 37 | 16.1 | 257 | 283 |
| 78 | 40 53 | 10 36 | 16.0 | 39 55 | 10 15 | 15.7 | 38 57 | 9 54 | 15.5 | 38 00 | 9 33 | 15.3 | 37 02 | 9 14 | 15.1 | 36 04 | 8 54 | 14.9 | 258 | 282 |
| 79 | 41 04 | 9 45 | 14.7 | 40 05 | 9 25 | 14.4 | 39 07 | 9 06 | 14.2 | 38 09 | 8 47 | 14.0 | 37 11 | 8 29 | 13.9 | 36 13 | 8 11 | 13.7 | 259 | 281 |
| 80 | 41 13 | 8 53 | 13.3 | 40 15 | 8 35 | 13.2 | 39 16 | 8 17 | 13.0 | 38 18 | 8 00 | 12.8 | 37 19 | 7 44 | 12.6 | 36 21 | 7 27 | 12.5 | 260 | 280 |
| 81 | 41 22 | 8 01 | 12.0 | 40 23 | 7 45 | 11.9 | 39 25 | 7 29 | 11.7 | 38 26 | 7 13 | 11.5 | 37 27 | 6 58 | 11.4 | 36 28 | 6 43 | 11.2 | 261 | 279 |
| 82 | 41 30 | 7 09 | 10.7 | 40 31 | 6 54 | 10.5 | 39 32 | 6 40 | 10.4 | 38 33 | 6 26 | 10.3 | 37 34 | 6 12 | 10.1 | 36 35 | 5 59 | 10.0 | 262 | 278 |
| 83 | 41 37 | 6 16 | 9.4 | 40 38 | 6 03 | 9.2 | 39 39 | 5 50 | 9.1 | 38 39 | 5 38 | 9.0 | 37 40 | 5 26 | 8.9 | 36 41 | 5 15 | 8.7 | 263 | 277 |
| 84 | 41 43 | 5 23 | 8.1 | 40 44 | 5 12 | 7.9 | 39 44 | 5 01 | 7.8 | 38 45 | 4 50 | 7.7 | 37 45 | 4 40 | 7.6 | 36 46 | 4 30 | 7.5 | 264 | 276 |
| 85 | 41 48 | 4 29 | 6.7 | 40 49 | 4 20 | 6.6 | 39 49 | 4 11 | 6.5 | 38 49 | 4 02 | 6.4 | 37 50 | 3 53 | 6.3 | 36 50 | 3 45 | 6.3 | 265 | 275 |
| 86 | 41 52 | 3 36 | 5.4 | 40 53 | 3 28 | 5.3 | 39 53 | 3 21 | 5.2 | 38 53 | 3 14 | 5.1 | 37 53 | 3 07 | 5.1 | 36 54 | 3 01 | 5.0 | 266 | 274 |
| 87 | 41 56 | 2 42 | 4.0 | 40 56 | 2 36 | 4.0 | 39 56 | 2 31 | 3.9 | 38 56 | 2 26 | 3.9 | 37 56 | 2 20 | 3.8 | 36 56 | 2 16 | 3.8 | 267 | 273 |
| 88 | 41 58 | 1 48 | 2.7 | 40 58 | 1 44 | 2.6 | 39 58 | 1 41 | 2.6 | 38 58 | 1 37 | 2.6 | 37 58 | 1 34 | 2.5 | 36 58 | 1 30 | 2.5 | 268 | 272 |
| 89 | 42 00 | 0 54 | 1.3 | 41 00 | 0 52 | 1.3 | 40 00 | 0 50 | 1.3 | 39 00 | 0 49 | 1.3 | 38 00 | 0 47 | 1.3 | 37 00 | 0 45 | 1.3 | 269 | 271 |
| 90 | 42 00 | 0 00 | 0.0 | 41 00 | 0 00 | 0.0 | 40 00 | 0 00 | 0.0 | 39 00 | 0 00 | 0.0 | 38 00 | 0 00 | 0.0 | 37 00 | 0 00 | 0.0 | 270 | 270 |

N. Lat.: for LHA > 180°....$Z_n = Z$
for LHA < 180°....$Z_n = 360° - Z$

S. Lat.: for LHA > 180°....$Z_n = 180° - Z$
for LHA < 180°....$Z_n = 180° + Z$

# SIGHT REDUCTION TABLE

317

| A' +/− | Z₂° | 30 | 29/31 | 28/32 | 27/33 | 26/34 | 25/35 | 24/36 | 23/37 | 22/38 | 21/39 | 20/40 | 19/41 | 18/42 | 17/43 | 16/44 | 15/45 | 14/46 | 13/47 | 12/48 | 11/49 | 10/50 | 9/51 | 8/52 | 7/53 | 6/54 | 5/55 | 4/56 | 3/57 | 2/58 | 1/59 | F' +/− P° |
|---|---|---|---|---|---|---|---|---|---|---|---|---|---|---|---|---|---|---|---|---|---|---|---|---|---|---|---|---|---|---|---|---|
| | 49 | 20 | 19 | 18 | 18 | 17 | 16 | 16 | 15 | 14 | 14 | 13 | 12 | 12 | 11 | 10 | 10 | 9 | 9 | 8 | 7 | 7 | 6 | 5 | 5 | 4 | 3 | 3 | 2 | 1 | 1 | 41 |
| | 48 | 20 | 19 | 19 | 18 | 17 | 16 | 16 | 15 | 15 | 14 | 13 | 13 | 12 | 11 | 11 | 10 | 9 | 9 | 8 | 7 | 7 | 6 | 5 | 5 | 4 | 3 | 3 | 2 | 1 | 1 | 42 |
| | 47 | 21 | 20 | 19 | 18 | 18 | 17 | 16 | 16 | 15 | 14 | 14 | 13 | 12 | 12 | 11 | 10 | 10 | 9 | 8 | 8 | 7 | 6 | 5 | 5 | 4 | 3 | 3 | 2 | 1 | 1 | 43 |
| | 46 | 21 | 20 | 20 | 19 | 18 | 17 | 17 | 16 | 15 | 15 | 14 | 13 | 13 | 12 | 11 | 10 | 10 | 9 | 8 | 8 | 7 | 6 | 6 | 5 | 4 | 3 | 3 | 2 | 1 | 1 | 44 |
| | 45 | 21 | 21 | 20 | 19 | 19 | 18 | 17 | 17 | 16 | 15 | 14 | 14 | 13 | 12 | 12 | 11 | 10 | 9 | 8 | 8 | 7 | 6 | 6 | 5 | 4 | 4 | 3 | 2 | 1 | 1 | 45 |
| | 44 | 22 | 21 | 20 | 20 | 19 | 18 | 18 | 17 | 16 | 16 | 15 | 14 | 13 | 13 | 12 | 11 | 10 | 9 | 9 | 8 | 7 | 6 | 6 | 5 | 4 | 4 | 3 | 2 | 1 | 1 | 46 |
| | 43 | 22 | 22 | 21 | 20 | 20 | 19 | 18 | 17 | 17 | 16 | 15 | 15 | 14 | 13 | 12 | 11 | 11 | 10 | 9 | 8 | 7 | 7 | 6 | 5 | 4 | 4 | 3 | 2 | 2 | 1 | 47 |
| | 42 | 22 | 22 | 21 | 21 | 20 | 19 | 19 | 18 | 17 | 17 | 16 | 15 | 14 | 14 | 13 | 12 | 11 | 10 | 9 | 8 | 8 | 7 | 6 | 5 | 5 | 4 | 3 | 2 | 2 | 1 | 48 |
| | 41 | 23 | 22 | 22 | 21 | 21 | 20 | 19 | 19 | 18 | 17 | 16 | 16 | 15 | 14 | 13 | 12 | 11 | 11 | 10 | 9 | 8 | 7 | 6 | 6 | 5 | 4 | 3 | 3 | 2 | 1 | 49 |
| | 40 | 23 | 23 | 22 | 21 | 21 | 20 | 20 | 19 | 19 | 18 | 17 | 16 | 15 | 14 | 14 | 13 | 12 | 11 | 10 | 9 | 8 | 7 | 7 | 6 | 5 | 4 | 4 | 3 | 2 | 1 | 50 |
| | 39 | 24 | 23 | 22 | 22 | 22 | 21 | 20 | 20 | 19 | 18 | 18 | 17 | 16 | 15 | 14 | 13 | 12 | 11 | 10 | 9 | 8 | 7 | 7 | 6 | 5 | 5 | 4 | 3 | 2 | 1 | 51 |
| | 38 | 24 | 23 | 23 | 22 | 22 | 21 | 21 | 20 | 20 | 19 | 18 | 17 | 16 | 16 | 15 | 14 | 13 | 12 | 11 | 10 | 9 | 7 | 7 | 6 | 5 | 5 | 4 | 3 | 2 | 1 | 52 |
| | 37 | 24 | 24 | 23 | 23 | 22 | 22 | 21 | 21 | 20 | 19 | 18 | 18 | 17 | 16 | 15 | 14 | 13 | 12 | 11 | 10 | 9 | 8 | 7 | 6 | 6 | 5 | 4 | 3 | 2 | 1 | 53 |
| | 36 | 25 | 24 | 24 | 23 | 23 | 22 | 22 | 21 | 20 | 20 | 19 | 18 | 17 | 17 | 16 | 14 | 13 | 12 | 11 | 10 | 9 | 8 | 7 | 6 | 6 | 5 | 4 | 3 | 2 | 1 | 54 |
| | 35 | 25 | 25 | 24 | 23 | 23 | 23 | 22 | 22 | 21 | 20 | 19 | 19 | 18 | 17 | 16 | 14 | 13 | 13 | 12 | 10 | 9 | 8 | 7 | 6 | 6 | 5 | 4 | 3 | 2 | 1 | 55 |
| | 34 | 25 | 25 | 25 | 24 | 24 | 23 | 23 | 22 | 22 | 21 | 20 | 19 | 18 | 18 | 17 | 15 | 14 | 13 | 12 | 11 | 9 | 8 | 7 | 6 | 6 | 5 | 4 | 3 | 2 | 1 | 56 |
| | 33 | 26 | 26 | 25 | 24 | 24 | 24 | 23 | 23 | 22 | 21 | 21 | 20 | 19 | 18 | 17 | 15 | 14 | 13 | 12 | 11 | 10 | 8 | 7 | 6 | 6 | 5 | 4 | 3 | 2 | 1 | 57 |
| | 32 | 26 | 26 | 26 | 25 | 25 | 24 | 24 | 23 | 23 | 22 | 21 | 20 | 19 | 19 | 17 | 15 | 14 | 13 | 12 | 11 | 10 | 8 | 8 | 7 | 6 | 5 | 4 | 3 | 2 | 1 | 58 |
| | 31 | 27 | 26 | 26 | 26 | 25 | 25 | 24 | 24 | 23 | 23 | 22 | 21 | 20 | 19 | 18 | 16 | 15 | 13 | 12 | 11 | 10 | 8 | 8 | 7 | 6 | 5 | 4 | 3 | 2 | 1 | 59 |
| | 30 | 27 | 27 | 27 | 26 | 26 | 25 | 25 | 24 | 23 | 23 | 22 | 22 | 21 | 20 | 18 | 16 | 15 | 14 | 13 | 11 | 10 | 8 | 8 | 7 | 6 | 5 | 4 | 3 | 2 | 1 | 60 |
| | 29 | 27 | 27 | 27 | 26 | 26 | 26 | 25 | 25 | 24 | 23 | 23 | 22 | 21 | 20 | 19 | 16 | 15 | 14 | 13 | 11 | 10 | 8 | 8 | 7 | 6 | 5 | 4 | 3 | 2 | 1 | 61 |
| | 28 | 28 | 27 | 27 | 27 | 26 | 26 | 26 | 25 | 24 | 24 | 23 | 22 | 22 | 20 | 19 | 17 | 15 | 14 | 13 | 12 | 10 | 9 | 8 | 7 | 6 | 5 | 4 | 3 | 2 | 1 | 62 |
| | 27 | 28 | 28 | 28 | 27 | 27 | 27 | 26 | 26 | 25 | 24 | 23 | 23 | 22 | 21 | 19 | 17 | 15 | 14 | 13 | 12 | 10 | 9 | 8 | 7 | 6 | 5 | 4 | 3 | 2 | 1 | 63 |
| | 26 | 28 | 28 | 28 | 27 | 27 | 27 | 27 | 26 | 25 | 25 | 24 | 23 | 22 | 21 | 20 | 17 | 16 | 14 | 13 | 12 | 10 | 9 | 8 | 7 | 6 | 5 | 4 | 3 | 2 | 1 | 64 |
| | 25 | 28 | 28 | 28 | 28 | 27 | 27 | 27 | 26 | 26 | 25 | 24 | 24 | 22 | 21 | 20 | 17 | 16 | 14 | 13 | 12 | 10 | 9 | 8 | 7 | 6 | 5 | 4 | 3 | 2 | 1 | 65 |
| | 24 | 29 | 29 | 28 | 28 | 28 | 28 | 27 | 27 | 26 | 25 | 25 | 24 | 23 | 22 | 20 | 18 | 16 | 15 | 13 | 12 | 11 | 9 | 8 | 7 | 6 | 5 | 4 | 3 | 2 | 1 | 66 |
| | 23 | 29 | 29 | 28 | 28 | 28 | 28 | 28 | 27 | 26 | 26 | 25 | 24 | 23 | 22 | 21 | 18 | 16 | 15 | 13 | 12 | 11 | 9 | 8 | 7 | 6 | 5 | 4 | 3 | 2 | 1 | 67 |
| | 22 | 29 | 29 | 29 | 28 | 28 | 28 | 28 | 27 | 27 | 26 | 25 | 24 | 23 | 22 | 21 | 18 | 17 | 15 | 14 | 13 | 11 | 9 | 8 | 7 | 6 | 5 | 4 | 3 | 2 | 1 | 68 |
| | 21 | 29 | 29 | 29 | 29 | 28 | 28 | 28 | 28 | 27 | 26 | 25 | 25 | 23 | 22 | 21 | 18 | 17 | 15 | 14 | 13 | 11 | 9 | 8 | 7 | 6 | 5 | 4 | 3 | 2 | 1 | 69 |
| | 20 | 29 | 29 | 29 | 29 | 29 | 29 | 28 | 28 | 27 | 27 | 26 | 25 | 24 | 22 | 21 | 18 | 17 | 15 | 14 | 13 | 12 | 9 | 8 | 7 | 6 | 5 | 4 | 3 | 2 | 1 | 70 |
| | 19 | 29 | 28 | 27 | 26 | 25 | 24 | 23 | 22 | 21 | 20 | 19 | 18 | 17 | 16 | 15 | 14 | 13 | 12 | 11 | 10 | 9 | 9 | 8 | 7 | 6 | 5 | 4 | 3 | 2 | 1 | 71 |
| | 18 | 29 | 28 | 27 | 26 | 25 | 24 | 23 | 22 | 21 | 20 | 19 | 18 | 17 | 16 | 15 | 14 | 13 | 12 | 12 | 10 | 9 | 9 | 8 | 7 | 6 | 5 | 4 | 3 | 2 | 1 | 72 |
| | 17 | 29 | 28 | 27 | 26 | 25 | 24 | 23 | 23 | 21 | 20 | 19 | 18 | 18 | 17 | 16 | 14 | 14 | 13 | 12 | 11 | 10 | 9 | 8 | 7 | 6 | 5 | 4 | 3 | 2 | 1 | 73 |
| | 16 | 29 | 28 | 27 | 26 | 25 | 25 | 24 | 23 | 22 | 20 | 20 | 19 | 18 | 17 | 16 | 15 | 14 | 13 | 12 | 11 | 10 | 9 | 8 | 7 | 6 | 5 | 4 | 3 | 2 | 1 | 74 |
| | 15 | 30 | 28 | 27 | 27 | 25 | 25 | 24 | 23 | 22 | 21 | 20 | 19 | 18 | 17 | 16 | 15 | 14 | 13 | 12 | 11 | 10 | 9 | 8 | 7 | 6 | 5 | 4 | 3 | 2 | 1 | 75 |
| | 14 | 29 | 28 | 27 | 26 | 25 | 24 | 23 | 22 | 21 | 20 | 19 | 17 | 16 | 15 | 14 | 13 | 12 | 11 | 10 | 9 | 8 | 7 | 6 | 5 | 4 | 3 | 2 | 1 | 76 |
| | 13 | 29 | 28 | 27 | 26 | 25 | 24 | 23 | 22 | 21 | 20 | 19 | 18 | 17 | 16 | 15 | 14 | 13 | 12 | 11 | 10 | 9 | 8 | 7 | 6 | 5 | 4 | 3 | 2 | 1 | 77 |
| | 12 | 29 | 28 | 27 | 26 | 25 | 24 | 23 | 22 | 21 | 20 | 19 | 18 | 17 | 16 | 15 | 14 | 13 | 12 | 11 | 10 | 9 | 8 | 7 | 6 | 5 | 4 | 3 | 2 | 1 | 78 |
| | 11 | 30 | 28 | 28 | 27 | 25 | 25 | 24 | 23 | 22 | 21 | 19 | 18 | 17 | 16 | 15 | 14 | 13 | 12 | 11 | 10 | 9 | 8 | 7 | 6 | 5 | 4 | 3 | 2 | 1 | 79 |
| | 10 | 30 | 29 | 28 | 27 | 26 | 25 | 24 | 23 | 22 | 21 | 20 | 19 | 18 | 17 | 16 | 15 | 14 | 13 | 12 | 11 | 10 | 9 | 8 | 7 | 6 | 5 | 4 | 3 | 2 | 1 | 80 |

For Z₂ < 10°, use 10°

# ADJUSTMENT TO TABULAR ALTITUDE

## AUXILIARY TABLE

*Sign for corr₂ for A'.* → *− A' / + A'*

| $Z_2^\circ$ | 30 □ | 29/31 | 28/32 | 27/33 | 26/34 | 25/35 | 24/36 | 23/37 | 22/38 | 21/39 | 20/40 | 19/41 | 18/42 | 17/43 | 16/44 | 15/45 | 14/46 | 13/47 | 12/48 | 11/49 | 10/50 | 9/51 | 8/52 | 7/53 | 6/54 | 5/55 | 4/56 | 3/57 | 2/58 | 1/59 |
|---|---|---|---|---|---|---|---|---|---|---|---|---|---|---|---|---|---|---|---|---|---|---|---|---|---|---|---|---|---|---|
| 89 | ′ | ′ | ′ | ′ | ′ | ′ | ′ | ′ | ′ | ′ | ′ | ′ | ′ | ′ | ′ | ′ | ′ | ′ | ′ | ′ | ′ | ′ | ′ | ′ | ′ | ′ | ′ | ′ | ′ | ′ |
| 88 | | | 0 | 0 | 0 | 0 | 0 | 0 | 0 | 0 | 0 | 0 | 0 | 0 | 0 | 0 | 0 | 0 | 0 | 0 | 0 | 0 | 0 | 0 | 0 | 0 | 0 | 0 | 0 | 0 |
| 87 | 1 | 1 | 1 | 1 | 1 | 1 | 1 | 1 | 1 | 1 | 1 | 1 | 1 | 1 | 1 | 1 | 0 | 0 | 0 | 0 | 0 | 0 | 0 | 0 | 0 | 0 | 0 | 0 | 0 | 0 |
| 86 | 1 | 1 | 1 | 1 | 1 | 1 | 1 | 1 | 1 | 1 | 1 | 1 | 1 | 1 | 1 | 1 | 1 | 1 | 1 | 1 | 1 | 0 | 0 | 0 | 0 | 0 | 0 | 0 | 0 | 0 |
| 85 | 2 | 2 | 2 | 2 | 2 | 2 | 2 | 2 | 2 | 2 | 2 | 2 | 1 | 1 | 1 | 1 | 1 | 1 | 1 | 1 | 1 | 1 | 1 | 1 | 0 | 0 | 0 | 0 | 0 | 0 |
| 84 | 3 | 3 | 3 | 3 | 3 | 3 | 3 | 3 | 3 | 3 | 2 | 2 | 2 | 2 | 2 | 2 | 2 | 1 | 1 | 1 | 1 | 1 | 1 | 1 | 1 | 1 | 0 | 0 | 0 | 0 |
| 83 | 3 | 3 | 3 | 3 | 3 | 3 | 3 | 3 | 3 | 3 | 3 | 3 | 2 | 2 | 2 | 2 | 2 | 2 | 2 | 2 | 1 | 1 | 1 | 1 | 1 | 1 | 1 | 1 | 0 | 0 |
| 82 | 4 | 4 | 4 | 4 | 4 | 3 | 3 | 4 | 3 | 4 | 3 | 3 | 3 | 3 | 3 | 3 | 3 | 3 | 2 | 2 | 2 | 2 | 2 | 2 | 2 | 1 | 1 | 1 | 1 | 0 |
| 81 | 4 | 4 | 4 | 4 | 4 | 4 | 4 | 4 | 4 | 4 | 4 | 4 | 4 | 4 | 3 | 3 | 3 | 3 | 3 | 3 | 3 | 2 | 2 | 2 | 2 | 2 | 1 | 1 | 1 | 1 |
| 80 | 5 | 5 | 5 | 5 | 5 | 4 | 4 | 4 | 4 | 5 | 5 | 4 | 5 | 4 | 4 | 4 | 4 | 4 | 4 | 3 | 3 | 3 | 3 | 2 | 2 | 2 | 1 | 1 | 1 | 1 |
| 79 | 6 | 6 | 5 | 5 | 5 | 5 | 5 | 5 | 5 | 5 | 5 | 5 | 5 | 5 | 5 | 4 | 4 | 4 | 4 | 4 | 4 | 3 | 3 | 3 | 2 | 2 | 2 | 1 | 1 | 1 |
| 78 | 6 | 6 | 6 | 6 | 6 | 6 | 5 | 5 | 6 | 6 | 6 | 6 | 5 | 5 | 5 | 5 | 5 | 5 | 4 | 4 | 4 | 3 | 3 | 3 | 2 | 2 | 2 | 1 | 1 | 1 |
| 77 | 7 | 7 | 6 | 6 | 6 | 6 | 6 | 6 | 7 | 6 | 6 | 6 | 6 | 6 | 6 | 5 | 5 | 5 | 5 | 4 | 4 | 4 | 3 | 3 | 2 | 2 | 2 | 2 | 1 | 1 |
| 76 | 7 | 7 | 7 | 7 | 7 | 6 | 7 | 7 | 7 | 7 | 7 | 7 | 6 | 6 | 6 | 6 | 6 | 5 | 5 | 5 | 4 | 4 | 3 | 3 | 3 | 2 | 2 | 2 | 1 | 1 |
| 75 | 8 | 8 | 7 | 7 | 7 | 7 | 8 | 7 | 8 | 8 | 7 | 7 | 7 | 7 | 7 | 6 | 6 | 5 | 5 | 5 | 5 | 4 | 4 | 3 | 3 | 3 | 2 | 2 | 1 | 1 |
| 74 | 8 | 8 | 8 | 7 | 7 | 7 | 8 | 8 | 8 | 8 | 8 | 7 | 7 | 7 | 7 | 7 | 6 | 6 | 5 | 5 | 5 | 4 | 4 | 3 | 3 | 3 | 2 | 2 | 1 | 1 |
| 73 | 9 | 8 | 8 | 8 | 8 | 8 | 8 | 8 | 8 | 8 | 8 | 8 | 7 | 7 | 7 | 7 | 7 | 6 | 6 | 6 | 5 | 5 | 4 | 3 | 3 | 3 | 2 | 2 | 1 | 1 |
| 72 | 9 | 9 | 9 | 9 | 9 | 9 | 8 | 8 | 9 | 9 | 8 | 8 | 8 | 8 | 7 | 7 | 7 | 7 | 6 | 6 | 5 | 5 | 4 | 3 | 3 | 3 | 2 | 2 | 1 | 1 |
| 71 | 10 | 9 | 9 | 9 | 9 | 9 | 9 | 9 | 9 | 9 | 9 | 9 | 8 | 8 | 8 | 7 | 7 | 7 | 7 | 6 | 5 | 5 | 4 | 4 | 3 | 3 | 2 | 2 | 1 | 1 |
| 70 | 10 | 10 | 10 | 10 | 10 | 10 | 10 | 9 | 9 | 9 | 10 | 9 | 9 | 9 | 8 | 8 | 7 | 7 | 7 | 6 | 5 | 5 | 4 | 4 | 3 | 3 | 2 | 2 | 1 | 1 |
| 69 | 11 | 10 | 10 | 10 | 11 | 11 | 11 | 10 | 10 | 10 | 10 | 10 | 9 | 9 | 8 | 8 | 8 | 7 | 7 | 6 | 6 | 5 | 4 | 4 | 3 | 3 | 2 | 2 | 1 | 1 |
| 68 | 11 | 11 | 11 | 11 | 11 | 11 | 11 | 11 | 11 | 11 | 11 | 10 | 10 | 10 | 9 | 9 | 8 | 8 | 7 | 7 | 6 | 5 | 5 | 4 | 3 | 3 | 2 | 2 | 1 | 1 |
| 67 | 12 | 12 | 11 | 12 | 12 | 12 | 11 | 11 | 11 | 11 | 11 | 11 | 10 | 10 | 10 | 9 | 9 | 8 | 8 | 7 | 6 | 5 | 5 | 4 | 4 | 3 | 2 | 2 | 1 | 1 |
| 66 | 12 | 12 | 12 | 12 | 12 | 12 | 12 | 12 | 12 | 12 | 11 | 11 | 11 | 10 | 10 | 9 | 9 | 8 | 8 | 7 | 6 | 6 | 5 | 4 | 4 | 3 | 2 | 2 | 1 | 1 |
| 65 | 13 | 13 | 13 | 13 | 13 | 12 | 12 | 12 | 12 | 12 | 12 | 11 | 11 | 11 | 10 | 10 | 9 | 8 | 8 | 7 | 7 | 6 | 5 | 4 | 4 | 3 | 2 | 2 | 1 | 1 |
| 64 | 13 | 13 | 13 | 14 | 13 | 13 | 13 | 13 | 12 | 12 | 12 | 12 | 11 | 11 | 10 | 10 | 9 | 9 | 8 | 8 | 7 | 6 | 5 | 4 | 4 | 3 | 2 | 2 | 1 | 1 |
| 63 | 14 | 14 | 14 | 14 | 14 | 13 | 13 | 13 | 13 | 13 | 12 | 12 | 12 | 11 | 11 | 10 | 9 | 9 | 8 | 8 | 7 | 6 | 5 | 4 | 4 | 3 | 2 | 2 | 1 | 1 |
| 62 | 14 | 14 | 14 | 15 | 14 | 14 | 14 | 14 | 13 | 13 | 13 | 13 | 12 | 12 | 11 | 10 | 10 | 9 | 9 | 8 | 7 | 6 | 5 | 4 | 4 | 3 | 2 | 2 | 1 | 1 |
| 61 | 15 | 14 | 14 | 15 | 15 | 14 | 15 | 14 | 14 | 14 | 13 | 13 | 12 | 12 | 11 | 10 | 10 | 9 | 9 | 8 | 7 | 6 | 5 | 4 | 4 | 3 | 2 | 2 | 1 | 1 |
| 60 | 15 | 15 | 15 | 15 | 15 | 15 | 15 | 14 | 14 | 14 | 14 | 13 | 12 | 12 | 11 | 10 | 10 | 9 | 9 | 8 | 7 | 6 | 5 | 4 | 4 | 3 | 2 | 2 | 1 | 1 |
| 59 | 15 | 15 | 16 | 16 | 15 | 15 | 15 | 15 | 14 | 14 | 14 | 14 | 13 | 13 | 12 | 11 | 10 | 10 | 9 | 8 | 7 | 6 | 5 | 4 | 4 | 3 | 2 | 2 | 1 | 1 |
| 58 | 16 | 16 | 16 | 16 | 16 | 15 | 15 | 15 | 15 | 15 | 14 | 14 | 13 | 13 | 12 | 11 | 10 | 10 | 9 | 8 | 7 | 6 | 5 | 5 | 4 | 3 | 2 | 2 | 1 | 1 |
| 57 | 17 | 17 | 17 | 17 | 16 | 16 | 15 | 15 | 15 | 15 | 14 | 14 | 13 | 13 | 12 | 11 | 10 | 10 | 9 | 8 | 7 | 6 | 5 | 5 | 4 | 3 | 2 | 2 | 1 | 1 |
| 56 | 18 | 17 | 17 | 17 | 17 | 16 | 16 | 16 | 15 | 15 | 14 | 14 | 13 | 13 | 12 | 11 | 10 | 10 | 9 | 8 | 7 | 6 | 5 | 5 | 4 | 3 | 2 | 2 | 1 | 1 |
| 55 | 18 | 18 | 17 | 17 | 17 | 16 | 16 | 16 | 15 | 15 | 14 | 14 | 13 | 13 | 12 | 11 | 10 | 10 | 9 | 8 | 7 | 6 | 5 | 5 | 4 | 3 | 2 | 2 | 1 | 1 |
| 54 | 18 | 18 | 18 | 17 | 17 | 17 | 16 | 16 | 15 | 15 | 14 | 14 | 13 | 13 | 12 | 11 | 10 | 10 | 9 | 8 | 7 | 6 | 5 | 5 | 4 | 3 | 2 | 2 | 1 | 1 |
| 53 | 18 | 18 | 18 | 18 | 17 | 17 | 17 | 16 | 15 | 15 | 14 | 14 | 13 | 13 | 12 | 11 | 10 | 10 | 9 | 8 | 7 | 6 | 5 | 5 | 4 | 3 | 2 | 2 | 1 | 1 |
| 52 | 19 | 19 | 18 | 18 | 18 | 17 | 17 | 16 | 16 | 15 | 14 | 14 | 13 | 13 | 12 | 11 | 10 | 10 | 9 | 8 | 7 | 6 | 5 | 5 | 4 | 3 | 3 | 2 | 1 | 1 |
| 51 | 19 | 19 | 19 | 18 | 18 | 17 | 17 | 16 | 16 | 15 | 14 | 14 | 13 | 13 | 12 | 11 | 10 | 10 | 9 | 8 | 7 | 6 | 5 | 5 | 4 | 3 | 3 | 2 | 1 | 1 |
| 50 | 19 | 19 | 18 | 17 | 17 | 16 | 15 | 15 | 14 | 13 | 13 | 12 | 12 | 11 | 10 | 10 | 9 | 8 | 8 | 7 | 6 | 6 | 5 | 4 | 4 | 3 | 3 | 2 | 1 | 1 |

*Sign of corr₁ for F'. Reverse sign if F > 90°.*

| F'/+ − | 1/59 | 2/58 | 3/57 | 4/56 | 5/55 | 6/54 | 7/53 | 8/52 | 9/51 | 10/50 | 11/49 | 12/48 | 13/47 | 14/46 | 15/45 | 16/44 | 17/43 | 18/42 | 19/41 | 20/40 | 21/39 | 22/38 | 23/37 | 24/36 | 25/35 | 26/34 | 27/33 | 28/32 | 29/31 | 30 □ |
|---|---|---|---|---|---|---|---|---|---|---|---|---|---|---|---|---|---|---|---|---|---|---|---|---|---|---|---|---|---|---|
| P° | | | | | | | | | | | | | | | | | | | | | | | | | | | | | | |

P° = 1, 2, 3, ... 40

316

Thanks to all those who helped to un-confuse, and proofread:
Jim Glenn, Judy Rouse, Johan DeBruin, Noemi Ybarra, Don Siddall, Jim Weaver, David Wrate, CT, and anyone else I forgot to mention.
Thanks also to Steve Bell and Catherine Hohenkirk from HM Nautical Almanac Office, and Sean Urban from the U.S. Naval Observatory.

If you find any errors, typos, confusing spots, etc. please let me know so I can correct them in future editions of this book. Email capn@ncsail.org with anything that bugs you.

Future editions of this book should be available at
http://www.ncsail.org/publications.html

Made in the USA